ONE-STORY HOMES

470 Designs
For All Lifestyles

860 to 5,400 square feet

HOME PLANNERS, INC.

Contents

Note: Many of the homes featured in this book have a matching or corresponding Landscape or Deck plan available from Home Planners, Inc. Some have both. These plans have a **L** or a **D** following their design number and square-footage notations. For information on how to order plans for landscapes and decks, see pages 366-373.

Published by Home Planners, Inc.
3275 West Ina Road, Suite 110
Tucson, Arizona 85741
Chairman: Charles W. Talcott
President and Publisher: Rickard D. Bailey
Publications Manager: Cindy J. Coatsworth
Editor: Paulette Mulvin
Front Cover Graphic Design: Paul Fitzgerald

First Printing December 1990
10   9   8   7   6   5   4   3   2   1

Library of Congress Number: 90-084444
ISBN: 0-918894-85-9

ON THE COVER: Plans for this Traditional Cape Cod Rambler, Design V12921, can be found on page 166.
Home of Charles and Catherine Talcott, Northville, Michigan.
Photographer: Laszlo Regos

How To Read
Floor Plans and Blueprints

Selecting the most suitable house plan for your family is a matter of matching your needs, tastes, and lifestyle against the many designs we offer. When you study the floor plans in this book, and the blueprints that you may subsequently order, remember that they are a two-dimensional representation of what will be a three-dimensional reality.

Floor plans are easy to read. Rooms are clearly labeled, with dimensions given in feet and inches. Most symbols are logical and self-explanatory: The location of bathroom fixtures, fireplaces, planters, tile floors, cabinets and counters, sinks, appliances, closets, and sloped or beamed ceilings will be obvious.

A blueprint, although much more detailed, is also easy to read; all it demands is concentration. The blueprints that we offer come in many large sheets, each one of which contains a different kind of information. One sheet contains foundation and excavation drawings, another has a precise plot plan. An elevations sheet deals with the exterior walls of the house; section drawings show precise dimensions, fittings, doors, windows, and roof structures. This provides all the construction information needed by your contractor. Also available is a helpful materials list with size and quantities of all necessary components. Using this list, your contractor and suppliers can make a start at calculating costs for you.

When you first study a floor plan or blueprint, imagine that you are walking through the house. By mentally visualizing each room in three dimensions, you can transform the technical data and symbols into something more real. Interior space should be organized in a logical way, based on the intended use of such space. Usually the space is divided into rooms which fall into one of three categories. The sleeping area includes bedrooms and bathrooms; the work area includes the kitchen, laundry, utility room, garage and other functional rooms; the living area includes the living and dining rooms, family room, and other gathering areas as well as entrance ways.

To begin a mental tour of the home, start at the front door. It's preferable to have a foyer or entrance hall in which to receive guests. A closet here is desirable; a powder room is a plus.

Look for good traffic circulation as you study the floor plan. You should not have to pass all the way through one main room to reach another. From the entrance area you should have direct access to the three principal areas of a house—the living, work, and sleeping zones. For example, a foyer might provide separate entrances to the living room, kitchen, patio, and a hallway or staircase leading to the bedrooms.

Study the layout of each zone. Most people expect the living room to be protected from cross traffic. The kitchen, on the other hand, should connect with the dining room—and perhaps also the utility room, basement, garage, patio or deck, or a secondary entrance. A homemaker whose workday centers in the kitchen may have special requirements: a window that faces the backyard; a clear view of the family room where children play; a garage or driveway entrance that allows for a short trip with groceries; laundry facilities close at hand. Check for efficient placement of kitchen cabinets, counter, and appliances. Is there enough room in the kitchen for additional appliances, for eating in? Is there a dining nook?

Perhaps this part of the house contains a family room or a den/bedroom/office. It's advantageous to have a bathroom or powder room in this section.

As you study the plan, you may encounter a staircase, indicated by a group of parallel lines, the number of lines equaling the number of steps. Arrows labeled "up" mean that the staircase leads to a higher level, and those pointing down mean it leads to a lower one. Staircases in a split-level will have both up and down arrows on one staircase because two levels are depicted in one drawing and an extra level in another.

Notice the location of the stairways. Is too much floor space lost to them? Will you find yourself making too many trips?

Study the sleeping quarters. Are the bedrooms situated as you like? You may want the master bedroom near the kids, or you may want it as far away as possible. Is there at least one closet per person in each bedroom or a double one for a couple? Bathrooms should be convenient to each bedroom—if not adjoining, then with hallway access and on the same floor.

Once you are familiar with the relative positions of the rooms, look for such structural details as:

- Sufficient uninterrupted wall space for furniture arrangement.
- Adequate room dimensions.
- Potential heating or cooling problems— i.e., a room over a garage or next to the laundry.
- Window and door placement for good ventilation and natural light.
- Location of doorways—avoid having a basement staircase or a bathroom in view of the dining room.
- Adequate auxiliary space—closets, storage, bathrooms, countertops.
- Separation of activity areas (will noise from the recreation room disturb sleeping children or a parent at work?).

As you complete your mental walk through the house, bear in mind your family's long-range needs. A good house plan will allow for some adjustments now and additions in the future.

Take time to notice special amenities: fireplaces and raised hearths, work islands in the kitchen, pass-through countertops between kitchen and breakfast nook, whirlpool baths. Note the placement of decks and balconies. Your family may find the listing of favorite features a most helpful exercise. Why not try it?

How To Shop
For Mortgage Money

Most people who are in the market for a new home spend months searching for the right house plan and building site. Ironically, these same people often invest very little time shopping for the money to finance their new home, though the majority will have to live with the terms of their mortgage for as long as they live in the home.

The fact is that not all lending institutions are alike, nor are the loans that they offer.

- Lending practices vary from one city and state to another. If you are a first-time builder or are new to an area, it is wise to hire a real estate (not divorce or general practice) attorney to help you unravel the maze of your area's laws and customs.
- Before talking with a lender, write down all your questions and take notes so you can make accurate comparisons.
- Do not be intimidated by financial officers. Do not hesitate to reveal what other institutions are offering; they may be challenged to meet or better the terms.

A GUIDE TO LENDERS

Where can you turn for home financing? Here is a list of sources for you to contact:

Savings and Loan Associations
Savings Banks/Mutual Savings Banks
Commercial Banks
Mortgage Banking Companies
Some Credit Unions

Each of the above institutions generally offers a variety of loan types, interest rates, and fees. It is recommended that you survey each type of institution in your area to determine exactly what type of financing is available so that you can make an intelligent and informed decision.

A GUIDE TO LOAN TYPES

Conventional Loans

These types of loans usually require a minimum down payment of 10% of the lower of the purchase price or appraised value of the property. However, in many cases, this down payment requirement has been increased to 15% to 20% depending on the type of loan and the requirements of the lending institution. Often, the minimum down payment requirement is applied to owner-occupied residences and is usually increased if the property is purchased as a vacation home or investment.

The most common type of conventional loan is the **fixed-rate loan** which has a fixed interest rate and fixed monthly payments. The term of the loan may vary, but such loans generally are available in fifteen- and thirty-year terms. The obvious advantage of a fifteen-year term is an earlier loan payoff as well as reduced interest charges.

Other types of conventional loans are called **adjustable rate mortgages (ARM's)**. This type of loan usually has a lower initial interest rate than the fixed-rate loan, but the interest rate of payment may change depending on the loan terms and economic conditions. The frequency of these interest/payment adjustments depends on the individual loan, but they usually occur every twelve months.

Some key terms to understanding ARM loans are listed below:

Adjustment Period - The period between one rate change and the next. Therefore, a loan with an adjustment period of one year is known as a One Year ARM.

Index - The interest rate change is tied to an index rate. These indexes usually go up and down with the general movement of interest rates. If the index rate moves up, so does your monthly payment. If the index rate goes down, your monthly payment may also go down. There are a variety of indexes. Among the most common is the weekly average yield on U.S. Treasury securities adjusted to a constant maturity of one, three, or five years.

Margin - To determine the interest rate on an ARM, lenders add a few percentage points to the index rate. These percentage points are called the margin. The amount of the margin can differ from one lender to the next, but is usually constant through the life of the loan.

Caps - Most ARM loans limit the amount that the interest rate can increase. There are periodic caps which limit the increase from one adjustment period to the next and overall caps which limit the interest rate increase over the life of the loan.

Negative Amortization - Several ARM loans contain negative amortization which means that your mortgage balance can increase even though you are making regular monthly payments. This happens when the interest rate of the loan increases while your monthly payment remains the same.

Convertibility or Conversion Option - This is a clause in your agreement that allows you to convert the ARM to a fixed-rate mortgage at designated times. Not all ARM loans contain this option.

There are other types of less-common conventional loans which are offered by many institutions: Graduated Payment Mortgages, Reverse Annuity Mortgages, and Bi-Weekly Mortgages. Consult with a financial officer of a lending institution for details on these other loan types.

Government Loans

FHA loans are government insured and have substantially lower down payments than conventional loans; however, there are maximum allowable loan amounts for these loans depending on the location of the property.

Another type of government loan is through the Veteran's Administration (VA). Like the FHA, the VA guarantees loans for eligible veterans and the spouses of those veterans who died while in the service. Down payment requirements are also extremely low on these types of loans.

There are a variety of loan types available under these government programs including fixed rate, ARM's and graduated payment mortgages. The financial officer of the lending institution will be able to explain these various loan types and the qualification standards.

The Cost of a Mortgage

Monthly principal and interest per $1,000 of mortgage

Mortgage rate	15-year loan	20-year loan	25-year loan	30-year loan
9.00%	10.15	9.00	8.40	8.05
9.10%	10.21	9.07	8.47	8.12
9.20%	10.27	9.13	8.53	8.20
9.30%	10.33	9.20	8.60	8.27
9.40%	10.39	9.26	8.67	8.34
9.50%	10.45	9.33	8.74	8.41
9.60%	10.51	9.39	8.81	8.49
9.70%	10.57	9.46	8.88	8.56
9.80%	10.63	9.52	8.95	8.63
9.90%	10.69	9.59	9.02	8.71
10.00%	10.75	9.66	9.09	8.78
10.10%	10.81	9.72	9.16	8.85
10.20%	10.87	9.79	9.23	8.93
10.30%	10.94	9.85	9.30	9.00
10.40%	11.00	9.92	9.38	9.08
10.50%	11.06	9.99	9.45	9.15
10.60%	11.12	10.06	9.52	9.23
10.70%	11.18	10.12	9.59	9.30
10.80%	11.25	10.19	9.66	9.38
10.90%	11.31	10.26	9.73	9.45
11.00%	11.37	10.33	9.81	9.53
11.10%	11.43	10.40	9.88	9.60
11.20%	11.50	10.46	9.95	9.68
11.30%	11.56	10.53	10.02	9.76
11.40%	11.62	10.60	10.10	9.83
11.50%	11.69	10.67	10.17	9.91
11.60%	11.75	10.74	10.24	9.98
11.70%	11.81	10.81	10.32	10.06
11.80%	11.88	10.88	10.39	10.14
11.90%	11.94	10.95	10.46	10.21

Note: Multiply the cost per $1,000 by the size of the mortgage (in thousands). The result is the monthly payment, including principal and interest. For example, for an $80,000 mortgage for 30 years at 10 percent, multiply 80 x 8.78 = $702.40.

How To Choose A Contractor

Contractors are part craftsmen, part businessmen, and part magicians. Transforming your dreams and drawings into a finished house, they are responsible for the final cost of the structure, for the quality of the workmanship, and for the solving of all problems that occur quite naturally in the course of construction.

There are two types of residential contractors: the construction company and the carpenter-builder, often called a general contractor. Each of these has its advantages and disadvantages.

Carpenter-builders work directly on the job as field foremen. Because their background is that of a craftsman, their workmanship is probably good—but their paperwork may be slow or sloppy. Their overhead—which you pay for—is less than that of a large construction company. However, if the job drags on for any reason, their interest may flag because your project is overlapping their next job and eroding profits.

Construction companies that handle several projects concurrently have an office staff to keep the paperwork moving and an army of reliable subcontractors. Though you can be confident that they will meet deadlines, they may sacrifice workmanship in order to do so. Emphasizing efficiency, they are less personal to work with than a general contractor and many will not work with an individual unless there is representation by an architect.

To find a reliable contractor, start by asking friends who have built homes for recommendations. Check with local lumberyards and building supply outlets for names of possible candidates and call departments of consumer affairs. Keep in mind that these watchdog organizations can give only the number of complaints filed; they cannot tell you what percent of those claims were valid. Remember, too, that a large-volume operation is logically going to have more registered complaints against it than will an independent contractor.

Interview each of the potential candidates. Find out about specialties—custom houses, development houses, remodeling, or office buildings. Ask each to take you into—not just to the site of—current projects. Ask to see projects that are complete as well as work in progress, emphasizing that you are interested in projects comparable to yours. A $300,000 dentist's office will give you little insight into a contractor's craftsmanship.

Ask each contractor for bank references from both a commercial bank and any other appropriate lender. If in good financial standing, the contractor should have no qualms about giving you this information. Also ask about warranties. Most will give you a one-year warranty on the structure; some offer as much as a ten-year warranty.

Ask for references, even though no contractor will give you the name of a dissatisfied customer. Ask about follow-through. Was the building site cleaned up or did the owner have to dispose of the refuse? Ask about the organization of business. Did the paperwork go smoothly, or was there a delay in hooking up the sewer because of a failure to apply for a permit?

Talk to each of the candidates about fees. Most work on a "cost plus" basis; that is, the basic cost of the project—materials, subcontractors' services, wages of those working directly on the project, but not office help—plus a fee. Some have a fixed fee; others work on a percentage of the basic cost. A fixed fee is usually better for you if you can get one. If a contractor works on a percentage, ask for a cost breakdown of the best estimate and keep very careful track as the work progresses. A crafty contractor can always use a cost overrun to good advantage when working on a percentage.

Do not be overly suspicious of a contractor who won't work on a fixed fee. One who is very good and in great demand may not be willing to do so and may also be reluctant to submit a competitive bid.

Give the top two or three candidates each copies of the plans and your specifications for materials. If they are not each working from the same guidelines, the competitive bids will be of little value. Give each the same deadline for turning in a bid; two or three weeks is a reasonable period of time. Make an appointment with each of them and open the envelopes at this time.

If one bid is remarkably low, the contractor may have made an honest error in the estimate. Don't insist that the contractor hold to a bid if it is in error. Forcing a building price that is too low could be disastrous for both of you. You may want to review the bids with your architect, if you have one, or with your lender to discuss which to accept. They may not recommend the lowest. A low bid does not necessarily mean that you will get the best quality with economy.

If the bids are relatively close, the most important consideration may not be money at all. A bid from a contractor who is easy to talk to and inspires confidence may be the best choice. Any sign of a personality conflict between you and a contractor should be weighed when making a decision.

Once you have financing, you can sign a contract with the builder. Most have their own contract forms, but it is advisable to have a lawyer draw one up or, at the very least, review the standard contract. This usually costs a small flat fee.

A good contract should include:
• Plans and sketches of the work to be done, subject to your approval.
• A list of materials, including quantity, brand names, style or serial numbers. (Do not permit any "or equal" clause that will allow the contractor to make substitutions.)
• The terms—who (you or the lender) pays whom and when.
• A production schedule.
• The contractor's certification of insurance for workmen's compensation, damage, and liability.
• A rider stating that all changes, whether or not they increase the cost, must be submitted and approved in writing.

Of course, this list represents the least a contract should include. Once you have signed it, your plans are on the way to becoming a home.

A Checklist For Plan Selection

Developing an architectural plan from the various wants and needs of an individual or family that fits into lifestyle demands and design elegance is the most efficient way to assure a livable plan. It is not only possible but highly desirable to design a plan around such requirements as separate bedrooms for each member of the family, guest suites, a quiet study area, an oversized entertainment area, a two-car garage, a completely private master suite, and a living room fireplace. Incorporated into this can be such wants as Tudor styling, 1½-stories, a large entry hall, decks and balconies, and a basement.

While it is obviously best to begin with wants and needs and then design a home to fit these criteria, this is not always practical or even possible. A very effective way around this problem is to select a professionally prepared home plan which meets all needs and incorporates as many wants as possible. With careful selection, it will be possible to modify sizes and make other design adjustments to make the home as close to custom as can be. It is important to remember that some wants may have to be compromised in the interest of meeting budgetary limitations. The trick is to build the best possible home for the available money while satisfying all absolute needs.

Following are some cost-controlling ideas that can make a big difference in the overall price of a home:
1. Square or rectangular homes are less expensive to build than irregularly shaped homes.
2. It is less expensive to build on a flat lot than on a sloping or hillside lot.
3. The use of locally manufactured or produced materials cuts costs greatly.
4. Using stock materials and stock sizes of components takes advantage of mass production cost reductions.
5. The use of materials that can be quickly installed cuts labor costs. Prefabricating large sections or panels eliminates much time on the site.
6. The use of prefinished materials saves significantly on labor costs.
7. Investigating existing building codes before beginning construction eliminates unnecessary changes as construction proceeds.
8. Refraining from changing the design or any aspect of the plan after construction begins will help to hold down cost escalation.
9. Minimizing special jobs or custom-built items keeps costs from increasing.
10. Designing the house for short plumbing lines saves on piping and other materials.
11. Proper insulation saves heating and cooling costs.
12. Utilizing passive solar features, such as correct orientation, reduces future maintenance costs.

To help you consider all the important factors in evaluating a plan, the following checklist should be reviewed carefully. By comparing its various points to any plan and a wants-and-needs list, it will be possible to easily recognize the deficiencies of a plan or determine its appropriateness. Be sure to include family members in the decision-making process. Their ideas and desires will help in finding exactly the right plan.

CHECKLIST

The Neighborhood

1. _____ Reasonable weather conditions
2. No excess
   - _____ *a.* wind
   - _____ *b.* smog or fog
   - _____ *c.* odors
   - _____ *d.* soot or dust
3. _____ The area is residential
4. There are no
   - _____ *a.* factories
   - _____ *b.* dumps
   - _____ *c.* highways
   - _____ *d.* railroads
   - _____ *e.* airports
   - _____ *f.* apartments
   - _____ *g.* commercial buildings
5. _____ City-maintained streets
6. No hazards in the area
   - _____ *a.* quarries
   - _____ *b.* storage tanks
   - _____ *c.* power stations
   - _____ *d.* unprotected swimming pools

7. Reasonably close to
   - _____ *a.* work
   - _____ *b.* schools
   - _____ *c.* churches
   - _____ *d.* hospital
   - _____ *e.* shopping
   - _____ *f.* recreation
   - _____ *g.* public transportation
   - _____ *h.* library
   - _____ *i.* police protection
   - _____ *j.* fire protection
   - _____ *k.* parks
   - _____ *l.* cultural activities
8. _____ Streets are curved
9. _____ Traffic is slow
10. _____ Intersections are at right angles
11. _____ Street lighting
12. _____ Light traffic
13. _____ Visitor parking
14. _____ Good design in street
15. _____ Paved streets and curbs
16. _____ Area is not deteriorating
17. _____ Desirable expansion
18. _____ Has some open spaces

19. _____ Numerous and healthy trees
20. _____ Pleasant-looking homes
21. _____ Space between homes
22. _____ Water drains off
23. _____ Near sewerage line
24. _____ Storm sewers nearby
25. _____ Mail delivery
26. _____ Garbage pickup
27. _____ Trash pickup
28. _____ No city assessments

The Lot

1. _____ Title is clear
2. _____ No judgments against the seller
3. _____ No restrictions as to the use of the land or the deed
4. _____ No unpaid taxes or assessments
5. _____ Minimum of 70 feet of frontage
6. _____ House does not crowd the lot
7. _____ Possible to build on
8. _____ Few future assessments (sewers, lights, and so forth)
9. _____ Good top soil and soil percolation
10. _____ Good view
11. _____ No low spots to hold water
12. _____ Water drains off land away from the house
13. _____ No fill
14. _____ No water runoff from high ground
15. _____ If cut or graded there is substantial retaining wall
16. _____ Permanent boundary markers
17. _____ Utilities available at property line
18. _____ Utility hookup is reasonable
19. _____ Utility rates are reasonable
20. _____ Taxes are reasonable
21. _____ Water supply is adequate
22. _____ Regular, simply shaped lot
23. _____ Trees
24. _____ Do not have to cut trees
25. _____ Privacy for outside activities
26. _____ Attractive front yard
27. _____ Front and rear yards are adequate
28. _____ Front yard is not divided up by walks and driveway
29. _____ Outdoor walks have stairs grouped

The Floor Plan

1. _____ Designed by licensed architect
2. _____ Purchased from a reputable stock plan company
3. _____ Supervised by skilled contractor
4. Orientation
    _____ *a.* sun
    _____ *b.* view
    _____ *c.* noise
    _____ *d.* breeze
    _____ *e.* contour of land
5. _____ Entry
6. _____ Planned for exterior expansion
7. Planned for interior expansion
    _____ *a.* attic
    _____ *b.* garage
    _____ *c.* basement
8. _____ Simple but functional plan
9. _____ Indoor recreation area
10. _____ Wall space for furniture in each room
11. Well-designed hall
    _____ *a.* leads to all areas
    _____ *b.* no congestions

_____ *c.* no wasted space
_____ *d.* 3' minimum widths
12. _____ Easy to clean
13. _____ Easy to keep orderly
14. _____ Plan meets family's needs
15. _____ All rooms have direct emergency escape
16. Doorways functional
    _____ *a.* no unnecessary doors
    _____ *b.* wide enough for moving furniture through
    _____ *c.* can see visitors through locked front door
    _____ *d.* do not swing out into halls
    _____ *e.* swing open against a blank wall
    _____ *f.* do not bump other subjects
    _____ *g.* exterior doors are solid
17. Windows are functional
    _____ *a.* not too small
    _____ *b.* enough but not too many
    _____ *c.* glare-free
    _____ *d.* roof overhang protection where needed
    _____ *e.* large ones have the best view
    _____ *f.* easy to clean
    _____ *g.* no interference with furniture placement
    _____ *h.* over kitchen sink
    _____ *i.* open easily
18. _____ No fancy gadgets
19. _____ Room sizes are adequate
20. _____ Well-designed stairs
    _____ *a.* treads are 9" minimum
    _____ *b.* risers are 8" maximum
    _____ *c.* 36" minimum width
    _____ *d.* 3' minimum landings
    _____ *e.* attractive
    _____ *f.* easily reached
21. _____ Overall plan "fits" family requirements
22. _____ Good traffic patterns
23. _____ Noisy areas separated from quiet areas
24. _____ Rooms have adequate wall space for furniture
25. _____ Halls are 3'6" minimum

The Living Area

1. _____ Minimum space 12' x 16'
2. _____ Front door traffic does not enter
3. _____ Not in a traffic pattern
4. _____ Windows on two sides
5. _____ Has a view
6. _____ Storage for books and music materials
7. _____ Decorative lighting
8. _____ Whole family plus guests can be seated
9. _____ Desk area
10. _____ Fireplace
11. _____ Wood storage
12. _____ No street noises
13. _____ Privacy from street
14. _____ Acoustical ceiling
15. _____ Cannot see or hear bathroom
16. _____ Powder room
17. _____ Comfortable for conversation
18. Dining room
    _____ *a.* used enough to justify
    _____ *b.* minimum of 3' clearance around table
    _____ *c.* can be opened or closed to kitchen and patio
    _____ *d.* can be opened or closed to living room
    _____ *e.* electrical outlets for table appliances

19. Family room
     _____ a. minimum space 10' x 12'
     _____ b. room for family activities
     _____ c. room for noisy activities
     _____ d. room for messy activities
     _____ e. activities will not disturb sleeping area
     _____ f. finish materials are easy to clean and durable
     _____ g. room for expansion
     _____ h. separate from living room
     _____ i. near kitchen
     _____ j. fireplace
     _____ k. adequate storage
20. _____ Dead-end circulation
21. _____ Adequate furniture arrangements

The Entry

1. _____ The entry is a focal point
2. _____ The outside is inviting
3. _____ The landing has a minimum depth of 5'
4. _____ Protected from the weather
5. _____ Has an approach walk
6. _____ Well planted
7. _____ Coat closet
8. _____ Leads to living, sleeping, and service areas
9. _____ Floor material attractive and easy to clean
10. _____ Decorative lighting
11. _____ Space for table
12. _____ Space to hang mirror
13. _____ Does not have direct view into any room

The Bedrooms

1. _____ Adequate number of bedrooms
2. _____ Adequate size—10' x 12' minimum
3. _____ Open into a hall
4. _____ Living space
5. _____ Children's bedroom has study and play area
6. _____ Oriented to north side
7. In quiet area
     _____ a. soundproofing
     _____ b. acoustical ceiling
     _____ c. insulation in walls
     _____ d. thermal glass
     _____ e. double doors
     _____ f. closet walls
8. _____ Privacy
9. _____ 4' minimum wardrobe rod space per person
10. Master bedroom
     _____ a. bath
     _____ b. dressing area
     _____ c. full-length mirror
     _____ d. 12' x 12' minimum
11. Adequate windows
     _____ a. natural light
     _____ b. cross-ventilation
     _____ c. windows on two walls
12. _____ Room for overnight guests
13. _____ Bathroom nearby
14. _____ Wall space for bed, nightstands, and dresser
15. _____ Quiet reading area

The Bathroom

1. _____ Well designed
2. _____ Plumbing lines are grouped
3. _____ Fixtures have space around them for proper use
4. _____ Doors do not interfere with fixtures
5. _____ Noises are insulated from other rooms

6. _____ Convenient to bedrooms
7. _____ Convenient to guests
8. _____ Ventilation
9. _____ Heating
10. _____ Attractive fixtures
11. _____ No windows over tub or shower
12. _____ Wall area around tub and shower
13. _____ Light fixtures are water tight
14. _____ Large medicine cabinet
15. _____ Children cannot open medicine cabinet
16. _____ No bathroom tie-ups
17. _____ Good lighting
18. _____ Accessible electrical outlets
19. _____ No electric appliance or switch near water supply
20. _____ Towel and linen storage
21. _____ Dirty clothes hamper
22. _____ Steamproof mirrors
23. _____ Wall and floor materials are waterproof
24. _____ All finishes are easy to maintain
25. _____ Curtain and towel rods securely fastened
26. _____ Grab bar by tub
27. _____ Mixing faucets
28. _____ Bath in service area
29. _____ No public view into open bathroom door
30. _____ Clean-up area for outdoor jobs and children's play

The Kitchen

1. _____ Centrally located
2. _____ The family can eat informally in the kitchen
3. _____ At least 20' of cabinet space
     _____ a. counter space on each side of major appliances
     _____ b. minimum of 8' counter work area
     _____ c. round storage in corners
     _____ d. no shelf is higher than 72"
     _____ e. floor cabinets 24" deep and 36" high
     _____ f. wall cabinets 15" deep
     _____ g. 15" clearance between wall and floor cabinets
4. _____ Work triangle is formed between appliances
     _____ a. between 12' and 20'
     _____ b. no traffic through the work triangle
     _____ c. refrigerator opens into the work triangle
     _____ d. at least six electric outlets in work triangle
     _____ e. no door between appliances
5. _____ No space between appliances and counters
6. _____ Window over sink
7. _____ No wasted space in kitchen
8. _____ Can close off kitchen from dining area
9. _____ Snack bar in kitchen
10. _____ Kitchen drawers are divided
11. _____ Built-in chopping block
12. _____ Writing and telephone desk
13. _____ Indoor play area visible from kitchen
14. _____ Outdoor play area visible from kitchen
15. _____ Exhaust fan
16. _____ Natural light
17. _____ Good lighting for each work area
18. _____ Convenient access to service area and garage
19. _____ Durable surfaces
20. _____ Dishwasher
21. _____ Disposal
22. _____ Built-in appliances
23. _____ Bathroom nearby

24. _____ Room for freezer
25. _____ Pantry storage

The Utility Room

1. _____ Adequate laundry area
2. _____ Well-lighted work areas
3. _____ 240-volt outlet
4. _____ Gas outlet
5. _____ Sorting area
6. _____ Ironing area
7. _____ Drip-drying area
8. _____ Sewing and mending area
9. _____ On least desirable side of lot
10. _____ Exit to outdoor service area
11. _____ Exit near garage
12. _____ Sufficient cabinet space
13. _____ Bathroom in area
14. _____ Accessible from kitchen
15. _____ Adequate space for washer and dryer
16. _____ Laundry tray
17. _____ Outdoor exit is protected from the weather
18. _____ Window

Working Areas

1. _____ Home repair area
2. _____ Work area for hobbies
3. _____ Storage for paints and tools
4. _____ Garage storage
5. _____ Incinerator area
6. _____ Refuse area
7. _____ Delivery area
8. _____ Near parking
9. _____ 240-volt outlet for power tools

Storage

1. _____ General storage space for each person
2. _____ 4' of rod space for each person
3. _____ Closet doors are sealed to keep out dust
4. _____ Minimum wardrobe closet size is 40" x 22"
5. _____ Cedar closet storage for seasonal clothing
6. _____ Bulk storage area for seasonal paraphernalia
7. _____ Closets are lighted
8. _____ Walk-in closets have adequate turnaround area
9. Storage for:
_____ a. linen and towels
_____ b. cleaning materials
_____ c. foods
_____ d. bedding
_____ e. outdoor furniture
_____ f. sports equipment
_____ g. toys—indoor
_____ h. toys—outdoor
_____ i. bicycles
_____ j. luggage
_____ k. out-of-season clothes
_____ l. storm windows and doors
_____ m. garden tools
_____ n. tools and paints
_____ o. hats
_____ p. shoes
_____ q. belts
_____ r. ties
_____ s. bridge tables and chairs
_____ t. camping equipment
_____ u. china
_____ v. silver
_____ w. minor appliances
_____ x. books

10. _____ Closets are ventilated
11. _____ Closets do not project into room
12. _____ Toothbrush holders in bathrooms
13. _____ Soap holders in bathrooms
14. _____ Adequate built-in storage
15. _____ Drawers cannot pull out of cabinet
16. _____ Drawers slide easily
17. _____ Drawers have divided partitions
18. _____ Adult storage areas easy to reach
19. _____ Children storage areas easy to reach
20. _____ Guest storage near entry
21. _____ Heavy storage areas have reinforced floors
22. _____ Sides of closets easy to reach
23. _____ Tops of closets easy to reach
24. _____ No wasted spaces around stored articles
25. _____ Sloping roof or stairs do not render closet useless
26. _____ Entry closet

The Exterior

1. _____ The design looks "right" for the lot
2. _____ Design varies from other homes nearby
3. _____ Design fits with unity on its site
4. _____ Definite style architecture—not mixed
5. _____ Simple, honest design
6. _____ Garage design goes with the house
7. _____ Attractive on all four sides
8. _____ Colors in good taste
9. _____ Finish materials in good taste
10. _____ Has charm and warmth
11. _____ Materials are consistent on all sides
12. _____ No false building effects
13. _____ Well-designed roof lines—not chopped up
14. _____ Window tops line up
15. _____ Bathroom windows are not obvious
16. _____ Does not look like a box
17. _____ Easy maintenance of finish materials
18. _____ Windows are protected from pedestrian view
19. _____ Attractive roof covering
20. _____ Gutters on roof
21. _____ Downspouts that drain into storm sewer
22. _____ Glass area protected with overhang or trees
23. _____ Dry around the house
24. _____ Several waterproof electric outlets
25. _____ Hose bib on each side
26. _____ Style will look good in the future

Outdoor Service Area

1. _____ Clothes hanging area
2. _____ Garbage storage
3. _____ Can storage
4. _____ On least desirable side of site
5. _____ Next to indoor service area
6. _____ Near garage
7. _____ Delivery area for trucks
8. _____ Fenced off from rest of site

Outdoor Living Area

1. _____ Area for dining
2. _____ Area for games
3. _____ Area for lounging
4. _____ Area for gardening
5. _____ Fenced for privacy
6. _____ Partly shaded
7. _____ Concrete deck at convenient places
8. _____ Garden walks

9. _____ Easy access to house
10. _____ Paved area for bikes and wagons
11. _____ Easy maintenance

Landscaping

1. _____ Planting at foundation ties
2. _____ Garden area
3. _____ Well-located trees
4. _____ Healthy trees
5. _____ Plants of slow-growing variety
6. _____ Landscaping professionally advised
7. _____ Garden walks
8. _____ Easy maintenance
9. _____ Extras as trellis or gazebo

Construction

1. _____ Sound construction
2. _____ All work complies to code
3. _____ Efficient contractor and supervision
4. _____ Honest builders
5. _____ Skilled builders
6. _____ Constructed to plans
7. Floors are well constructed
   _____ a. resilient
   _____ b. subfloor diagonal to joints
   _____ c. flat and even
   _____ d. slab is not cold
   _____ e. floor joists rest on 2" of sill—minimum
   _____ f. girder lengths are joined under points of support
8. Foundation is well constructed
   _____ a. level
   _____ b. sill protected from termites
   _____ c. vapor barrier
   _____ d. no cracks
   _____ e. no water seepage
   _____ f. no dryrot in sills
   _____ g. garage slab drains
   _____ h. waterproofed
   _____ i. walls are 8" thick
   _____ j. basement height 7'6" minimum
   _____ k. sills bolted to foundation
   _____ l. adequate vents
9. Walls are well constructed
   _____ a. plumb
   _____ b. no waves
   _____ c. insulation
   _____ d. flashing at all exterior joints
   _____ e. solid sheathing
   _____ f. siding is neat and tight
   _____ g. drywall joints are invisible
10. Windows are properly installed
   _____ a. move freely
   _____ b. weatherstripped
   _____ c. caulked and sealed
   _____ d. good-quality glass
11. Doors properly hung
   _____ a. move freely
   _____ b. exterior doors weatherstripped
   _____ c. exterior doors are solid-core
   _____ d. interior doors are hollow-core
12. Roof is well constructed
   _____ a. rafters are straight
   _____ b. all corners are flashed
   _____ c. adequate vents in attic
   _____ d. no leaks
   _____ e. building paper under shingles
13. _____ Tile work is tight

14. _____ Hot water lines are insulated
15. _____ Mortar joints are neat
16. _____ Mortar joints do not form shelf to hold water
17. _____ Ceiling is 8'0" minimum
18. _____ No exposed pipes
19. _____ No exposed wires
20. _____ Tight joints at cabinets and appliances
21. _____ Stairs have railings
22. _____ Neat trim application
23. _____ Builder responsible for new home flaws

The Fireplace

1. _____ There is a fireplace
2. _____ Wood storage near the fireplace
3. _____ Draws smoke
4. _____ Hearth in front (minimum 10" on sides; 20" in front)
5. _____ Does not project out into the room
6. _____ Has a clean-out
7. _____ Chimney top 2' higher than roof ridge
8. _____ No leaks around chimney in roof
9. _____ No wood touches the chimney
10. _____ 2" minimum air space between framing members and masonry
11. _____ No loose mortar
12. _____ Has a damper
13. _____ Space for furniture opposite fireplace
14. _____ Doors minimum of 6' from fireplace
15. _____ Windows minimum of 3' from fireplace
16. _____ On a long wall
17. _____ Install "heatilator"
18. _____ Install glass doors to minimize heat loss

Equipment

1. _____ All equipment listed in specifications and plans
2. _____ All new equipment has warranty
3. _____ All equipment is up to code standards
4. _____ All equipment is functional and not a fad
5. _____ Owner's choice of equipment meets builder's allowance
6. _____ Public system for utilities
7. _____ Private well is deep; adequate and healthy water
8. Electrical equipment is adequate
   _____ a. inspected and guaranteed
   _____ b. 240 voltage
   _____ c. 120 voltage
   _____ d. sufficient electric outlets
   _____ e. sufficient electric circuits—minimum of six
   _____ f. circuit breakers
   _____ g. television aerial outlet
   _____ h. telephone outlets
   _____ i. outlets in convenient places
9. Adequate lighting
   _____ a. all rooms have general lighting
   _____ b. all rooms have specific lighting for specific tasks
   _____ c. silent switches
   _____ d. some decorative lighting
   _____ e. light at front door
   _____ f. outdoor lighting
10. _____ Plumbing equipment is adequate
   _____ a. inspected and guaranteed
   _____ b. adequate water pressure
   _____ c. hot water heater—50-gallon minimum
   _____ d. shut-off valves at fixtures

_____ e. satisfactory city sewer or septic tank
_____ f. septic tank disposal field is adequate
_____ g. septic tank is large enough for house (1000 gallons for three-bedroom house, plus 250 gallons for each additional bedroom)
_____ h. water softener for hard water
_____ i. siphon vertex or siphon reverse-trap water closet
_____ j. clean-out plugs at all corners of waste lines
_____ k. water lines will not rust
_____ l. water pipes do not hammer
_____ m. waste lines drain freely
_____ n. cast iron with vitreous enamel bathtub

11. _____ Good ventilation through house and attic

12. Heating and cooling systems are adequate
_____ a. insulation in roof, ceiling, walls
_____ b. air conditioning system
_____ c. heating and cooling outlets under windows
_____ d. air purifier
_____ e. thermostatic control
_____ f. walls are clean over heat outlets
_____ g. comfortable in hot or cold weather
_____ h. automatic humidifier
_____ i. furnace blower is belt-driven
_____ j. quiet-heating plant
_____ k. ducts are tight

13. _____ Windows are of good quality
_____ a. storm windows
_____ b. secure locks
_____ c. screened
_____ d. double glazed in extreme weather (thermal)
_____ e. glass is ripple-free
_____ f. safety or safe thickness of glass
_____ g. moisture-free
_____ h. frost-free

14. Doors are of good quality
_____ a. secure locks on exterior doors
_____ b. attractive hardware
_____ c. hardware is solid brass or bronze

15. All meters easily accessible to meter readers
16. _____ Fire extinguisher in house and garage
17. _____ Acoustical ceiling
18. _____ Facilities to lock mail box
19. _____ Facilities to receive large packages
20. _____ Gas or electric incinerator
21. Adequate small hardware
_____ a. soap dishes
_____ b. toilet-paper holders
_____ c. toothbrush holders
_____ d. towel holders
_____ e. bathtub grab bars
_____ f. door and drawer pulls

The Garage

1. _____ Same style as the house
2. _____ Fits with house
3. _____ Single garage 12' x 22' minimum
4. _____ Double garage 22' x 22' minimum
5. _____ Larger than minimum size if used for storage or workshop
6. _____ Protected passage to house
7. _____ Doors are safe
8. _____ Access to overhead storage

Financial Checklist

1. _____ Do you understand conveyancing fees (closing costs)?
2. _____ Is the house a good investment?
3. _____ Is the total cost approximately three times your annual income?
4. _____ Have you shopped for the best loan?
5. _____ Do you have a constant payment plan (sliding principal and interest)?
6. _____ Is there a prepayment penalty?
7. _____ Will a week's salary cover the total housing expense for one month?
8. _____ Are all the costs itemized in the contract?
9. Do you understand the following closing costs?
_____ a. title search
_____ b. lawyer
_____ c. plot survey
_____ d. insurance, fire, and public liability
_____ e. mortgage tax
_____ f. recording mortgage
_____ g. recording deed
_____ h. bank's commitment fee
_____ i. state and county taxes
_____ j. state and government revenue stamps
_____ k. title insurance (protects lender)
_____ l. homeowner's policy (protects owner)
_____ m. transferring ownership
_____ n. mortgage service charge
_____ o. appraisal
_____ p. notarizing documents
_____ q. attendant fee (paying off previous mortgage)
_____ r. personal credit check

10. _____ Do you have extra cash to cover unforeseen expenses?

11. Can you afford to pay the following?
_____ a. closing costs
_____ b. old assessments or bonds
_____ c. new assessments or bonds
_____ d. downpayment
_____ e. immediate repairs
_____ f. immediate purchases (furniture, appliances, landscape, tools, fences, carpets, drapes, patio)
_____ g. adequate insurance
_____ h. mortgage payments
_____ i. general maintenance
_____ j. utilities (water, heat, electricity, phone, gas, trash pickup)
_____ k. special design features wanted
_____ l. extras not covered in plans and contract
_____ m. prepayment of interest and taxes for first month of transition
_____ n. moving
_____ o. gardener
_____ p. travel to work
_____ q. interest on construction loan
_____ r. advances to contractors

12. _____ Who will pay for the following?
_____ a. supervision costs of architect or contractor
_____ b. inspection fees
_____ c. increased costs during building
_____ d. building permits
_____ e. difficulties in excavation
_____ f. dry wells
_____ g. extra features the building inspector insists upon

The above Checklist is used with permission. It is taken from Home Planners' Guide to Residential Design _by Charles Talcott, Don Hepler, and Paul Wallach; 1986; McGraw-Hill, Inc._

ENGLISH TUDOR VERSIONS . . .

have become increasingly popular in recent years. This style has emanated from the more massive two-story with its many gabled roofs, exposed half-timber work, stucco and muntined windows. More correctly identified as Elizabethan style, the Tudor term of reference has become an accepted misnomer. Other distinguishing features include large sculptured chimneys, brick and stone exterior surfaces and panelled doors. Of interest in this section are the houses which feature complete one-story livability, including first floor bedrooms, but deliver bonus sleeping facilities either upstairs or on a lower level. Truly an impressive and distinctive style.

Design V12785
Square Footage: 2,375

D

● Exceptional Tudor design! Passersby will take a second glance at this fine home wherever it may be located. And the interior is just as pleasing. As one enters the foyer and looks around, the plan will speak for itself in the areas of convenience and efficiency.

Cross room traffic will be avoided. There is a hall leading to each of the three bedrooms and study of the sleeping wing and another leading to the living room, family room, kitchen and laundry with washroom. The formal dining room can be entered from both

the foyer and the kitchen. Efficiency will be the by-word when describing the kitchen. Note the fine features: a built-in desk, pantry, island snack bar with sink and pass-thru to the family room. The fireplace will be enjoyed in the living and family rooms.

TERRACE

55'-4"

TERRACE

MASTER
BEDROOM
11⁰ x 15⁰

LIVING RM.
18⁸ x 14⁰

DINING RM.
10⁴ x 10⁰

BATH

VANITY

DRESS. RM.

CL.

CL.

CHINA

KITCHEN
12⁴ x 12⁸

LEDGE

BATH

CL.

LIN.

CL.

BRM
CL.

P'TRY

REF'G

STORAGE

DESK

OVENS

CL.

DN.

46'-4"

FOYER

CURB

MEDIA RM.
13⁸ x 11⁴

CABINET
BOOKS

PORCH

BEDROOM
11⁰ x 13⁰

GARAGE
21⁴ x 22⁰

LEDGE

Design V12929
Square Footage: 1,608

● Here is a cozy Tudor exterior with a contemporary interior for those who prefer the charm of yesteryear combined with the convenience and practicality of today. This efficient floor plan will cater nicely to the living patterns of the small family; be it a retired couple or newlyweds. The efficient kitchen is strategically located handy to the garage, dining room, dining terrace and the front door. The spacious living area has a dramatic fireplace that functions with the rear terrace. A favorite spot will be the media room. Just the place for the TV, VCR and stereo systems. The master bedroom is large and has plenty of wardrobe storage along with a master bath featuring twin lavatories and a tub plus stall shower. Don't miss the extra guest room (or nursery). This affordable home has a basement for the development of additional recreational facilities and storage.

Design V12962

Square Footage: 2,112

● A Tudor exterior with an efficient floor plan favored by many. Each of the three main living zones - the sleeping zone, living zone, and the working zone - are but a couple steps from the foyer. This spells easy, efficient traffic patterns. Open planning, sloping ceiling and plenty of glass create a nice environment for the living-dining area. Its appeal is further enhanced by the open staircase to the lower level recreation/hobby area. The L-shaped kitchen with its island range and work surface is delightfully opened to the large breakfast room. Again, plenty of glass area adds to the feeling of spaciousness. Nearby is the step-saving first floor laundry. The sleeping zone has the flexibility of functioning as a two or three bedroom area. Notice the economical back-to-back plumbing.

Design V12605
Square Footage: 1,775

● Here are three modified L-shaped Tudor designs with tremendous exterior appeal and efficient floor plans. While each plan features three bedrooms and 2½ baths, the square footage differences are interesting. Note that each design may be built with or without a basement. This appealing exterior is highlighted by a variety of roof planes, patterned brick, wavy-edged siding and a massive chimney. The garage is oversized and has good storage potential. In addition to the entrance court, there are two covered porches and two terraces for outdoor living. Most definitely a home to be enjoyed by all family members.

Design V12206
Square Footage: 1,769

D

● The charm of Tudor adaptations has become increasingly popular in recent years. And little wonder. Its freshness of character adds a unique touch to any neighborhood. This interesting one-story home will be a standout wherever you choose to have it built. The covered front porch leads to the formal front entry—the foyer. From this point traffic flows freely to the living and sleeping areas. The outstanding plan features a separate dining room, a beamed ceiling living room, an efficient kitchen and an informal family room.

OPTIONAL BASEMENT

Design V12604
Square Footage: 1,956

D

● A feature that will set the whole wonderful pattern of true living will be the 26 foot wide country kitchen. The spacious, L-shaped kitchen has its efficiency enhanced by the island counter work surface. Beamed ceilings, fireplace and sliding glass doors add to the cozy atmosphere of this area. The laundry, dining room and entry hall are but a step or two away. The big keeping room also has a fireplace and can function with the terrace. Observe the 2½ baths.

90'-10"

32'-10"

TERRACE

MASTER BED RM. 15⁰ x 13⁶

BATH

FAMILY RM. 21⁴ x 12⁶

BEAMED CEILING

SNACK

KIT. 12⁰ x 13⁶

MUD RM.

BATH

RAISED HEARTH

CL

AIR COND.

OVEN

BAR

RANGE

PNTRY.

CL

CURB

FOYER

BED RM. 11⁶ x 15²

BED RM. 13⁶ x 11⁶

LIVING RM. 19⁸ x 13⁶

DINING RM. 11³ x 13⁶

GARAGE 21⁸ x 23⁴

PORCH

OPTIONAL BASEMENT

CL

FOYER

LIVING RM.

PORCH

Design V12318
Square Footage: 2,029

D

● Warmth and charm are characteristics of Tudor adaptations. This modest sized home with its twin front-facing gabled roofs represents a great investment. While it will be an exciting and refreshing addition to any neighborhood, its appeal will never grow old.

The covered, front entrance opens to the center foyer. Traffic patterns flow in an orderly and efficient manner to the three main zones — the formal dining zone, the sleeping zone and the informal living zone. The sunken living room with its fireplace is separated

from the dining room by an attractive trellis divider. A second fireplace, along with beamed ceiling and sliding glass doors, highlights the family room. Note snack bar, mud room, cooking facilities, two full baths and optional basement.

Design V12515
Square Footage: 2,363

● Another Tudor adaptation with all the appeal that is inherent in this design style. The brick veneer exterior is effectively complimented by the beam work, the stucco and the window treatment. The carriage lamp, perched on the planter wall, adds a delightful touch as do the dovecotes of the bedroom wing and over the garage door. The livability of the interior is just great. The kitchen, nook and dining room overlook the front yard. The laundry is around the corner from the kitchen. An extra washroom is not far away. Sloping, beamed ceiling and raised hearth fireplace are highlights of the family room. Like the living room and master bedroom, it functions with the rear terrace. Note vanity outside main bath. Wood posts separate the living room and hall.

Design V12859
Square Footage: 1,599

● Incorporated into the extremely popular basic one-story floor plan is a super-insulated structure. This means that it has double exterior walls separated by R-33 insulation and a raised roof truss that insures ceiling insulation will extend to the outer wall. More popularity is shown in the always popular Tudor facade. Enter the home through the air-locked vestibule to the foyer. To the left is the sleeping area. To the right of the foyer is the breakfast room, kitchen and stairs to the basement. Viewing the rear yard are the gathering and dining rooms. Study the technical details described in the blueprints of the wall section so you can better understand this super-insulated house.

Design V12606
Square Footage: 1,499

● This modest sized house with its 1,499 square feet could hardly offer more in the way of exterior charm and interior livability. Measuring only 60 feet in width means it will not require a huge, expensive piece of property. The orientation of the garage and the front drive court are features which promote an economical use of property. In addition to the formal, separate living and dining rooms, there is the informal kitchen/family room area. Note the beamed ceiling, the fireplace, the sliding glass doors and the eating area of the family room.

OPTIONAL BASEMENT

20

Design V12737

Square Footage: 1,796

L

● You will be able to build this distinctive, modified U-shaped one-story home on a relatively narrow site. But, then, if you so wished, with the help of your architect and builder you may want to locate the garage to the side of the house. Inside, the living potential is just great. The interior U-shaped kitchen handily services the dining and family rooms and nook. A rear covered porch functions ideally with the family room while the formal living room has its own terrace. Three bedrooms and two baths highlight the sleeping zone (or make it two bedrooms and a study). Notice the strategic location of the washroom, laundry, two storage closets and the basement stairs.

Design V12573
Square Footage: 2,747

L **D**

● A Tudor ranch! Combining brick and wood for an elegant look. It has a living/dining room measuring 32' by 13', large indeed. It is fully appointed with a traditional fireplace and built-in shelves, flanked by diagonally paned windows. There's much more! There is a family room with a raised hearth fireplace and sliding glass doors that open onto the terrace. A U-shaped kitchen has lots of built-ins . . . a range, an oven, a desk. Plus a separate breakfast nook. The sleeping facilities consist of three family bedrooms plus an elegant master bedroom suite. A conveniently located laundry with a folding counter is in the service entrance. Adjacent to the laundry is a washroom. The corner of the plan has a study or make it a fifth bedroom if you prefer.

Design V12746
Square Footage: 2,790

D

● This impressive one-story will be the talk-of-the-town. And not surprisingly, either. It embodies all of the elements to assure a sound investment and years of happy family livability. The projecting living room with its stucco, simulated wood beams and effective window treatment adds a dramatic note. Sunken by two steps, this room will enjoy privacy. The massive double front doors are sheltered by the covered porch and lead to the spacious entry hall. The interior is particularly well-zoned. The large, rear gathering room will cater to the family's gregarious instincts. Outdoor enjoyment can be obtained on the three terraces. Also, a study is available for those extra quiet moments. Be sure to observe the plan closely for all of the other fine features.

Design V11989

Square Footage: 2,282

L D

● High style with a plan as contemporary as today and tomorrow. There is, indeed, a feeling of coziness that emanates from the ground-hugging qualities of this picturesque home. Inside, there is livability galore. There's the sunken living room and the separate dining room to function as the family's formal living area. Then, over-looking the rear yard, there's the informal living area with its beamed ceiling family room, kitchen and adjacent breakfast room.

Design V12378

Square Footage: 2,580

● If yours is a preference for an exterior that exudes both warmth and formality, the styling of English Tudor may suit your fancy. A host of architectural features blend together to produce this delightfully appealing exterior. Notice the interesting use of contrasting exterior materials. Don't overlook the two stylish chimneys. The manner in which the interior functions to provide the fine living patterns is outstanding. Each of four main rooms — look out on the rear terrace.

Design V12129
Square Footage: 2,057

● This four bedroom home is zoned for convenient living. The sleeping area, with its two full baths and plenty of closets, will have a lot of privacy. The formal living and dining rooms function together and may be completely by-passed when desired. The informal living areas are grouped together and overlook the rear yard. The family room with its beamed ceiling is but a step from the kitchen. The U-shaped kitchen is handy to both the breakfast and dining rooms.

TERRACE

FAMILY RM.
11⁴ x 17⁰

LIVING RM.
18⁰ x 12⁰

BED RM.
10⁰ x 13⁰

MASTER
BED RM.
13⁰ x 11⁰

RAISED HEARTH

BEAMED CEILING

SLIDING DOOR

ENTRY

BATH

KIT.
11⁴ x 10⁴

DINING
11⁸ x 11⁰

STUDY
BED RM.
9⁶ x 10⁰

BED RM.
10⁸ x 10⁰

MUD RM.

P.R.

ENTRANCE
COURT

GARAGE
21⁴ x 23⁴

60'-0"

60'-0"

Design V12170

Square Footage: 1,646

● An L-shaped home with
an enchanting Olde English
styling. The wavy-edged siding, the similated beams, the
diamond lite windows, the
unusual brick pattern and
the interesting roof lines all
are elements which set the
character of authenticity.
The center entry routes traffic directly to the formal living and sleeping zones of the
house. Between the kitchen-
family room area and the attached two-car garage is the
mud room. Here is the
washer and dryer with the
extra powder room nearby.
The family room is highlighted by the beamed ceilings,
the raised hearth fireplace
and sliding glass doors to the
rear terrace. The work center with its abundance of
cupboard space will be fun
in which to function. Four
bedrooms, two full baths and
good closet space are features of the sleeping area.

Design V12678
Square Footage: 1,971

L **D**

● If you've ever desired to have a large country kitchen in your home then this is the design for you. The features of this room are many, indeed. Begin your long list with the island range with snack bar, pantry and broom closets, eating area with sliding glass doors leading to a covered porch, adjacent mud room with laundry facilities and access to the garage, raised hearth fireplace and conversation area with built-in desk on one side and shelves on the other. Now that is some multi-purpose room! There are formal living and dining rooms, too. Two and a half baths, all grouped around the living and sleeping areas. Review the rest of this plan which is surrounded by a delightful Tudor facade. It will surely prove to be a remarkable home to live in for the entire family.

Design V12728
Square Footage: 1,825

L **D**

● Your family's new lifestyle will surely flourish in this charming, L-shaped English adaptation. The curving front driveway produces an impressive approach. A covered front porch shelters the centered entry hall which effectively routes traffic to all areas. The fireplace is the focal point of the spacious, formal living and dining area. The kitchen is strategically placed to service the dining room and any informal eating space developed in the family room. In addition to the two full baths of the sleeping area, there is a handy washroom at the entrance from the garage. A complete, first floor laundry is nearby and has direct access to the yard. Sliding glass doors permit easy movement to the outdoor terrace and side porch. Don't overlook the basement and its potential for the development of additional livability and/or storage.

Design V12286

First Floor: 1,496 square feet
Second Floor: 751 square feet
Total: 2,247 square feet

● Here is a subtly styled Tudor design with complete one-floor livability plus two bonus bedrooms upstairs. It retains all the appearance of a one-story with a living room and family/dining room to accommodate all occasions. The convenient kitchen has a pass-through to the nook, which features sliding glass doors to the terrace. The two first-floor bedrooms have an abundance of closet space.

Design V12374

Square Footage: 1,919

● This English adaptation will never grow old. There is, indeed, much here to please the eye for many a year to come. The wavy-edged siding contrasts pleasingly with the diagonal pattern of brick below. The diamond lites of the windows create their own special effect. The projecting brick wall creates a pleasant court outside the covered front porch. The floor plan is well-zoned with the three bedrooms and two baths comprising a distinct sleeping wing. Flanking the entrance hall is the formal living room and the informal, multi-purpose family room. The large dining room is strategically located. The mud room area is adjacent to the extra washroom and the stairs to the basement.

Design V12245
First Floor: 2,855 square feet
Second Floor: 955 square feet
Total: 3,810 square feet

D

● The graciousness of this impressive English country house will endure for generations. The fine proportions, the exquisite architectural detailing and the interesting configuration are among the elements that create such an overwhelming measure of true character. The interior of this home will be as dramatic as the exterior. The recessed front entrance opens into a spacious, formal entrance hall. From here traffic patterns flow efficiently to all areas of the house. The garden view shows the three spacious outdoor terrace areas.

Design V12317

Square Footage: 3,161

● Here's a rambling English manor with its full measure of individuality. Its fine proportions and irregular shape offer even the most casual of passers-by delightful views of fine architecture. The exterior boasts an interesting use of varying materials. In addition to the brick work, there is vertical siding, wavy-edged horizontal siding and stucco. Three massive chimneys provide each of the three major wings with a fireplace. The overhanging roof provides the cover for the long front porch. Note the access to both the foyer as well as the service hall. The formal living room, with its sloping beamed ceiling, and fireplace flanked by bookshelves and cabinets, will be cozy, indeed. Study rest of plan. It's outstanding. Don't miss the three fireplaces and three full baths.

Design V12387
Square Footage: 2,744

● This rambling Tudor design will not fail to excite even the most casual of visitors. Its inviting facade is enhanced by its distinctive configuration. But such an appealing exterior is only a prelude to what the interior has to offer. Zoned for privacy, the four bedroom, 2½ bath sleeping area is outstanding. To the right of the entrance hall is the sunken living room which has a most commanding fireplace. The efficient kitchen effectively services the sunken dining room and the spacious breakfast room. Far removed from the sleeping and formal living areas is the beamed ceiling family room. Indoor-outdoor living relationships are delightfully maintained with utilization of those sliding glass doors to the strategically located terrace. Observe laundry, washroom and basement.

Design V12385
Square Footage: 2,100

● The charm of Tudor styled exterior adaptations is difficult to beat. Here is a hip-roof version which highlights the effective use of stucco, patterned brick and exposed beam work. The varying roof planes and the massive chimney, along with the recessed front entrance enhance the appeal. A study of the floor plan is most revealing. Excellent zoning is readily apparent.

Design V12613
Square Footage: 2,132

● A classic Tudor! With prominent wood and stucco styling. And unique features throughout. Start with the sunken living room where an attractive railing has replaced the anticipated hallway wall. For more good looks, a traditional fireplace with an attached woodbox and sliding glass doors that open onto the terrace. There's a formal dining room, too, also with access onto the terrace. Together these rooms form a gracious center for entertaining! For casual times, a family room with a beamed ceiling, fireplace and summer porch. And a work-efficient kitchen plus a roomy breakfast nook.

Design V12629

First Floor: 1,555 square feet
Second Floor: 1,080 square feet
Total: 2,635 square feet

● This home will really be fun in which to live. In addition to the sizeable living, dining and family rooms, many extras will be found. There are two fireplaces one to serve each of the formal and the informal areas. The back porch is a delightful extra. It will be great to relax in after a long hard day. Note two half baths on the first floor and two full baths on the second floor to serve the three bedrooms. Count the number of closets in the spacious upstairs. The door from the bedroom leads to storage over garage.

Design V12630

First Floor: 1,491 square feet
Second Floor: 788 square feet
Total: 2,279 square feet

● This distinctive version of Tudor styling will foster many years of prideful ownership and unique, yet practical living patterns. The main portion of the facade is delightfully symmetrical. Inside, the family living will focus on the 29 foot great room with its dramatic fireplace and beamed ceiling. The kitchen is outstanding with snack bar and dining nook nearby. Note the three large bedrooms each having its own dressing room. Extra storage space is available above the garage or may be developed into another room. Oversized garage includes a built-in workbench. Study plan carefully. It has much to offer.

Design V12273

First Floor: 1,357 square feet
Second Floor: 1,065 square feet
Total: 2,422 square feet

● Note the traditional charm of this design. Formal/informal dining areas are offered in this plan. The large living room with fireplace will provide a lot of enjoyment. A full bath, storage area and your option of a library/bedroom also are featured on this floor. The second floor has a large master bedroom with a full bath. Two bedrooms and another full bath will serve the rest of the family.

This is an exquisitely styled Tudor tri-level designed to serve its happy occupants for many years. The contrasting use of material surely makes the exterior eye-catching.

Design V12847

Main Level: 1,874 square feet
Lower Level: 1,131 square feet
Total: 3,005 square feet

L **D**

Design V12773

Main Level: 1,157 square feet
Upper Level: 950 square feet
Lower Level: 912 square feet
Total: 3,019 square feet

● Here is an exquisitely styled Tudor tri-level which retains the low-slung characteristics of a one-story house. The contrasting use of material surely makes the exterior eye-catching. Another outstanding feature will be the covered front porch. A delightful way to enter this home. Many fine features also will be found inside this design. Formal living and dining room, U-shaped kitchen with snack bar and family room find themselves located on the main level. Two of the three bedrooms are on the upper level with two baths. Activities room, third bedroom and hobby/sewing room are on the lower level — a real bonus. Notice the built-in planter on the lower level which is visible from the other two levels. A powder room and a washroom both are on the main level. A study is on the upper level which is a great place for a quiet retreat. The basement will be convenient for storage of any bulk items.

Design V13346

Square Footage: 2,032

● This home boasts a delightful Tudor exterior with a terrific interior floor plan. Though compact, there's plenty of living space: large study with fireplace, gathering room, dining room, and breakfast room. The master bedroom has an attached bath with whirlpool tub. Note the double walk-in closets.

Design V12961

Square Footage: 3,049

● Another interesting and charming L-shaped one-story. This time with Tudor exterior styling. Contributing to the pleasing eye-appeal are the varying roof planes, the cornice detailing, the brick exterior with those accents of stucco and beam-work, the window treatment, and that dramatic front door with its surrounding glass area. The brick wall forming the front courtyard is a nice touch. Inside, the spacious foyer with its slate floor routes traffic most effectively. Highlights include the media room, the clutter room, the country kitchen, the 29 foot formal living-dining room area, and the large master bedroom with its luxurious master bath. Functioning with the country kitchen and clutter room is the glass-walled greenhouse. Its 130 sq. ft. is included in the total above.

Design V12278

First Floor: 1,804 square feet
Second Floor: 939 square feet
Total: 2,743 square feet

● The Tudor charm is characterized in each of these three one-and-a-half story designs. Study each of them for its own special features.

Design V12674

First Floor: 1,922 square feet
Second Floor: 890 square feet
Total: 2,812 square feet

● This delightful Tudor design's configuration permits a flexible orientation on its site with either the garage doors or the front doors facing the street. One-and-a-half-story designs offer great flexibilty in their livability. Complete livability is offered on the first floor; by utilizing the second floor another three bedrooms and bath are available. First floor features include a sunken family room with fireplace and built-in bookshelves, rear living room with sliding glass doors to the terrace, large formal dining room, first floor laundry and two washrooms.

● This is a most interesting home; both inside and out. Its L-shape with covered front porch and diamond-lite windows is appealing. Its floor plan with extra bedroom, lounge and storage room is exceptional.

Design V12241

First Floor: 1,617 square feet
Second Floor: 1,348 square feet
Total: 2,965 square feet

Design V12372
First Floor: 2,634 square feet
Second Floor: 819 square feet
Total: 3,453 square feet

● What a wonderfully unique design — one-story livability with bonus space upstairs. The Tudor styling and the varying roof planes, along with its U-shape, add to the air of distinction. From the driveway, steps lead past a big raised planter up to the enclosed entrance court. A wide overhanging roof shelters the massive patterned double doors flanked by diamond paned sidelites. The living room is outstanding. It is located a distance from other living areas and is quite spacious. The centered fireplace is the dominant feature, while sliding glass doors open from each end onto out-door terraces. The kitchen, too, is spacious and functions well. Two eating areas are nearby. It is worth noting that each of the major first floor rooms have direct access to the outdoor ter-races. Note second floor suite which includes a lounge with built-in book cabinets.

Design V12391

First Floor: 2,496 square feet
Second Floor: 958 square feet
Total: 3,454 square feet

● This impressive English adaptation allows complete one-story convenience with additional sleeping and study space on a second floor. Note the large living areas: family room with raised hearth fireplace and beamed ceiling, L-shaped living/dining room area with bay window — all arranged around the kitchen and breakfast room. Three first floor bedrooms have access to two full baths while an entry hall powder room serves guests nicely. The large three-car garage means no lack of space for the family vehicles and provides a service entrance to the laundry.

84' - 8"

53' - 0"

TERRACE

MASTER BEDROOM
12⁴ x 20⁶

TUB

BATH

VANITY

SLOPED CEILING

SLOPED CEILING

SEAT

DRESSING RM.

FAMILY RM.
19¹⁰ x 13⁴ + BAY

DW   S

KITCHEN
10⁰ x 13⁴

REFG.

BRKFST.
8⁰ x 10⁰

LT W. D.

BEDROOM
11⁰ x 11⁰

WALK-IN CLOSET

SHELVES

MUD RM.

STORAGE

RAISED HEARTH

OVENS

COOK TOP

PANTRY

DN

CL

WASH RM.

BATH

VANITY

CONSOLE

RAILING

LIVING RM.
19⁴ x 13⁴

RAIL

SLOPED CEILING

DN

DINING RM.
12⁰ x 13⁴

CURB

LINEN

CL

DN

RAIL

CL

BEDROOM
11⁰ x 13⁶

BEDROOM STUDY
11⁸ x 10²

FOYER

SLOPED CEILING

CL

PORCH

GARAGE
21⁰ x 21²

Design V12877
Square Footage: 2,612

D

● Here's a dramatic, Post-Modern exterior with a popular plan featuring an outstanding master bedroom suite. The bedroom itself is spacious, has a sloped ceiling, a large walk-in closet and sliding glass doors to the terrace. Now examine the bath and dressing area. Two large closets, twin vanities, built-in seat and a dramatically presented corner tub are present. The tub will be a great place to spend the evening hours after a long, hard day. Along with this bedroom, there are three more served by a full bath. The living area of this plan has the formal areas in the front and the informal areas in the rear. Both have a fireplace. The spacious work center is efficiently planned.

Design V12966
Square Footage: 3,403

● This Tudor adaptation is as dramatic inside as it is outside. As a visitor approaches the front courtyard there is much that catches the eye. The interesting roof lines, the appealing window treatment, the contrasting exterior materials and their textures, the inviting panelled front door and the massive twin chimneys with their protruding clay pots. Inside, the spacious foyer with its sloping ceiling looks up into the balcony-type lounge. It also looks down the open stairwell to the lower level area. From the foyer, traffic flows conveniently to other areas. The focal point of the living zone is the delightful atrium. Both the formal living room and the informal family room feature a fireplace. Each of the full baths highlights a tub and shower, a vanity and twin lavatories. Note the secondary access to the basement adjacent to the door to three car garage. Lounge adds an additional 284 sq. ft.

76'-10"
76'-0"

TERRACE

TERRACE

MASTER
BED RM.
15⁰ x 14⁰

WALK-IN
CL.

FAMILY RM.
13⁴ x 23⁴

KIT.
14⁴ x 10⁰

BREAKFAST
10⁴ x 10⁰

DINING RM.
13⁰ x 10⁴

TERRACE

SLIDING
DOORS

BATH

REFG.

D.W.

S

PANTRY DESK

PANTRY

VANITY

RANGE

OVEN

CHINA

47'-10"
44'-0"

BED RM.
11⁰ x 11⁰

LIN.

W. T D.

LAUNDRY

RAISED
HEARTH

PDR.
RM.

LIVING RM.
23⁴ x 13⁰

BATH

WOOD
BOX

DN.

CL.

BED RM.
11⁰ x 15⁴

LIN.

CL.

ENTRY

VEST.

BED RM.
12⁰ x 12⁰

CURB

GARAGE
23⁴ x 22⁸

Design V12142
Square Footage: 2,450

● Adaptations of Old England have become increasingly popular in today's building scene. And little wonder; for many of these homes when well-designed have a very distinctive charm. Here is certainly a home which will be like no other in its neighborhood. Its very shape adds an extra measure of uniqueness. And inside, there is all the livability the exterior seems to fortell. The sleeping wing has four bedrooms, two full baths and the laundry room — just where the soiled linen originates. The location of the family room is an excellent one. It is convenient for children because their traffic usually flows between family room and bedrooms. The spacious formal living and dining area will enjoy its privacy and be great fun to furnish.

FRENCH FACADES ...

have an outstanding charm of their own. Their exterior appeal seems to announce a graciously formal lifestyle. The hip-roof is a distinguishing characteristic of the one-story French house. Shuttered casement windows, brick quoins at the corners of the house, cornice dentils, double front doors with raised panels, massive chimneys and cupolas are among other features that establish the style. In many cases arched window heads and shutters, recessed front entrances, wrought iron grillwork, carriage lamps and entry courts add an extra measure of appeal. In addition to the variety of interior living features, it is worth noting the outdoor living potential.

Design V12220
Square Footage: 2,646

L D

● The gracious formality of this home is reminiscent of a popularly accepted French styling. The hip-roof, the brick quoins, the cornice details, the arched window heads, the distinctive shutters, the recessed double front doors, the massive center chimney, and the delightful flower court are all features which set the dramatic appeal of this home. This floor plan is a favorite of many. The four bedroom, two bath sleeping wing is a zone by itself. Further, the formal living and dining rooms are ideally located. For entertaining they function well together and look out upon the pleasant flower court. Overlooking the raised living terrace at the rear are the family and breakfast rooms and work center. Don't miss the laundry, extra wash room and work shop in garage.

● You'll want life's biggest investment — the purchase of a home — to be a source of everlasting enjoyment. To assure such a rewarding dividend, make every effort to match your family's desired living patterns with a workable plan. Of course, you'll want your plan enveloped by a stunning exterior. Consider both the interior and exterior of this design. Each is impressive. The sleeping zone comprises a separate wing and is accessible from both living and kitchen areas. There are four bedrooms, two full baths and plenty of closets. The 32 foot wide living and dining area will be just great fun to decorate. Then, there is the large family room with its raised hearth fireplace and sliding glass doors to the terrace. Note the fine laundry with wash room nearby. The extra curb area in the garage is great for storing small garden equipment.

● This French design is surely impressive. The exterior appearance will brighten any area with its French roof, paned-glass windows, masonry brick privacy wall and double front doors. The inside is just as appealing. Note the unique placement of rooms and features. The entry hall is large and leads to each of the areas in this plan. The formal dining room is outstanding and guests can enter through the entry hall. While serving one can enter by way of the butler's pantry (notice it's size and that it has a sink). To the right of the entry is a sizable parlor. Then there is the gathering room with fireplace, sliding glass doors and adjacent study. The work center is also outstanding. There is the U-shaped kitchen, island range, snack bar, breakfast nook, pantry plus wash room and large laundry near service entrance. Basement stairs are also nearby.

Design V12740
Square Footage: 2,535

Design V12779
Square Footage: 3,225

L D

49

Design V12851
Square Footage: 2,739

● This spacious one-story has a classic Country French hip roof. The front entrance creates a charming entry. Beyond the covered porch is an octagonal foyer. A closet, shelves and powder room are contained in the foyer. All of the living areas overlook the rear yard.

Sliding glass doors open each of these areas to the rear terrace. Their features include a fireplace in the living room, skylight in the dining room and a second set of sliding glass doors in the family room leading to a side covered porch. An island range and other built-

ins are featured in the spacious, front kitchen. Adjacent is the breakfast room which will be used for informal dining. The four bedrooms and bath facilities are all clustered in one wing. Note the bay windows in the master bedroom, breakfast room and the three-car garage.

90'-10"

32'-10"

TERRACE

TERRACE

MASTER BED RM. 15⁰ x 13⁶

BATH

BATH

FAMILY RM. 21⁴ x 12⁶

KIT. 12⁰ x 13⁶

MUD RM.

GARAGE 23⁸ x 23⁴

CURB

CL

CL

BEAMED CEILING

RAISED HEARTH

AIR COND.

OVEN

BAR

FOYER

LIVING RM. 19⁸ x 13⁶

DINING RM. 11⁸ x 13⁶

BED RM. 11⁶ x 15²

BED RM. 13⁶ x 11⁶

PORCH

ENTRY COURT

OPTIONAL BASEMENT

CL

FOYER

LIVING RM.

DN.

DN.

PORCH

Design V11892

Square Footage: 2,036

L **D**

● The romance of French Provincial is captured here by the hip-roof masses, the charm of the window detailing, the brick quoins at the corners, the delicate dentil work at the cornices, the massive centered chimney, and the recessed double front doors. The slightly raised entry court completes the picture. The basic floor plan is a favorite of many. And little wonder, for all areas work well together, while still maintaining a fine degree of separation of functions. The highlight of the interior, perhaps, will be the sunken living room. The family room, with its beamed ceiling, will not be far behind in its popularity. The separate dining room, mud room, efficient kitchen, complete the livability.

Design V11797
Square Footage: 1,618

● A house to be looked at and lived in —that's what this impressively formal French Provincial adaptation represents. The front court, just inside the brick wall with its attractive iron gate, sets the patterns of formality that are so apparent inside. The formal living and dining rooms separate the sleeping area from the kitchen/family room area. A pass-thru facilitates serving of informal snacks in family room. The three bedrooms will serve the average sized family perfectly. Details for an optional basement are included with this plan.

Design V11272
Square Footage: 1,690

● Designed for the family who wants the refinement of French Provincial, but on a small scale. Keynoting its charm are the long shutters, the delightful entrance porch with its wood posts, the interesting angles of the hip roof and the pair of paneled garage doors. Behind this formal facade is a simple, efficient, up-to-date floor plan. The living patterns for the family occupying this house will be toward the rear where the long living terrace is just a step outside the glass sliding doors of the formal and informal living areas. The two bathrooms in the sleeping area share back-to-back plumbing, which is economical.

Design V11362
Square Footage: 1,896

● This dramatic L-shaped French adaptation is distinctive indeed. The projecting bedroom wing, consisting of three bedrooms, adds to the exterior appeal. Inside, the traffic patterns are excellent. The blueprints show optional basement details as well as an optional fireplace in the living room. This is most definitely a design to please all family members.

52

● Here are three delightful French Provincial adaptations, any one of which would surely be an impressive addition to a neighborhood. Each design features a sleeping wing of four bedrooms, two full baths, and plenty of closets. Further, each design has a separate first floor laundry with an adjacent wash room. Observe the sunken living room . . .

Design V11345
Square Footage: 2,026

Design V12134
Square Footage: 2,530

. . . and the beamed ceiling family room of Design V12134 above. Don't miss its big dressing room or raised hearth fire-place. Design V11345 has both its family and living rooms located to the rear and functioning with the terrace. Design V11054 has an efficient work area and a large formal dining room.

Design V11054
Square Footage: 2,080

Design V11330
Square Footage: 1,820

● A dramatic, formal exterior uses strong horizontal cornice lines to accentuate its low-slung qualities. The brick quoins at the corners, the paneled shutters, the ornamental iron and the hip-roof contribute to a distinctly continental flavor. Inside, the various areas are clearly defined. The bedrooms and living room are away from the noise of the family and service areas. The living room can double as a den-study. The U-shaped kitchen with pass-thru counters serves both the family room and dining area conveniently. The sleeping wing is highlighted by three sizable bedrooms, two baths and an abundance of wardrobe storage facilities. Optional fireplace details are included with the plan.

Design V11326

Square Footage: 2,014

● This pleasing, French Provincial adaptation has an extremely practical basic floor plan which contains many of those "extras" that contribute so much to good living. Among the features that make this such an outstanding home are: two fireplaces—one with raised hearth and wood box, first floor laundry, extra washroom, powder room, snack bar, separate dining room, partial basement, garage storage and workbench. With the four bedrooms and the formal and informal living areas, there is plenty of space in which the large family may move around and enjoy their surroundings.

Design V12342

First Floor: 2,824 square feet
Second Floor: 1,013 square feet
Total: 3,837 square feet

Design V11228

First Floor: 2,583 square feet
Second Floor: 697 square feet
Total: 3,280 square feet

L **D**

● This beautiful house has a wealth of detail taken from the rich traditions of French Regency design. The roof itself is a study in pleasant dormers and the hips and valleys of a big flowing area. A close examination of the plan shows the careful arrangement of space for privacy as well as good circulation of traffic. The spacious formal entrance hall sets the stage for good zoning. The informal living area is highlighted by the updated version of the old country kitchen. Observe the fireplace, built-in wood box, and china cabinet. While there is a half-story devoted to the master bedroom suite, this home functions more as a one-story country estate design than as a 1½ story.

Design V11784
Square Footage: 2,686

● Truly impressive, and surely a home of which dreams are made. Yet, its basic rectangular shape, its economical use of space, its tremendous livability and its outstanding design make it a worthy lifetime investment. Consider the features which will serve you so well and make you such a proud home-owner for so many years to come. The pleasant formality of the front entrance invites one through the double front doors to a spacious interior. Study the zoning. The formal living and dining rooms will enjoy their deserved privacy and function with their own rear outdoor living facilities. The family room and kitchen function together and have an enclosed court.

● The elegance of pleasing proportion and delightful detailing has seldom been better exemplified than by this classic French country manor adaptation. Approaching the house across the drive court, the majesty of this multi-roofed structure is breathtaking, indeed. An outstanding feature is the maid's suite. It is located above the garage and is easily reached by use of the covered porch connecting the laundry room's service entrance to the garage. If desired, it would make an excellent studio, quiet retreat or even a game room.

Design V11993
First Floor: 2,658 square feet
Master Suite: 840 square feet
Maid's Suite: 376 square feet
Total: 3,874 square feet

Design V12212

Square Footage: 3,577

L

● From the graceful, curving drive court to the formal living room, this expansive, hospitable French country house welcomes the visitor. Truely a house for gracious living. List your favorite features.

TERRACE

DINING RM.
11⁰ x 13⁰

GATHERING RM.
18⁰ x 17⁴

TERRACE

MASTER BED RM.
14⁴ x 13⁰

NOOK
11⁰ x 8⁰

TERRACE

KITCHEN
11⁰ x 9⁸

BATH

LAUNDRY
9⁴ x 7⁰

SERVICE ENTRANCE

ENTRY

STUDY-BED RM.
12⁴ · 10⁰ x 12⁰

BATH

CURB

PORCH

BED RM.
14⁴ x 11⁰

GARAGE
20⁸ x 21⁸

57'-4"

58'-0"

Design V12738
Square Footage: 1,898

● Impressive architectural work is indeed apparent in this three bedroom home. The three foot high entrance court wall, the high pitched roof and the paned glass windows all add to this home's exterior appeal. It is also apparent that the floor plan is very efficient with the side, U-shaped kitchen and nook with two pantry closets. Overlooking the backyard, the dining and gathering rooms will serve your every family occasion. Three (or make it two with a study) bedrooms and two baths are in the sleeping wing. Indoor-outdoor living also will be enjoyed in this home with a dining terrace off the nook and a living terrace off the gathering room and master bedroom. Note the fireplace in the gathering room and bay window in dining room. This design will be very livable.

SPANISH & WESTERN VARIATIONS . . .

can be found to offer a delightful change of pace wherever built. The appealing exterior design highlights include stucco surfaces, arched window heads, porch or courtyard columns, flared chimneys, exposed rafter tails, tiled roofs, window grilles, massive panelled doors, wide overhanging roofs, covered porches and private courtyards. Sloping and beamed ceilings are often among the focal points of these spacious interiors. The rambling nature of the floor plan configurations is consistent with the wide, open spaces from which these designs emanated. This, of course, results in a selection of houses with virtually unlimited livability potential.

Design V12236
Square Footage: 2,307

● Living in this Spanish adaptation will truly be fun for the whole family. It will matter very little whether the backdrop matches the mountains above, becomes the endless prairie, turns out to be the rolling farmland, or is the backdrop of a suburban area. A family's flair for distinction will be satisfied by this picturesque exterior, while its requirements for everyday living will be gloriously catered to. The hub of the plan will be the kitchen-family room area. The beamed ceiling and raised hearth fireplace will contribute to the cozy, informal atmosphere. The separate dining room and the sunken living room function together formally. The master bedroom will enjoy its privacy from the three children's rooms located at the opposite end of the plan.

Design V12820
Square Footage: 2,261

L D

● A privacy wall around the courtyard with pool and trellised planter area is a gracious area by which to enter this one-story design. The Spanish flavor is accented by the grillework and the tiled roof. Interior livability has a great deal to offer. The front living room has sliding glass doors which open to the entrance court; the adjacent dining room features a bay window. Informal activities will be enjoyed in the rear family room. Its many features include a sloped, beamed ceiling, raised hearth fireplace, sliding glass doors to the terrace and a snack bar for those very informal meals. A laundry and powder room are adjacent to the U-shaped kitchen. The sleeping wing can remain quiet away from the plan's activity centers. Notice the three-car garage with an extra storage area.

Design V12670

Square Footage: 3,058

L **D**

● A centrally located interior atrium is one of the most interesting features of this Spanish design. The atrium has a built-in seat and will bring light to its adjacent rooms; living, dining and breakfast. Beyond the foyer, sunken one step, is a tiled reception hall that includes a powder room. This area leads to the sleeping wing and up one step to the family room. Overlooking the family room is a railed lounge, 279 square feet, which can be used for various activities. The work center area will be convenient to work in.

Design V12950
Square Footage: 2,559

● A natural desert dweller, this stucco, tile-roofed beauty is equally comfortable in any clime. Inside, there's a well-planned design. Common living areas — gathering room, formal dining room, and breakfast room — are offset by a quiet study that could be used as a bedroom or guest room. A master suite features two walk-in closets, a double vanity, and whirlpool spa. The two-car garage has a service entrance; close by is an adequate laundry area and a pantry. Notice the warming hearth in the gathering room and the snack bar area for casual dining.

Design V13421
Square Footage: 2,145

● Split-bedroom planning makes the most of a one-story design. In this case the master suite is on the opposite side of the house from two family bedrooms. Gourmets can rejoice at the abundant work space in the U-shaped kitchen and will appreciate the natural light afforded by the large bay window in the breakfast room. A formal living room has a sunken conversation area with a cozy fireplace as its focus. The rear covered porch can be reached through sliding glass doors in the family room.

Design V13413
Square Footage: 2,517

● Though distinctly Southwest in design, this home has some features that are universally appealing. Note, for instance, the central gallery, perpendicular to the raised entry hall, and running almost the entire width of the house. An L-shaped, angled kitchen serves the breakfast room and family room in equal fashion. A cozy study is nearby. Sleeping areas are found in three bedrooms and exquisite master suite.

Design V12949

Square Footage: 2,922

D

● Spanish and western influences take center stage in a long, low stucco design. You'll enjoy the Texas-sized gathering room that opens to a formal dining area and has a snack bar through to the kitchen. More casual dining is accommodated in the nook. A luxurious master suite is graced by plenty of closet space and a soothing whirlpool spa. Besides another bedroom and full bath, there is a media room that could easily double as a third bedroom or guest room.

Design V12922
Square Footage: 3,505

● Loaded with custom features, this plan seems to have everything imaginable. There's an enormous sunken gathering room and cozy study. The country-style kitchen contains an efficient work area, as well as space for relaxing in the morning and sitting rooms. Two nice-sized bedrooms and a luxurious master suite round out the plan.

Design V13416
Square Footage: 1,375

● Here's a Southwestern design that will be economical to build and a pleasure to occupy. The front door opens into a spacious living room with corner fireplace and dining room with coffered ceiling. The near-by kitchen serves both easily. A few steps away is the cozy media room with built-in space for audio-visual equipment. Down the hall are two bedrooms and two baths; the master features a whirlpool. A guest room is found across the entry court and includes a fireplace and sloped ceiling.

Design V13419

Square Footage: 1,965

BRKFST RM
11⁸ x 7⁸

COVERED PORCH

WHIRLPOOL

MASTER
BEDROOM
14⁸ x 15¹⁰

KITCHEN
11⁸ x 11⁸

REF'G

DW

RANGE

DINING
7⁸ x 10⁰

LIVING RM
12² x 15⁸

BATH

UP

S

WALK-IN
CLOSET

SNACK BAR
S

BEDROOM
10⁶ x 10⁰

BATH

LEDGE

LIN CL

CL

FAMILY RM
19⁴ x 13⁰

CL

FOYER

CL

CL

PORCH

CURB

WASH
RM

COVERED
PORCH

BEDROOM
9¹⁰ x 10¹⁰

BEDROOM
10⁶ x 11⁴

W D

LAUND/
MECH

GARAGE
19⁴ x 20⁰

WH

FURN

54'-0"

56'-4"

● This attractive, multi-gabled exterior houses a compact, livable interior. The entry foyer effectively routes traffic to all areas: left to the family room and kitchen, straight back to the dining room and living room, and right to the four-bedroom sleeping area. The spacious family room provides an informal gathering space while the living and dining rooms are perfect for formal occasions. The highlight of the sleeping area is the master bedroom with its whirlpool, walk-in closet and view of the back yard.

Design V13400 Square Footage: 2,784

Design V13401
Square Footage: 2,850

● This Southwestern design caters to families who enjoy outdoor living and entertaining. Doors open onto shaded terraces from the master bedroom and living room, while a sliding glass door in the family room accesses a smaller terrace. Also notice the outdoor bar with pass-through window to the kitchen.

● Abundant terrace space favors an outdoor lifestyle in this charming one-story. Each room has access to a porch or terrace; think of the added entertainment possibilities! Interior highlights include corner fireplaces in the master suite and family room, a dining room with bay window, and a regal master bath. Note the dramatic two-story foyer.

Design V13402

Square Footage: 3,212

● This one-story pairs the customary tile and stucco of Spanish design with a livable floor plan. The sunken living room with its open-hearth fireplace promises to be a cozy gathering place. For more casual occasions, there's a family room with fireplace off the entry foyer. Also noteworthy: a sizable kitchen and a sumptuous master suite.

66'-0"

62'-0"

TERRACE

COVERED PORCH

GATHERING RM.
16⁸ x 19⁴

MASTER BEDROOM
13⁰ x 13⁸

VANITY

DRSG. RM.

BATH

WALK-IN CLOSET

DINING RM.
12⁸ x 11⁰

SLOPED CEILING

6'-0" FLAT CEILING

BATH

TERRACE

BRKFST. RM.
10⁰ x 10⁸

OVENS

PASS THRU

REF'G

P'TRY

DN.

CL.

LIV.

CL.

KITCHEN
13⁸ x 10⁸

SNACK BAR

SLOPED CEILING

FOYER

CL.

OPEN

BEDROOM
10⁸ x 11⁴

BEDROOM
11⁴ x 11⁴

BC

DESK

DW

PORCH

PLANT LEDGE

W.R.

MUD RM.

D W

GARAGE
21⁴ x 21⁴

SLOPED CEILING

SLOPED CEILING

PLANT LEDGE

Design V12912
Square Footage: 1,864

● This modern design with smart Spanish styling incorporates careful zoning by room functions with lifestyle comfort. All three bedrooms, including a master bedroom suite, are isolated at one end of the one-story home for privacy and out of traffic patterns. Entry to a breakfast room and kitchen is possible through a mud room off the garage. That's good news for people carrying groceries from car to kitchen or people with muddy shoes during inclement weather. The modern kitchen includes a snack bar and cook top with multiple access to breakfast room, side foyer, and pass-thru to hallway. There's also a nearby formal dining room. A large rear gathering room features sloped ceiling and its own fireplace. Note the two-car garage and built-in plant ledge in front. Gabled end window treatment plus varied roof lines further enhance the striking appearance of this efficient design.

Design V12875

Square Footage: 1,913

L **D**

● This elegant Spanish design incorporates excellent indoor-outdoor living relationships for modern families who enjoy the sun and comforts of a well-planned new home. Note the overhead openings for rain and sun to fall upon a front garden, while a twin arched entry leads to the front porch and foyer. Inside the floor plan features a modern kitchen with pass-thru to a large gathering room with fireplace. Other features include a dining room, laundry room, a study off the foyer, plus three bedrooms including master bedroom with its own whirlpool.

Design V13412
Square Footage: 2,150

● Although typically Southwestern in design,
this home will bring style to any neighborhood.
Huge bay windows flood the front living and
dining rooms with plenty of natural light. An
amenity-filled kitchen with attached family room
will be the main gathering area, where the family works and relaxes together. Notice the fireplace, the island snack bar and walk-in pantry. A
split sleeping zone separates the master suite
with luxurious bath from the two family bedrooms. Also notice the covered porch off the
family room.

Design V13430
Square Footage: 2,394

● This dramatic design benefits from open planning. The centerpiece of the living area is a
sunken conversation pit which shares a through-
fireplace with the family room. The living room
and dining room share space beneath a sloped
ceiling. The open kitchen features a snack bar
and breakfast room and conveniently serves all
living areas. Split zoning in the sleeping area
places the private master suite to the left of the
plan and three more bedrooms, including one
with a bay window, to the right.

Design V12948

Square Footage: 1,830

● Styled for Southwest living, this home is a good choice in any region. Its highlights include: gathering room/dining room combination with fireplace, a uniquely shaped kitchen, luxurious master suite, and a study or alternate third bedroom. Notice the covered porch with open skylights.

Design V13423 Square Footage: 2,571

● This spacious Southwestern home will be a pleasure to come home to. Immediately off the foyer are the dining room and step-down living room with bay window. The highlight of the four-bedroom sleeping area is the master suite with porch access and a whirlpool for soaking away the day's worries. The informal living area features an enormous family room with fireplace and bay-windowed kitchen and breakfast room. Notice the snack bar pass-through to the family room.

COVERED PORCH

MASTER
BATH

WHIRLPOOL

MASTER
BEDROOM
13⁰ x 13⁸

SLOPED CEILING

FAMILY RM
12⁸ x 18⁶

SLOPED CEILING

BREAKFAST
7⁶ x 9⁴

WALK-IN
CLOSET

SLOPED CEILING

OVENS

SNACK BAR

KIT.
9⁴ x 13⁴

DW

COOK TOP

BEDROOM
9⁸ x 9¹⁰

CL

SLOPED CEILING

PANTRY

REFS

BATH

PDR
RM

CL

HALF WALL

DINING
13⁴ x 9⁶

BAR

LINEN

BEDROOM
12⁰ x 10⁰

LT

LAUND

STUDY
9⁸ x 9⁶

W
D

SLOPED CEILING

WH   FURN   CL

CURB

DN

FOYER

HALF WALL

LIVING RM
13⁴ x 13⁴

COVERED PORCH

GARAGE
21⁴ x 19⁸

60'-0"

50'-0"

Design V13422

Square Footage: 1,932

● An enclosed entry garden
greets visitors to this charming
Southwestern home. Inside, the
foyer is flanked by formal and
informal living areas — a living
room and dining room to the
right and a cozy study to the
left. To the rear, a large family
room, breakfast room and open
kitchen have access to a
covered porch and overlook the
back yard. Notice the fireplace
and bay window. The three-
bedroom sleeping area includes
a master with a spacious bath
with whirlpool.

Design V13411

Square Footage: 2,441

● You'll love the entry to this Southwestern home — it creates a dramatic first impression and leads beautifully to the formal living and dining rooms. Beyond, look for an open family room and dining area in the same proximity as the kitchen. Sliding glass doors here open to a backyard patio. Take your choice of four bedrooms or five, depending on how you wish to use the optional room. The huge master suite is not to be missed.

COVERED TERRACE

MASTER BEDROOM
13⁶ x 20⁶

SLOPED CEILING

SLOPED CEILING

S WHIRLPOOL

MASTER BATH

WALK-IN CLOSET

CL

BEDROOM
11² x 10⁰

BREAKFAST
9⁰ x 5⁰

OVEN DW S

KIT.
11⁸ x 16⁰

SNACK BAR

BOOK TOP

REFG

PANTRY

CL

BEDROOM
11² x 13¹⁰

SLOPED CEILING

BATH

LINEN

FAMILY RM
19⁸ x 14⁰

SLOPED CEILING

DESK

LAUNDRY

D W

WASH RM

WH FURN

MECH RM

CL

CL

BEDROOM
11⁶ x 10⁰

SLOPED CEILING

NICHE

CURB

GARAGE
26⁴ x 21²

DINING RM
10⁴ x 10¹⁰

SLOPED CEILING

DN

DN DN

SLOPED CEILING

FOYER

COVERED PORCH

LIVING RM
15⁰ x 14⁰

64'-0"

60'-0"

Design V13415

Square Footage: 2,406

● Relax and enjoy the open floor plan of this lovely one-story. Its family room with fireplace and space for eating are a suitable complement to the formal living and dining rooms to the front of the house. There are four bedrooms, or three if you choose to make one a den, and 2½ baths. Don't miss the large pantry and convenient laundry area.

81

Design V12671
Square Footage: 1,589

L **D**

● A rustic exterior of this one-story home features vertical wood siding. The entry foyer is floored with flagstone and leads to the three areas of the plan: sleeping, living and work center. The sleeping area has three bedrooms, the master bedroom has sliding glass doors to the rear terrace. The living area, consisting of gathering and dining rooms, also has access to the terrace. The work center is efficiently planned. It houses the kitchen with snack bar, breakfast room with built-in china cabinet and stairs to the basement. This is a very livable plan.

Design V12594 Square Footage: 2,294

D

● A spectacular foyer! Fully 21' long, it offers double entry to the heart of this home . . . a 21' by 21' gathering room, complete with sloped ceiling, raised-hearth fireplace and sliding glass doors onto the terrace. There's a formal dining room, too. Plus a well-located study for solitude or undisturbed work. The kitchen features a snack bar and a breakfast nook with sliding doors onto the terrace. For more convenience, a pantry and first-floor laundry. In the master suite, a dressing room with entry to the bath, four closets and sliding doors onto the terrace! Two more bedrooms if you wish to convert the study, or one easily large enough for two children with a dressing area and private entry to the second bath.

Design V12528
Square Footage: 1,754

D

● This inviting, U-shaped western ranch adaptation offers outstanding living potential behind its double, front doors and flanking glass panels. In but 1,754 square feet there are three bedrooms, 2½ baths, a formal living room and an informal family room, an excellently functioning interior kitchen, an adjacent breakfast nook and good storage facilities. The open stairwell to the lower level basement can be an interesting, interior feature. Note raised-hearth fireplace and sloped ceiling.

Design V11223
Square Footage: 2,568

113'-4"

71'-0"

SWIMMING POOL

TERRACE

PORCH
8'9 x 16'0

LIVING RM.
17'6 x 28'0

DINING TERRACE

DINING RM.
12'0 x 13'6

FAMILY RM.
17'9 x 18'0

COOK PORCH

BAR-B-Q

PORCH
10'4 x 14'0

TERRACE

BED RM.
12'0 x 13'6

STORAGE

SNACK BAR

STORAGE

OVEN RANGE

WOOD GRILLE SCREEN

ENTRANCE HALL

MASTER BED RM.
15' x 13'6

KITCHEN
19'8 x 9'6

WASH RM.

BREAKFAST

DRY WASH.

D.W.

BATH

BED RM.
11'6 x 10'0

BATH

GARAGE
23'4 x 27'4

STORAGE

GARDEN FLOWER COURT

BED RM.
11'9 x 13'0

Design V12879 Living Area Including Atrium: 3,173 square feet
Upper Lounge/Balcony: 267 square feet
Total: 3,440 square feet

● This plush modern design seems to have it all, including an upper lounge, upper family room, and upper foyer. There's also an atrium with skylight centrally located downstairs. A modern kitchen with snack bar service to a breakfast room also enjoys its own greenhouse window. A deluxe master bedroom includes its own whirlpool and bay window. Three other bedrooms also are isolated at one end of the house downstairs to allow privacy and quiet. A spacious family room in the rear enjoys its own raised-hearth fireplace and view of a rear covered terrace. A front living room with its own fireplace looks out upon a side garden court and the central atrium. There's also a formal dining room situated between the kitchen and living room, plus a three-car garage, covered porches, and sizable laundry with washroom just off the garage.

Design V12200
Square Footage: 1,695

● The two plans featured here are both housed in this L-shaped ranch home. Its exterior shows a Spanish influence by utilizing a stucco exterior finish, grilled windows and an arched entryway. Beyond the arched entryway is the private front court which leads to the tiled foyer. Interior livability has been well planned in both designs.

OPTIONAL BASEMENT PLAN

Design V12677
Square Footage: 1,634

● Notice the difference in these plan's livability. Design V12200 has a shared living dining room overlooking the backyard and a front master bedroom with a side terrace where Design V12677 has a separate front dining room, family room with access to the rear terrace and a rear master bedroom with an adjacent covered porch. Both designs have two additional bedrooms besides the master bedroom. Access to the basement varies in each plan.

TRADITIONAL DESIGNS 1,500-2,000 Sq. Ft.

Providing all the livability of much larger plans, the homes in this collection feature the elements that are most in demand: family rooms, breakfast rooms, separate living and dining rooms, and comfortable master bedroom suites. The appealing traditional styling includes amenities like covered porches, wide rear terraces, and lovely classic architectural details. A fine combination in one-story living.

Design V12878
Square Footage: 1,521

L **D**

● This charming one-story Traditional design offers plenty of livability in a compact size. Thoughtful zoning puts all bedroom sleeping areas to one side of the house apart from household activity in the living and service areas. The home includes a spacious gathering room with sloped ceiling, in addition to formal dining room and separate breakfast room. There's also a handy pass-thru between the breakfast room and an efficient, large kitchen. The laundry is strategically located adjacent to garage and breakfast/kitchen areas for handy access. A master bedroom enjoys its own suite with private bath and walk-in closet. A third bedroom can double as a sizable study just off the central foyer. This design offers the elegance of Traditional styling with the comforts of modern lifestyle.

Design V12672

Square Footage: 1,717

L **D**

● The traditional appearance of this one-story is emphasized by its covered porch, multi-paned windows, narrow clapboard and vertical wood siding. Not only is the exterior eye-appealing but the interior has an efficient plan and is very livable. The front U-shaped kitchen will work with the breakfast room and mud room, which houses the laundry facilities. An access to the garage is here. Outdoor dining can be enjoyed on the covered porch adjacent to the dining room. Both of these areas, the porch and dining room, are convenient to the kitchen. Sleeping facilities consist of three bedrooms and two full baths. Note the three sets of sliding glass doors leading to the terrace.

Design V12597
Square Footage: 1,515

L **D**

● Whether it be a starter house you are after, or one in which to spend your retirement years, this pleasing frame home will provide a full measure of pride in ownership. The contrast of vertical and horizontal lines, the double front doors and the coach lamp post at the garage create an inviting exterior. The floor plan functions in an orderly and efficient manner. The 26 foot gathering room has a delightful view of the rear yard and will take care of those formal dining occasions. There are two full baths serving the three bedrooms. There are plenty of storage facilities, two sets of glass doors to the terraces, a fireplace in the gathering room, a basement and an attached two-car garage to act as a buffer against the wind. A delightful home, indeed.

TERRACE

GATHERING RM
16⁰ x 20⁵

DINING RM
12⁰ x 10⁰

COVERED
DINING
PORCH

WALK-IN
CLOSET

MASTER
BEDROOM
11⁰ x 15⁴

SLOPED
CEILING

SLOPED
CEILING

S

BATH

BATH

KITCHEN
12⁰ x 11⁰

PANTRY

OVEN

LS

LAUND

BC
LT

STORAGE
12⁰ x 9⁰

REF'G

W

D

CL

RAILING

DN

COOK
TOP

SNACK BAR

CURB

LINEN

CL

CL

FOYER

DESK

BRKFST RM
14⁴ x 8⁰

BEDROOM
11⁰ x 12⁸

STUDY/
BEDROOM
10⁰ x 11⁰

COVERED PORCH

COVERED PORCH

GARAGE
21⁴ x 21⁴

68'-6"

49'-0"

Design V13345 Square Footage: 1,738

● This quaint shingled cottage offers an unexpected amount of living space in just over 1,700 square feet. The large gathering room with fireplace, dining room with covered porch, and kitchen with breakfast room handle formal parties as easily as they do the casual family get-together. Three bedrooms, one that could also serve as a study, are found in a separate wing of the house. Give special attention to the storage space in this home and the extra touches that set it apart from many homes of equal size.

TERRACE

COVERED PORCH

SKYLIGHT SKYLIGHT SKYLIGHT

BRKFST RM
13² x 11⁸

LIVING RM
13⁰ x 17²

DINING
8⁸ x 9¹⁰

SLOPED CEILING SLOPED CEILING

DESK

SNACK BAR

LAUNDRY
8⁴ x 7⁸

CL.

STORAGE
11⁰ x 8⁴

DW   S

KITCHEN
13² x 9⁶

LT   W   D

RAILING

P'TRY

COOK TOP

OVEN   REF'S

DN

BATH

SLOPED CEILING

FOYER

BATH

LINEN

WALK-IN CLOSET

STUDY/ BEDROOM
10⁰ x 10⁴

PORCH

GARAGE
19⁸ x 20⁴

CL.   CL.

SLOPED CEILING SLOPED CEILING

MASTER BEDROOM
13⁴ x 13⁰

BEDROOM
13⁴ x 10⁸

SEAT

52'-6"

58'-0"

Design V13340

Square Footage: 1,611

● You may not decide to build this design simply because of its delightful covered porch. But it certainly will provide its share of enjoyment if this plan is your choice. Notice also how effectively the bedrooms are arranged out of the traffic flow of the house. One bedroom could double nicely as a TV room or study. The living room/dining area is highlighted by a fireplace, sliding glass doors to the porch, and an open staircase with built-in planter to the basement.

Design V11337
Square Footage: 1,606

● A pleasantly traditional facade which captures a full measure of warmth. Its exterior appeal results from a symphony of such features as: the attractive window detailing; the raised planter; the paneled door, carriage light and cupola of the garage; the use of both horizontal siding and brick. The floor plan has much to recommend this design to the family whose requirements include formal and informal living areas. There is an exceptional amount of livability in this modest-sized design.

Design V11890
Square Footage: 1,628

● The pediment gable and columns help set the charm of this modestly sized home. Here is graciousness normally associated with homes twice its size. The pleasant symmetry of the windows and the double front doors complete the picture. Inside, each square foot is wisely planned to assure years of convenient living. There are three bedrooms, each with twin wardrobe closets. There are two full baths economically grouped with the laundry and heating equipment. A fine feature.

TERRACE

FAMILY RM.
13⁶ x 13⁶

KIT.
10⁰ x 11⁶

LAUNDRY

RANGE PANTRY

DINING RM.
10⁰ x 11⁶

WALK-IN CL.

BATH

LINEN

BED RM.
11⁰ x 11⁶

AIR COND.

BED RM.
11⁰ x 11⁶

STORAGE
CL.

LIVING RM.
20⁰ x 13⁶

ENTRY HALL

WALK IN CL.

WALK-IN CL.

GARAGE
19⁴ x 21⁶

PORCH

BATH

MASTER BED RM.
14⁴ x 12⁰

60'-0"
20'-0"
40'-0"
40'-0"
42'-0"

DN.

LIVING RM.

LINEN

CL.

OPTIONAL BASEMENT

Design V11920
Square Footage: 1,600

L **D**

● A charming exterior with a truly great floor plan. The front entrance with its covered porch seems to herald all the outstanding features to be found inside. Study the sleeping zone with its three bedrooms and two full baths. Each of the bedrooms has its own walk-in closet. Note the efficient U-shaped kitchen with the family and dining rooms to each side. Observe the laundry and the extra wash room. Blueprints for this design include details for both basement and non-basement construction.

Design V11100
Square Footage: 1,752

● This modest sized, brick veneer home has a long list of things in its favor—from its appealing exterior to its feature-packed interior. All of the elements of its exterior complement each other to result in a symphony of attractive design features. The floor plan features three bedrooms, two full baths, an extra wash room, a family room, kitchen eating space, a formal dining area, two sets of sliding glass doors to the terrace and one set to the covered porch, built-in cooking equipment, a pantry and vanity with twin lavatories. Further, there is the living room fireplace, attached two-car garage with a bulk storage unit and a basement for extra storage and miscellaneous recreational activities. A fine investment.

Design V11343
Square Footage: 1,620

L

● This is truly a prize-winner! The traditional, L-shaped exterior with its flower court and covered front porch is picturesque, indeed. The formal front entry routes traffic directly to the three distinctly zoned areas—the quiet sleeping area; the spacious; formal living and dining area; the efficient, informal family-kitchen. A closer look at the floor plan reveals four bedrooms, two full baths, good storage facilities, a fine snack bar and sliding glass doors to the rear terrace. The family-kitchen is ideally located. In addition to being but a few steps from both front and rear entrances, one will enjoy the view of both yards. Blueprints include basement and non-basement details.

Design V11896

Square Footage: 1,690

● Complete family livability is provided by this exceptional floor plan. Further, this design has a truly delightful traditional exterior. The fine layout features a center entrance hall with storage closet in addition to the wardrobe closet. Then, there is the formal, front living room and the adjacent, separate dining room. The U-shaped kitchen has plenty of counter and cupboard space. There is even a pantry. The family room functions with the kitchen and is but a step from the outdoor terrace. The mud room has space for storage and laundry equipment. The extra wash room is nearby. The large family will find those four bedrooms and two full baths just the answer to sleeping and bath accommodations.

Design V11130
Square Footage: 1,856

● A delightfully impressive and formal ranch home. The brick veneer, the ornamental iron columns supporting the overhanging gable, the window treatment and the cupola are among the features that contribute to the charm of this almost perfectly rectangular home. A study of the floor plan reveals excellent room relationships. The formal areas, the living and dining rooms, are adjacent to each other and overlook the front yard. The efficient kitchen is flanked by the informal breakfast area and the all-purpose family room.

Design V11091
Square Footage: 1,666

D

● What could be finer than to live in a delightfully designed home with all the charm of the exterior carried right inside. The interior points of interest are many. However, the focal point will surely be the family-kitchen. The work center is U-shaped and most efficient. The family activity portion of the kitchen features an attractive fireplace which will contribute to a feeling of warmth and fellowship. Nearby is the wash room and stairs to the basement.

Design V11919
Square Footage: 1,752

● Here is a real charmer and one which your large family will have fun living in for years to come. All the facilities are present to assure convenient living. There are four good sized bedrooms. Two full back-to-back baths service the sleeping area efficiently and economically. There is the wonderfully spacious L-shaped living and dining area which looks out upon the rear terrace through sliding glass doors. The kitchen is ideally located between the dining and family rooms.

Design V11384
Square Footage: 1,636

● Here, a wise and economical use of space results in a most practical plan with exceptional livability. There are four bedrooms, two full baths, a 25-foot formal living and dining area, a wonderful family kitchen, an attached two-car garage and a covered front porch. For those who wish to build with a basement there is the optional plan included with the blueprints. Features that are particularly noteworthy are the private bath for the master bedroom, the twin lavatories for the main bath, the island snack bar of the kitchen, the extra closets and the pantry in the kitchen.

Design V13144
Square Footage: 1,760

● If you are short on space and searching for a home that is long on both good looks and livability, search no more! This impressive L-shaped home measures merely 56'-5" in width. It, therefore, qualifies for placement on a relatively narrow building site. Of course with land costs so high, the purchase of a smaller and less expensive building site can significantly reduce the building budget. Whether you build with, or without, a basement (blueprints include details for both types of construction) the outstanding livability remains. There are three bedrooms, two baths, a formal rear living room, a big breakfast room, an excellent kitchen, a wash room and laundry and a huge bulk storage area projecting from the front of the garage. Note window treatment.

OPTIONAL BASEMENT PLAN

Design V11280
Square Footage: 1,730

● This medium-sized, L-shaped ranch home with its touch of traditional styling is, indeed, pleasing to the eye. Hub of this plan is the centrally located foyer which controls traffic to the bedrooms, living/dining room and family room. Economically planned circulation spends very little floor space on hallways. Back-to-back fireplaces in the family room and the living room are an effective sound barrier between the informal and formal areas. Strategically placed kitchen allows for a convenient observation post overlooking family room. The kitchen features a snack bar, built-in desk with shelves and adjacent mud room with washroom. This design includes a basement for future development or storage space.

Design V12261
Square Footage: 1,825

● This distinctive L-shaped home virtually exudes traditional warmth and charm. And little wonder, for the architectural detailing is, indeed, exquisite. Notice the fine window detailing, the appealing cornice work, the attractiveness of the garage door and the massive chimney. The dovecote and the weather vane add to the design impact. The covered front porch shelters the entry which is strategically located to provide excellent traffic patterns. A service entry from the garage is conveniently located handy to the laundry, washroom, kitchen and stairs to the basement. The beamed-ceilinged family room will naturally be everyone's favorite spot for family living.

Design V11758
Square Footage: 1,872

● Setting the delightful character of this L-shaped traditional one-story home are such design features as: the wood columns of the covered front porch; the pediment, gabled ends; the attractive window treatment and the front entrance detail. The floor plan is an exceptional one. The nicely sized formal entry hall routes traffic ideally to the major areas of the house. The two large living areas - the informal family-kitchen and the quiet, formal living room - look out upon the rear terrace through sliding glass doors. The work center is efficient.

Design V11346
Square Footage: 1,644

● Whether you enter through the service door of the attached garage, or through the centered front entry your appreciation of what this plan has to offer will grow. The mud room area is certainly an outstanding feature. Traffic flows from this area to the informal family room with its fireplace and access to the rear terrace.

Design V11949
Square Footage: 1,992

D

● Surely a prize winner. Whether the contest be to pick the best in exterior appeal, or the finest in true livability, this L-shaped home will score at the top. The curving drive is a charming approach to the inviting front doors of the center entrance. The traditionally styled windows, the cupola, the contrasting materials of masonry and wood (or make it aluminum, if you prefer), the interesting roof lines and the excellent proportions are the exterior features which catch the eye. Inside, the highlights are, indeed, numerous. Of particular interest is the family room and the living room. Both are sunken to a depth of two steps, are free from traffic and look out upon the rear yard. That is a beamed ceiling in the family room.

● The paneled, front door, flanked by attractive vertical glass panels, will welcome callers to this traditional exterior with a refreshingly different floor plan. The highlight of the interior is the unique location of the family room. While it functions conveniently with the kitchen, it is also easily accessible from the front entry hall, the attached two-car garage and the covered, rear porch. A raised hearth fireplace, snack bar and sliding glass doors are plus features of this multi-purpose area. The strategic location of the extra washroom will reduce thru-the-house traffic from the outdoors. Spaciousness, resulting from the open planning of the formal living and dining rooms, permits the creation of a most gracious atmosphere.

Design V11317
Square Footage: 1,930

Design V12947
Square Footage: 1,830

● This charming one-story Traditional home greets visitors with a covered porch. A galley-style kitchen shares a snack bar with the spacious gathering room where a fireplace is the focal point. An ample master suite includes a luxury bath with whirlpool tub and separate dressing room. Two additional bedrooms, one that could double as a study, are located at the front of the home.

Design V13336
Square Footage: 2,022

TERRACE

MASTER BEDROOM
13⁶ x 18⁰ + BAY

GATHERING RM
14⁴ x 17⁸

DINING RM
10⁸ x 11⁰

COVERED PORCH

SLOPED CEILING

WHIRLPOOL

VANITY

BATH

LINEN

CL

CL

BRKFST RM
12⁰ x 13⁰

KITCHEN
11⁴ x 11⁶

COOK TOP

S DW

DESK

REF'S

P'TRY

BC

LINEN

BATH

CL

DN RAILING

FOYER

PDR RM

D W LT

CL

BEDROOM
10⁴ x 11⁰

PORCH

CURB

BEDROOM
12⁰ x 12⁰

CL

GARAGE
21⁴ x 21⁸

55'-4"

62'-0"

Design V11252
Square Footage: 1,985

● Here is a traditional adaptation which embodies all the warmth and appeal to make its occupants swell with pride. The projection of the bedroom wing, the recessed front entrance, the boxed bay windows and the set-back attached two-car garage all contribute to the interesting lines of the front exterior. The floor plan is one which contains all the features an active family would require to assure years of exceptional livability. There are two full baths in the three bedroom sleeping area, a sunken formal living room, a separate dining room and a spacious rear family room.

Design V12550
Square Footage: 1,892

D

● An enchanting low-slung traditional ranch with exceptional appeal. The low-pitched roof has a wide overhang and exposed beams. Stone and vertical siding offer a pleasing contrast. However, you may wish to substitute other materials of your choice. The diamond lite windows, the fence with its lamp post, the double front doors and the dovecote above the carriage lamp of the garage are among the interesting exterior features. Inside, there are four bedrooms and two full baths in the sleeping wing. The L-shaped living area is spacious and features a sloping ceiling for the gathering and dining rooms. The open stairwell to the basement recreation area is attractive. The pleasant kitchen is flanked by the nook and laundry.

Design V11186
Square Footage: 1,872

● This appealing home has an interesting and practical floor plan. It is cleverly zoned to cater to the living patterns of both the children and the parents. The children's bedroom wing projects to the rear and functions with their informal family room. The master bedroom is ideally isolated and is located in a part of the plan's quietly formal wing. The efficient kitchen looks out upon the rear terrace and functions conveniently with the dining area and family room. A full bath serves each of the two main living areas. A built-in vanity highlights each bath. The mud room features laundry equipment, storage unit and stairs to the basement. The blueprints show details for basement and non-basement construction.

Design V12603

Square Footage: 1,949

L D

● Surely it would be difficult to beat the appeal of this traditional one-story home. Its slightly modified U-shape with the two front facing gables, the bay window, the covered front porch and the interesting use of exterior materials all add to the exterior charm. Besides, there are three large bedrooms serviced by two full baths and three walk-in closets. The excellent kitchen is flanked by the formal dining room and the informal family room. Don't miss the pantry, the built-in oven and the pass-thru to the snack bar. The handy first floor laundry is strategically located to act as a mud room. The extra wash room is but a few steps away. The sizable living room highlights a fireplace and a picture window. Note the location of the basement stairs.

Design V13177

Square Footage: 1,888

● It would certainly be difficult to pack more living potential into such a modestly sized home than this. The family's living patterns will be just great with "convenience" as the byword. Consider: three bedrooms serviced by two full baths; a formal living room and a formal dining room overlooking the rear terrace and free from unnecessary cross-room traffic; an interior kitchen functioning ideally with the dining room, the family room and the laundry; a powder room handy to living and family rooms and kitchen. Observe: stall shower, fireplace, abundant wardrobe closets, built-in planter, snack bar, family room storage wall and sliding glass doors. The exterior is charming.

Design V11282
Square Footage: 1,732

● If it is just good plain economical livability with an exterior that has a flair for distinction that you are seeking, you'll find this traditional home difficult to top. Within only 1,732 square feet there are all the features the average family could require, plus a few for good measure. Observe that there are two full baths with one compartmented in such a manner as to conveniently serve two distinct areas—the master bedroom and the family-kitchen. There won't be any lack of storage facilities with all that cupboard and closet space. The 21 foot living room has a fireplace and built-in book shelves. There is the formal dining room and then, the covered porch nearby for warm evening relaxation. The family-kitchen is ideal.

Design V12742
Square Footage: 1,907

● Colonial charm is expressed in this one-story design by the vertical siding, the post pillars, the cross fence, paned glass windows and the use of stone. A 19' wide living room, a sloped ceilinged family room with a raised hearth fireplace and its own terrace, a kitchen with many built-ins and a dining room with built-in china cabinets are just some of the highlights. The living terrace is accessible from the dining room and master bedroom. There are two more bedrooms and a full bath in addition to the master bedroom.

Design V11222
Square Footage: 1,657

● How will you call upon this home to function? As a three or four bedroom home? The study permits all kinds of flexibility in your living patterns. If you wish, the extra room could serve the family as a TV area or an area for sewing, hobbies or guests. The 27 foot living room features a formal dining area which is but a step from the secluded, covered dining porch and efficient kitchen. There is a strategically located mud room which houses the washer and dryer and adjacent washroom. The stairs leading to the basement are also in this area.

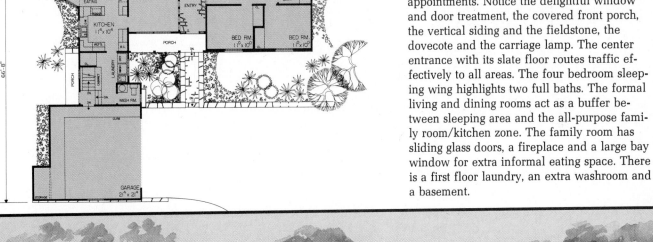

66'-4"

66'-8"

TERRACE   TERRACE

FAMILY RM.
11'x21'

LIVING RM.
18'x13'0"

BED RM.
11'x13'0"

BED RM.
13'4x11'0

DINING RM.
11'8x11'0

EATING

BATH

LINEN

KITCHEN
11'4x10'4

ENTRY

BATH

REF'S.

BED RM.
11'0x10'0

BED RM.
11'0x10'0

PORCH

PORCH

LAUNDRY

WASH RM.

GARAGE
21'4 x 21'4

STORAGE

Design V12533
Square Footage: 1,897

● The distinctive appeal of the traditional, L-shaped ranch home is indeed, hard to beat. Particularly, one with such exquisite exterior appointments. Notice the delightful window and door treatment, the covered front porch, the vertical siding and the fieldstone, the dovecote and the carriage lamp. The center entrance with its slate floor routes traffic effectively to all areas. The four bedroom sleeping wing highlights two full baths. The formal living and dining rooms act as a buffer between sleeping area and the all-purpose family room/kitchen zone. The family room has sliding glass doors, a fireplace and a large bay window for extra informal eating space. There is a first floor laundry, an extra washroom and a basement.

Design V11829
Square Footage: 1,800

L D

● All the charm of a traditional heritage is wrapped up in this U-shaped home with its narrow, horizontal siding, delightful window treatment and high-pitched roof. The massive center chimney, the bay window and the double front doors are plus features. Inside, the living potential is outstanding. The sleeping wing is self-contained and has four bedrooms and two baths. The large family and living rooms cater to the divergent age groups.

Design V11980
Square Footage: 1,901

● Planned for easy living, the daily living patterns of the active family will be pleasant ones, indeed. All the elements are present to assure a wonderful family life. The impressive exterior is enhanced by the recessed front entrance area with its covered porch. The center entry results in a convenient and efficient flow of traffic. A secondary entrance leads from the covered side porch, or the garage, into the first floor laundry. Note the powder room nearby.

Design V12360
Square Footage: 1,936

● There is no such thing as taking a fleeting glance at this charming home. Fine proportion and pleasing lines assure a long and rewarding study. Inside, the family's everyday routine will enjoy all the facilities which will surely guarantee pleasurable living. Note the sunken living room with its fireplace flanked by storage cabinets and book shelves. Observe the excellent kitchen just a step from the dining room and the nook.

Design V12931
Square Footage: 1,998

● Little details make the difference. Consider these that make this such a charming showplace: Picket fenced courtyard, carriage lamp, window boxes, shutters, muntined windows, multi-gabled roof, cornice returns, vertical and horizontal siding with corner boards, front door with glass side lites, etc. Inside this appealing exterior there is a truly outstanding floor plan for the small family or empty-nesters. The master bedroom suite is long on luxury, with a separate dressing room, private vanities, and whirlpool bath. An adjacent study is just the right retreat. There's room to move and - what a warm touch! - it has its own fireplace. Other attractions: roomy kitchen and breakfast area, spacious gathering room, rear and side terraces, and an attached two-car garage with storage.

Design V13314

Square Footage: 1,951

● Formal living areas in this plan are joined by a sleeping wing that holds three bedrooms. Two verandas and a screened porch enlarge the plan and enhance indoor/outdoor livability. Notice the abundant storage space.

TERRACE

SCREENED PORCH
11⁰ x 10¹⁰

BREAKFAST RM
13⁸ x 11⁴

VERANDA

RAILING

DINING RM
12⁰ x 13⁶

REF'G

SNACK BAR
D.W.

KITCHEN
14⁰ x 8⁴

MASTER BEDROOM
12⁰ x 15⁰

SLOPED CEILING

SLOPED CEILING

WHIRL POOL

S

VANITY

BATH

PANTRY

COOK TOP

OVENS

RAILING

DN

BC

DESK

WALK-IN CLOSET

LINEN

WALK-IN CLOSET

CL

CL

SLOPED CEILING | SLOPED CEILING

FOYER

GATHERING RM
17⁰ x 16⁴

CL

CL

BEDROOM
11⁰ x 12⁰ BAY

BATH

LINEN

SEAT

BEDROOM
11⁰ x 12⁰

VERANDA

RAILING

UP

48'-8"

56'-0"

RB

Design V11325
Square Footage: 1,942

L D

● The large front entry hall permits direct access to the formal living room, the sleeping area and the informal family room. Both of the living areas have a fireplace. When formal dining is the occasion of the evening the separate dining room is but a step from the living room. The U-shaped kitchen is strategically flanked by the family room and the breakfast areas.

Floor plan V11325 labels

92'-0"
28'-5"

QUIET TERRACE
LIVING TERRACE
SCREEN
MASTER BED RM. 15⁰ x 13⁶
BATH
VANITY
FAMILY RM. 18⁰ x 13⁶
KITCHEN 10⁸ x 11⁶
BRKFST 8⁰ x 11⁶
W.R.
GARAGE 19⁸ x 23⁴
BRM. CL.
LAUNDRY
DN
BED RM. 11⁸ x 13⁶
BED RM. 10⁸ x 10⁰
FOYER
COVERED PORCH
LIVING RM. 19⁴ x 13⁶
DINING RM. 12⁰ x 11⁶
STOR.
LIN. CL.

Design V11748
Square Footage: 1,986

D

● A sunken living room, two fireplaces, 2½ baths, a rear family room, a formal dining room, a mud room and plenty of storage facilities are among the features of this popular design. Blueprints include optional basement details.

Floor plan V11748 labels

90'-10"
26'-0"   40'-0"   24'-0"
32'-10"   32'-0"   24'-0"   4'-0"

QUIET TERRACE
LIVING TERRACE
SCREEN
MASTER BED RM. 15⁰ x 13⁶
BATH
BATH
VANITY
FAMILY RM. 21⁴ x 12⁶
KIT. 12⁰ x 13⁰
MUD RM.
W.R.
GARAGE 23⁸ x 23⁴
RAISED HEARTH
AIR COND.
BAR-B-Q RANGE
ENTRY HALL
DN
CL. LIN.
BED RM. 11⁶ x 15⁴
BED RM. 13⁶ x 11⁶
LIVING RM. 20⁰ x 13⁶
UP
DINING RM. 11⁴ x 13⁶
STORAGE
R
FENCE
LAMP POST

OPTIONAL BASEMENT
CL. CL. CL.
BED RM.
DN
LIVING RM.
ENTRY HALL
DN
P.

Shared Expense – Shared Livability

Design V12869
Square Footage: 1,986

● This traditional one-story design offers the economical benefits of shared living space without sacrificing privacy. The common area of this design is centrally located between the two private, sleeping wings. The common area, 680 square feet, is made up of the great room, dining room and kitchen. Sloping the ceiling in this area creates an open feeling as will the sliding glass doors on each side of the fireplace. These doors lead to a large covered porch with skylights above. Separate outdoor entrances lead to each of the sleeping wings. Two bedrooms, dressing area, full bath and space for an optional kitchenette occupy 653 square feet in each wing. Additional space will be found in the basement which is the full size of the common area. Don't miss the covered porch and garage with additional storage space.

Design V12698
Square Footage: 1,700

(Main plan labels)
BATH
SEAT
BATH
LINEN
CL
CL
MASTER BEDROOM
12⁸ x 13⁴

BEDROOM
16⁸ x 11⁰

TERRACE
DN
DN
CL

FAMILY RM.
21⁰ x 12⁰

SHELVES
OVENS
D.W.
KITCHEN
17⁰ x 9⁰
B.C.
REF'G
COOK TOP
CL

DN
CL

DINING RM.
14⁴ x 11⁰
CL

LIVING RM.
16⁸ x 13⁰

PORCH
UP

22'-0"
77'-4"

(Alternate plan labels)
WALK-IN CLOSET
LIN
BATH
MASTER BEDROOM
13⁰ x 15⁰

TERRACE
DN
DN
STORAGE

FAMILY RM.
21⁰ x 12⁰

SHELVES
OVENS
D.W.
KITCHEN
17⁰ x 9⁰
B.C.
REF'G
COOK TOP
CL

DINING RM.
14⁴ x 11⁰
CL

LIVING RM.
16⁸ x 13⁰

PORCH
UP

65'-4"

ALTERNATE ONE BEDROOM PLAN

● Here is the quintessential narrow lot house. It was found in 19th Century New Orleans and many other southern towns. Its origins go back to the West Indies and Africa and has been called, the "shotgun house". A name derived from the fact that a bullet could travel through the front door and exit the rear without striking a partition. For the sake of contemporary floor planning this version forsakes the rear door in favor of two full baths. Despite its small size, the facade with its projecting gable and columned front porch is charming, indeed. As a starter home, or even as a retirement home, this unique house will serve its occupants well. An alternate one bedroom version contains 1,436 sq. ft. Notice that all of the amenities to be found in the other rooms remain the same.

TRADITIONAL DESIGNS 2,000-3,000 Sq. Ft.

The larger one-story home offers a full measure of living potential. With all the pluses of the traditional two-story, it has the added advantage of complete livability on one level. Generally, a large home offers larger rooms and practical, efficient traffic patterns that accommodate not only the family's favorite pursuits but the demands of social gatherings as well.

Design V12777

Square Footage: 2,006

L **D**

● Many years of delightful living will be enjoyed in this one-story traditional home. The covered, front porch adds a charm to the exterior as do the paned windows and winding drive. Inside, there is livability galore. An efficient kitchen with island range and adjacent laundry make this work area very pleasing. A breakfast nook with bay window and built-in desk will serve the family when informal dining is called upon. A formal dining room with sliding glass doors leads to the rear terrace. The large gathering room with raised hearth fireplace can serve the family on any occasion gracefully. The sleeping wing consists of two bedrooms and a study (or make it three bedrooms). The master bedroom includes all of the fine features one would expect: a huge walk-in closet, a vanity, a bath and sliding glass doors to a private terrace.

TERRACE

68' - 0"

FAMILY RM.
13⁰ x 18⁸

DINING RM.
11⁰ x 13⁰

LIVING RM.
18⁸ x 13⁰

DRESS RM.

MASTER BED RM.
14⁴ x 13⁰

BEAMED CEILING

DN.

RAILING

BATH

SHOWER

VANITY

BED RM.
11⁰ x 11⁰

CL.

REF'G OVEN

CHINA DESK

DN.

PANTRY PANTRY

WOOD BOX

KIT.
10⁰ x 12⁰

STOR.

AIR COND.

W.R.

LAUND.

RANGE

DRY.

WASH.

D.W.

SINK

BREAKFAST
8⁰ x 12⁰

ENTRY

LIN.

BATH

VANITY

LIN.

CL.

CL.

42' - 0"

48' - 0"

GARAGE
21⁴ x 21⁸

CURB

ENTRY COURT

STUDY-BED RM.
10⁰ x 11⁰

BED RM.
11⁰ x 14⁰

Design V11950
Square Footage: 2,076

D

● If you were to count the various reasons that will cause excitement over the prospect of moving into this home, you would certainly be able to compile a long list. You might head your list with the grace and charm of the front exterior. You'd certainly have to comment on the delightful entry court, the picket fence and lamp post and the recessed front entrance. Comments about the interior obviously would begin with the listing of such features as: spaciousness galore; sunken living room; separate dining room; family room with beamed ceiling; excellent kitchen with pass-thru to breakfast room; two full baths, plus washroom, etc.

Design V11102
Square Footage: 2,348

● This quietly impressive home with curving front drive, covered front porch, delightful muntined windows, and panelled door flanked by patterned side-lites, houses a fine floor plan. The center entry hall joins another hall which runs the width of the home and routes traffic directly to each room. There are four bedrooms, two full baths, and plenty of storage potential in sleeping area. A covered rear porch off the master bedroom will be nice on hot, summer evenings. The living and dining rooms are sure to enjoy their privacy. The focal point of the plan, is perhaps the 27 foot family-kitchen. Don't miss the strategic location of the mud room. A snack bar provides a handy spot for the enjoyment of quick and easy meals.

Design V11149
Square Footage: 2,040

● The very shape of this traditional adaptation seems to spell, "welcome". A study of the floor plan reflects excellent zoning. The sleeping area consists of four bedrooms and two full baths. The formal area, located to the front of the house, consists of a separate dining room with built-in china cabinet and living room with fireplace and accompanying woodbox. Study the work center of the kitchen, laundry and wash room. An informal family room. It is only a couple of steps from the kitchen and functions with the outdoor terrace.

Design V12316
Square Footage: 2,000

L **D**

● Here is a basic floor plan which is the favorite of many. It provides for the location, to the front of the plan, of the more formal areas (living and dining rooms); while the informal areas (family room and kitchen) are situated to the rear of the plan and function with the terrace. To the left of the center entrance is the four bedroom, two bath sleeping zone. Adjacent to the kitchen is the utility room with a wash room nearby. The garage features a storage room and work shop area with more storage.

92'-10"

58'-0" 12'-0" 22'-0"

32'-0"

TERRACE

MASTER BED RM. 14⁴ x 13⁴

LIVING RM. 20⁰ x 14⁶

FAMILY RM. 14⁰ x 19⁴

RAISED HEARTH

DRESS. RM.

BATH

BATH

CL.

CL.

CL.

BOOKS

DN.

CL.

PORCH

WORK SHOP & STORAGE

W.T.

W.

W.R.

MUD RM.

DN.

BED RM. 12⁰ x 12⁰

BED RM. 11⁸ x 12⁰

CL.

ENTRY HALL

CL.

DINING RM. 12⁰ x 12⁰

REF'G DESK

RANGE

KIT. 20⁸ x 11⁸

GARAGE 21⁴ x 27⁴

D.W. S.

EATING

PANTRY

CL. LIN.

PORCH

Design V11788
Square Footage: 2,218

L D

● "Charm" is one of the many words which may be used to correctly describe this fine design. In addition to its eye-appeal, it has a practical and smoothly functioning floor plan. The detail of the front entrance, highlighted by columns supporting the projecting pediment gable, is outstanding. Observe the window treatment and the double, front doors. Perhaps the focal point of the interior will be the formal living room. It is, indeed, dramatic with its bay window overlooking the backyard. Three bedrooms and two baths are in the private area.

Design V12204
Square Footage: 2,016

● Your life's investment hardly could be more wisely made than for the choice of this delightful design as your family's next home. Over the years its charm will not diminish. This is a favorite plan of many. It establishes a quiet sleeping zone, a formal living-dining zone and an informal family-kitchen zone. Sliding glass doors permit the master bedroom, family room and breakfast nook to have easy access to the rear terrace. Entering the house from the garage, all will appreciate the proximity of the closets, the washroom and the basement stairs.

Design V12260
Square Footage: 2,041

● Upon entering this hip-roof traditional, you will view the built-in planter atop a practical storage cabinet. A look into the living room reveals an attractive fireplace flanked by bookshelves, cabinet and wood box. A step into the master bedroom brings into view the twin walk-in closets and sliding glass doors to the rear terrace. Moving into the kitchen, the fine counter and cupboard space will be appreciated. This efficient work area is but a step from the informal nook and the formal dining room. Behind the garage is a large, covered screened porch.

Design V12208
Square Footage: 2,522

● You really won't need a half acre to build this home. Its very breadth will guarantee plenty of space to the front, thus providing a fine setting. The pedimented gables, horizontal siding, corner boards, window and door treatment, two covered porches and the cupola set the note of distinction. An excellent feature is the service entrance, adjacent to the garage. The bedroom wing is positively outstanding. In addition to the three bedrooms and two baths, there is the private study. It has a sloping, beamed ceiling, bookshelves, cabinets and two closets.

70'-0

66'-8

TERRACE

TERRACE

GATHERING RM.
18⁰ x 15⁰

COUNTRY
KITCHEN
12⁰ x 27⁸

MASTER
BEDROOM
13⁰ x 13⁴

DRESS RM.

BATH

SLOPED   CEILING

TERRACE

EATING

WALK-IN
CLOSET

BAR

CL.

BATH

COOK
TOP

CL.

CL.

LIN.

CL.

DINING RM.
11⁸ x 10⁴

FOYER

OPEN

BEDROOM
10⁴ x 12⁴

BEDROOM
12⁰ x 14⁰

B.C.

CL.

ON

MUD RM.

W.R.

COVERED PORCH

SEAT

CURB

GARAGE
21⁴ x 21⁴

STORAGE

Design V12916
Square Footage: 2,129

● Pride of ownership will be forever yours as the occupant of this Early American styled one-story house. The covered front porch provides a shelter for the inviting panelled front door with its flanking side lites. Designed for fine family living, this three bed-room, 2½ bath home offers wonderful formal and informal living patterns. The 27 foot country kitchen has a beamed ceiling and a fireplace. The U-shaped work center is efficient. It is but a step from the mud room area with its laundry equipment, closets, cupboards, counter space and wash-room. There are two dining areas - an informal eating space and a formal separate dining room. The more formal gathering room is spacious with a slop-ing ceiling and two sets of sliding glass doors to the rear terrace.

Design V13332

Square Footage: 2,168

● Nothing completes a traditional-style home quite as well as a country kitchen with fireplace. Notice also the sloped-ceiling living room and well-appointed master suite. A handy wash-room is near the laundry, just off the garage.

Design V12353
Square Footage: 2,302

● Here is an inviting Colonial Ranch home with matching pediment gables projecting toward the street. Deep double-hung windows flanked by shutters enhance the exterior charm. The massive chimney, the raised planter, the panelled front door, and the patterned garage door add their extra measure of appeal. The interior offers loads of livability. Note the sunken living room, the beamed-ceilinged family room, and the efficient kitchen strategically located between the breakfast nook and the formal dining room.

Design V12362
Square Footage: 2,166

● Here is a ground-hugging, traditional adaptation with plenty of exterior appeal and a fine functioning floor plan. Observe the interior zoning. The sunken living room will have plenty of privacy. The four bedroom sleeping area is a wing by itself. The U-shaped kitchen is strategically flanked by the two eating areas. Study the exceptional family room. Note powder room. The indoor-outdoor living relationships are excellent. The covered rear porch will be a popular spot for summer outdoor eating and relaxation.

Design V12352
Square Footage: 2,179

● This enchanting hip-roof traditional has a distinctive air of its own. From the recessed gardening area between the living room and garage to the master bedroom vanity, this plan is replete with features. Notice the covered front porch, the spacious kitchen, the quiet living room, the beamed ceilinged family room, the laundry/mud room, the sliding glass doors to terrace, etc. The planting court, so completely visible from the formal living and dining rooms, will be great fun for the amateur horticulturist during the warm months.

Design V11835
Square Footage: 2,144

● Cedar shakes and quarried natural stone are the exterior materials which adorn this irregularly shaped traditional ranch home. Adding to the appeal of the exterior are the cut-up windows, the shutters, the pediment gable, the cupola and the double front doors. The detail of the garage door opening adds further interest. Inside, this favorite among floor plans, reflects all the features necessary to provide complete livability for the large family. The sleeping zone is a 24' x 40' rectangle which contains four bedrooms and two full baths. A dressing room with a vanity and a wall of wardrobe storage highlights the master bedroom. Both the informal family room and the formal living room have a fireplace.

● Whatever the setting, here is a traditional, one story home that is truly impressive. Zoned in a most practical manner, the floor plan features an isolated bedroom wing, formal living and dining rooms and, across the rear of the house, the informal living areas.

Design V11174
Square Footage: 2,292

OPTIONAL BASEMENT

Design V11786
Square Footage: 2,370

● Like this? If the answer is, yes, it is easy to understand. This is an extremely appealing design, highlighted by its brick masses, its window detailing, its interesting shape, and its inviting covered front entrance. The foyer is centrally located and but a step or two from all areas. The house, while it features all the facilities for family living, assures a full measure of privacy for all. The bedroom wing is distinctly defined. The quiet, sunken living room is off by itself. There is a separate, formal dining room. The family room is one which will function alone and cater to numerous activities. The kitchen, with its eating space, is of good size. The mud-room area is a true convenient living feature.

Design V12867
Square Footage: 2,388

● A live-in relative would be very comfortable in this home. This design features a self-contained suite (473 sq. ft.) consisting of a bedroom, bath, living room and kitchenette with dining area. This suite is nestled behind the garage away from the main areas of the house. The rest of this traditional, one-story house, faced with fieldstone and vertical wood siding, is also very livable. One whole wing houses the four family bedrooms and bath facilities. The center of the plan has a front, U-shaped kitchen and breakfast room. The formal dining room and large gathering room will enjoy the view, and access to, the backyard. The large, covered porch will receive much use.

TERRACE

COVERED PORCH

MASTER BEDROOM
13⁰ x 21⁴ + BAY

BATH

WHIRLPOOL

VANITY

FAMILY RM
19⁸ x 13⁴

BRKFST
8⁰ x 11⁰

KITCHEN
10⁰ x 13²

SEAT

MUD RM

LAUNDRY
9⁰ x 10⁰

HER WALK-IN CLOSET

HIS WALK-IN CLOSET

RAISED HEARTH

OVEN

COOK TOP

PANTRY

WR

BEDROOM
11² x 10⁰

BATH

LINEN

CONSOLE

RAILING

CURB

BEDROOM
11² x 13⁴

STUDY/ BEDROOM
11⁶ x 12⁰

FOYER

LIVING RM
20⁰ x 13⁴

DINING
11⁸ x 12⁶

STORAGE

GARAGE
21⁴ x 20⁶

COVERED PORCH

53'-6"

87'-0"

Design V13348 Square Footage: 2,549

● Covered porches front and rear will be the envy of the neighborhood when this house is built. The interior plan meets family needs perfectly in well- zoned areas: a sleeping wing with four bedrooms and two baths, a living zone with formal and informal gathering space, and a work zone with U-shaped kitchen and laundry with washroom. The two-car garage has a huge storage area.

Design V11929
Square Footage: 2,312

D

● There's more to this U-shaped, traditional adaptation than meets the eye. Much more! And, yet, what does meet the eye is positively captivating. The symmetry of the pediment gables, the window styling, the projecting garden wall, the iron gates, and the double front doors, are extremely pleasing. Once inside, a quick tour reveals plenty of space and a super-abundance of features. Each of the rooms is extra large and allows for fine furniture placement. In addition to the raised hearth fireplace, the family room highlights built-in book shelves, sliding glass doors and beamed ceilings.

Design V11931
Square Footage: 2,424

● This home will lead the hit parade in your new subdivision. Its sparkling, traditionally styled exterior will be the favorite of all that pass. And, once inside, friends will marvel at how the plan just seems to cater to your family's every activity. When it comes to eating, you can eat in the informal breakfast room or the formal dining room. As you come in the front door you may sit down and relax in the sunken living room or the beamed ceiling family room. Two full baths with built-in vanities, plus the extra wash room will more than adequately serve the family.

Design V11872
Square Footage: 2,212

● If exceptional exterior appeal means anything to interior living potential then this traditional home should have unlimited livability. And, indeed, it has! There are five bedrooms (and a study if you so wish), two full baths and loads of storage in the sleeping wing. The formal living zone highlights a quiet living room and separate dining room. Each completely free of cross-room traffic. For informal living there is the family-kitchen with a snack bar, fireplace and sliding glass doors to the terrace. The work center is outstanding with laundry and washroom nearby. There are plenty of cupboards and lots of counter space. The laundry, with more cupboards and twin closets, is nearby. Note washroom and covered side porch.

Design V11924 Square Footage: 2,504

Design V11851 Square Footage: 2,450

Design V11886
Square Footage: 2,352

● Here are three designs each featuring four bedrooms and two plus baths. While each home has a basement, it also highlights a first floor laundry. The differing arrangements of the living, dining, and family rooms are most interesting. The kitchen functions directly with the breakfast rooms, yet again, their locations vary. Raised hearth fireplaces are a focal point of the family rooms, while a second fireplace can be found in the living rooms. Note the side opening garages. Design V11851 has a handy tool room for heavy equipment.

TERRACE

GATHERING RM.
22⁰×18⁰

RAISED HEARTH

BEAMED CEILING

DINING RM.
12⁰×13⁴

SLOPED CEILING   SLOPED CEILING

DN.   DN.

STUDY
BED RM.
10⁰×11⁰

BED RM.
15⁸×11⁰

CL.   CL.

CL.   CL.   CL.

NOOK
12⁰×11⁰

SNACKS

D.W.   S.

KIT.
13⁰×11⁰

RANGE

CL.

PDR. RM.

LIN.

BED RM.
12⁰×11⁰

CL.

REF'G.   B.C.

FOYER

BATH

CL.

SER.
ENT.

PDR. RM.

PORCH

BATH

CL.

MASTER
BED RM.
15⁸×16⁴

DRESS'G.

CURB.

STOR.

GARAGE
23⁴×23⁴

67'-4"

61'-4"

Design V12527
Square Footage: 2,392

D

● Vertical boards and battens, field-stone, bay window, a dovecote, a gas lamp and a recessed front entrance are among the appealing exterior features of this U-shaped design. Through the double front doors, flanked by glass side lites, one enters the spacious foyer. Straight ahead is the cozy sunken gathering room with its sloping, beamed ceiling, raised hearth fireplace and two sets of sliding glass doors to the rear terrace. To the right of the foyer is the sleeping wing with its three bedrooms, study (make it the fourth bedroom if you wish) and two baths. To the left is the strategically located powder room and large kitchen with its delightful nook and bay window.

Design V12181

Square Footage: 2,612

D

● It is hard to imagine a home with any more eye-appeal than this one. It is the complete picture of charm. The interior is just as outstanding. Sliding glass doors permit the large, master bedroom, quiet, living room and all-purpose family room to function directly with the outdoors. Two fireplaces, built-in china cabinets, bookshelves, complete laundry and kitchen pass-thru to breakfast room are extra features. Although the illustration of this home shows natural quarried stone, you may wish to substitute brick or even siding.

Design V12675

Square Footage: 2,478

D

● Many extra features have been designed into this delightfully traditional home. Bookshelves and cabinets are in the family room, china cabinets and a window seat are in the dining room, a second window seat is in the breakfast room, a large dressing room with vanity is in the master bedroom and the list can go on. Two fireplaces, one in each of the living areas. If you like this design, but are in need of a four bedroom home, please order Design V12181 above.

Design V12209
Square Footage: 2,659

● Such an impressive home would, indeed, be difficult to top. And little wonder when you consider the myraid of features this one-story Colonial possesses. Consider the exquisite detailing, the fine proportions, and the symmetry of the projecting wings. The gracious and inviting double front doors are a prelude to the exceptional interior. Consider the four bedroom, two-bath sleeping wing. Formal entertaining can be enjoyed in the front living and dining rooms. For informal living there is the rear family room.

Design V12264
Square Footage: 2,352

● This U-shaped traditional will be a welcomed addition on any site. It has living facilities which will provide your family with years of delightful livability. The two living areas are located to the rear and function with the outdoor terrace. The outstanding kitchen is strategically located handy to the family room and the eating areas. A separate laundry area with fine storage and nearby powder room is a favorite feature. Note garage size and storage potential. Also notice stairway to attic.

Design V11761
Square Footage: 2,548

L **D**

● Low, strong roof lines and solid, enduring qualities of brick give this house a permanent, here-to-stay appearance. Bedroom wing is isolated, and the baths and closets deaden noise from the rest of the house. Center fireplaces in family and living rooms make furniture arrangement easy. There are a number of extras – a workshop, an unusually large garage, and an indoor barbecue. Garage has easy access to both basement and kitchen area. There are two eating areas – a formal dining room and a breakfast nook next to the delightful kitchen.

Design V12270
Square Footage: 2,505

● Four bedrooms and two baths make up the sleeping area of this delightful design. There are spacious living areas, too. The family room will serve the informal, family needs; while the living room is available for those more formal times. Both formal and informal dining areas are available to serve every family occasion. They both have easy access to the U-shaped kitchen. Complimenting the work center, an adjacent laundry and washroom will be appreciated. Outstanding storage facilities will be found throughout the plan. These are but some of the highlights of this family-oriented design.

Design V12271
Square Footage: 2,317

● Here's a plan with both formal and informal living areas functioning with the rear terrace. Why let the beauty of your backyard be wasted on the laundry room? This puts the kitchen in the front of the plan. Working in the kitchen, you will be able to see approaching visitors. Among the other features, there are two fireplaces, three full baths, three bedrooms, nook and snack bar and extra garage storage. List the other features that will serve your family.

Design V11201
Square Footage: 2,960

● If it's formal living you are after, then the elegance and spaciousness of this richly detailed design should meet your specifications. The large bow windows, the overhanging roof, the massive chimney and the ornamental cupola give this house a stately facade. As you study the plan, note the generous size of the various rooms. Observe the excellence of the zoning and how the elements of each zone - sleeping, formal and informal living and work area - function together smoothly.

86'-10"

64'-10"

MASTER
BED RM.
15⁰ x 15⁴

WALK-IN
CL.

WALK-IN
CL.

LIVING RM.
20⁰ x 15⁴

FAMILY RM.
15⁴ x 19⁰

RAISED
HEARTH

WOOD
BOX

BREAKFAST

REFG.

GARDEN
COURT

BEAMED
CEILING

FAMILY
KITCHEN
13⁴ x 15⁰

RANGE &
BAR B Q

BATH

VANITY

LINEN

OVEN

FREEZER

BATH

WALK-IN
CL.

CL.

CL.

ENTRANCE
HALL

CL.

LAUNDRY
14⁰ x 8⁴

LINEN

W. D.

CL.

DN.

BED RM.
13⁸ x 12⁰

CL.

CL.

DINING RM.
15⁴ x 12⁰

LINEN

W. R.

SERVICE
ENTRY

BED RM.
15⁴ x 11⁸

CL.

CL.

PORCH

STORAGE LOFT
ABOVE

UP

GARAGE
23⁴ x 23⁸

STORAGE
15⁴ x 9⁴

Design V11295
Square Footage: 2,520

● A custom home is one tailored to fit the needs and satisfy the living patterns of a particular family. Here is a traditional home which stands ready to serve its occupants ideally. The overhanging roof creates the covered porch with its attractive wood columns. The center entrance leads to an interior which will cater to the formal as well as the informal activities of the family. Two fireplaces, back-to-back, serve the master bedroom and the quiet, formal living room. Another two-way fireplace can be enjoyed from the large, family room and the gaily, informal family kitchen. Adjacent to the kitchen is the formal dining room, the spacious laundry and the powder room. No storage problems here. Of particular interest is the storage room and the storage balcony in the garage.

GARAGE
23⁴ x 23⁸

LAUNDRY

KITCHEN
10⁰ x 13⁰

NOOK
8⁸ x 11⁰

FAMILY RM.
18⁰ x 17⁴

BEAMED CEILING

SLOPED CEILING

SLOPED CEILING

BED RM.-STUDY
10⁰ x 13⁰

BATH

MASTER BED RM.
17⁸ x 13⁰

LINEN

VANITY

WALK IN CLOSET

RAISED HEARTH

PANTRY

BOOKS

BOOKS

CHINA

HALL

LINEN

VANITY

B.C. OVENS

STORAGE

DN.

WASH RM.

ENTRY

CL.

CL.

CL.

BATH

DINING RM.
12⁰ x 11⁸

PORCH

BED RM.
11⁰ x 11⁸

BED RM.
11⁰ x 11⁸

LIVING RM.
16⁰ x 16⁸

TERRACE

STEP

STEP

STEP

STEP

STEP

106'-8"

41'-10"

Design V12544
Square Footage: 2,527

D

● A blend of exterior materials enhance the beauty of this fine home. Here, the masonry material used is fieldstone to contrast effectively with the horizontal siding. You may substitute brick or quarried stone if you wish. Adding to the appeal are the various projections and their roof planes, the window treatment and the recessed front entrance. Two large living areas highlight the interior. Each has a fireplace. The homemaking effort will be easily and enjoyably dispatched with such features as the efficient kitchen, the walk-in pantry, the handy storage areas, the first floor laundry and extra washroom. The sleeping zone has four bedrooms, two baths with vanities and good closet accommodations. There's a basement for additional storage and recreation activities.

Clutter Room, Media Room To The Fore

Design V12880
Living Area: 2,758 square feet
Greenhouse: 149 square feet
Total: 2,907 square feet

L **D**

● This comfortable traditional home offers plenty of modern livability. A clutter room off the two-car garage is the perfect space for workbench, sewing, and hobbies. It includes a work island and bench space. Across the hall one finds a modern media room, the perfect place for stereo speakers, videos, and more. A spacious country kitchen off the greenhouse is a cozy gathering place for family and friends, as well as convenient work area. The 149-foot greenhouse itself easily could be the focal point of this home filled with modern amenities. The house also features a formal dining room, living room with fireplace, covered porch, and three bedrooms including a master bedroom suite.

Design V11952

Square Footage: 2,705

● This delightful home has been designed for country-estate living. L-shaped, this traditional will be a worthy addition to any building site. Its pleasing proportions are almost breathtaking. They seem to foretell the tremendous amount of livability its inhabitants are to enjoy. The interior zoning hardly could be improved upon. The children's bedrooms function together in a wing with their own bath. There is a large master bedroom suite. It features Mr. and Mrs. dressing rooms, each with a vanity, with a full bath in the middle. The dining room is nestled between the living and family rooms. Both of these living areas have a beamed ceiling and a fireplace. All of the work area, kitchen, breakfast room, laundry and washroom, is in the front of the plan.

Design V12766

Square Footage: 2,711

D

● A sizable master bedroom has a dressing area featuring two walk-in closets, a twin lavatory and compartmented bath. The two-bedroom children's area has a full bath and supporting study. Formal living and dining zone is separated by a thru-fireplace. A spacious kitchen-nook is cheerfully informal with a sun room just a step away through sliding glass doors. The service area has a laundry, storage, washroom and stairs to basement. An array of sliding glass doors lead to outdoor living on the various terraces. These are but some of the highlights of this appealing, L-shaped traditional home. Be sure to note the large number of sizable closets for a variety of uses.

Design V12778

Square Footage: 2,761

D

● No matter what the occasion, family and friends alike will enjoy this sizable gathering room. A spacious 20' x 23', this room has a thru fireplace to the study and two sets of sliding glass doors to the large, rear terrace. Indoor-outdoor living also can be enjoyed from the dining room, study and master bedroom. There is also a covered porch accessible through sliding glass doors in the dining room and breakfast nook.

Design V12784
Square Footage: 2,980

● The projection of the master bedroom and garage create an inviting U-shaped area leading to the covered porch of this delightful traditionally styled design. After entering through the double front doors, the gallery will lead to each of the three living areas: the sleeping wing of two bedrooms, full bath and study; the informal area of the family room with raised hearth fireplace and sliding glass doors to the terrace and the kitchen/nook area (the kitchen has a pass-thru snack bar to the family room); and the formal area consisting of a separate dining room with built-in china cabinets and the living room. Note the privacy of the master bedroom.

● What a pleasing, traditional exterior. And what a fine, convenient living interior! The configuration of this home leads to interesting roof planes and even functional outdoor terrace areas. The front court and the covered porch with its stolid pillars strike an enchanting note. The gathering room will be just that. It will be the family's multi-purpose living area. Sunken to a level of two steps, its already spacious feeling is enhanced by its open planning with the dining room and study. This latter room may be closed off for more privacy if desired. Just adjacent to the foyer is the open stairwell to the basement level. Here will be the possibility of developing recreation space.

Design V12519
Square Footage: 2,889

TRADITIONAL and CONTEMPORARY ..

as highlighted in this interesting section have both traditional and contemporary exteriors. Each design offers square footage over 3000 sq. ft. In a couple of designs, bonus square footage and livability are picked-up by the addition of the upstairs sleeping quarters. These houses deliver all the livability potential and amenities one would want in a house designed for the unrestricted budget. Provisions are made for both formal and informal living patterns. Flexible and varied indoor-outdoor living relationships have been provided. The configurations of these floor plans are important for they represent, with thoughtful siting, the opportunity to enjoy solar orientation.

Design V12888
Square Footage: 3,018

● This is an outstanding Early American design for the 20th-Century. The exterior detailing with narrow clap boards, multi-paned windows and cupola are the features of yesteryear. Interior planning, though, is for today's active family. Formal living room, in- formal family room plus a study are present. Every activity will have its place in this home. Picture yourself working in the kitchen. There's enough counter space for two or three helpers. Four bedrooms are in the private area. Stop and imagine your daily routine if you occupied the master bedroom. Both you and your spouse would have plenty of space and privacy. The flow-er porch, accessible from the master bedroom, living and dining rooms, is a very delightful "plus" feature. Study this design's every detail.

Design V11911
Square Footage: 3,107

● For luxurious, country-estate living it would be difficult to beat the livability offered by these two impressive traditional designs. To begin with, their exterior appeal is, indeed, gracious. Their floor plans highlight plenty of space, excellent room arrangements, fine traffic circulation, and an abundance of convenient living features. It is interesting to note that each design features similar livability facilities. Both may function as four bedroom homes . . .

Design V11916
Square Footage: 3,024

● . . . or three bedroom with a study or library. There are first floor laundries, two fireplaces, formal and informal living and dining areas, fine storage potential, and delightful indoor-outdoor living relationships. You'll have fun listing the built-in features. The two family rooms have beamed ceilings and sliding glass doors to the play terraces. The two living rooms are spacious and enjoy a full measure of privacy. They are but a step from outdoor living.

Design V12783
Square Footage: 3,210

● The configuration of this traditional design is outstanding indeed. The garage-bedroom wing on one side and the master bedroom on the other create an inviting U-shaped entry court. This area is raised two steps from the driveway and has a 6 foot high masonry wall with coach lamps for an added attraction. Upon entrance through the double front doors one will begin to enjoy the livability that this design has to offer. Each room is well planned and deserves praise. The sizeable master bedroom has a fireplace and sliding glass doors to the entry court. Another sizeable room, the gathering room, has access to the rear terrace along with the dining room, family room and rear bedroom. Note interior kitchen which is adjacent to each of the major rooms.

Design V12183 Square Footage: 3,074

● A great country-estate home with unsurpassed exterior appeal and positively outstanding interior livability. The enclosed front courtyard is just one of the many features that contribute to the air of distinction surrounding this pleasing traditional design. The floor plan includes everything one would require to guarantee his family the ultimate in gracious living. There are four bedrooms and two full baths in the sleeping wing, a large rear living room with bay window overlooking the back yard, formal and informal dining, family room with raised hearth fireplace and built-in book cabinets plus a study. The members of your family will have fun making their own lists of the features that are most appealing to them. What are your favorite highlights of this design?

OPTIONAL BASEMENT PLAN

Design V12767
Square Footage: 3,000

D

● What a sound investment this impressive home will be. And while its value withstands the inflationary pressures of ensuing years, it will serve your family well. It has all the amenities to assure truly pleasurable living. The charming exterior will lend itself to treatment other than the appealing fieldstone, brick and frame shown. Inside, the plan will impress you with large, spacious living areas, formal and informal dining areas, three large bedrooms, two full baths with twin lavatories, walk-in closets and a fine study. The kitchen features an island work center with range and desk. The two fireplaces will warm their surroundings in both areas. Two separate terraces for a variety of uses. Note laundry, wash room and three-car garage with extra curb area.

154

Design V12768

Square Footage: 3,436

● Besides its elegant traditionally styled exterior with its delightfully long covered front porch, this home has an exceptionally livable interior. There is the outstanding four bedroom and two-bath sleeping wing. Then, the efficient front kitchen with island range flanked by the formal dining room and the informal breakfast nook. Separated by the two-way, thru fireplace are the living and family rooms which look out on the rear yard. Worthy of particular note is the development of a potential live-in relative facility. These two rooms would also serve the large family well as a hobby room and library or additional bedrooms. A full bath is adjacent as well as the laundry. Note curb area in the garage for the storage of outdoor equipment.

Design V13344
Square Footage: 3,054

- WHIRLPOOL
- HER BATH
- HIS BATH
- S
- VANITY
- DRESSING RM
- MASTER BEDROOM 13⁰ x 17⁴
- QUIET TERRACE
- FLOWER PORCH 13⁰ x 11⁶
- SKYLIGHTS ABOVE
- DINING RM 13⁰ x 11⁰
- KITCHEN 10⁰ x 11⁴
- BRKFST RM 8⁴ x 11⁴
- LS
- S
- DW
- DESK
- REF'G
- OVEN
- COOK TOP
- S
- PLAY TERRACE
- HER WALK-IN CLOSET
- SHELVES
- SHELVES
- HIS WALK-IN CLOSET
- ETAGERE
- SLOPED CEILING
- SLOPED CEILING
- SLOPED CEILING
- SLOPED CEILING
- PDR RM
- BC
- PANTRY
- S BAR CL
- FAMILY RM 15⁴ x 19⁶
- RAISED HEARTH
- BEDROOM 10¹⁰ x 11⁰
- LINEN
- CL
- BATH
- SKYLIGHT
- ON
- SKYLIGHT
- DN
- FOYER
- STUDY 13⁰ x 11⁰
- BAR
- S
- LIVING RM 13⁰ x 19⁴
- CL
- LAUNDRY 7⁶ x 10⁰
- BEDROOM 11⁸ x 12⁰
- TRELLIS ABOVE
- COURTYARD
- CL
- CL
- LT
- W
- D
- P
- BEDROOM 10¹⁰ x 14⁴
- CURB
- GARAGE 21⁴ x 21⁴

70'-2"

85'-8"

● This home features interior planning for today's active family. Living areas include a living room with fireplace, a cozy study and family room with wet bar. Convenient to the kitchen is the formal dining room with attractive bay window overlooking the back yard. The four-bedroom sleeping area contains a sumptuous master suite. Also notice the cheerful flower porch with access from the master suite, living room and dining room.

Design V13315

Square Footage: 3,248

● Besides the covered front veranda, look for another full-width veranda to the rear of this charming home. The master bedroom, breakfast room, and gathering room all have French doors to this outdoor space. A handy wet bar/ tavern enhances entertainment options. The upper lounge could be a welcome haven.

157

Design V12739
Square Footage: 3,313

● If you and your family are looking for new living patterns, try to envision your days spent in this traditionally styled home. Its Early American flavor is captured by effective window and door treatment, cornice work and porch pillars. Its zoning is interesting.

The spacious interior leaves nothing to be desired. There are three bedrooms and two full baths in the sleeping area. A quiet, formal living room is separated from the other living areas. The gathering and dining rooms are adjacent to each other and function with

the excellent kitchen and its breakfast eating area. Note work island, pantry and pass-thru. Then, there is an extra guest room sunken one step. A live-in relative would enjoy the privacy of this room. Full bath is nearby. This is definitely a home for all to enjoy.

Design V11936
Square Footage: 3,280

● Country-estate living will be experienced in this 3,280 square foot home. The arrangement of the numerous rooms places the major living areas to the rear. They will enjoy their privacy and function with the outdoors. Count the sliding glass door units. Visualize the gracious indoor/outdoor living to be enjoyed by all the members of the family. Even the children's rooms have a terrace. The homemaker's work center overlooks the front yard and is efficient, indeed. There is a breakfast nook, a U-shaped kitchen, a separate laundry room, an extra washroom, and a whole wall of storage facilities. Be sure you notice the powder room near the entrance hall.

159

Created Especially For *Colonial Homes*

Design V12977
First Floor: 4,104 square feet
Second Floor: 979 square feet
Total: 5,083 square feet

● Beautifully balanced, both front and rear facades of this elegant brick manor depict classic Georgian symmetry. A columned, Greek entry opens to an impressive two-story foyer. Fireplaces, built-in shelves, and cabinets highlight each of the four main gathering areas: living room, dining room, family room, and library. The kitchen features a handy work island, pass-through to the dining room and snack bar that opens to the two-story family room. The master suite is located in its own wing and has a private atrium entrance and lounge/exercise room. A fifth fireplace graces the master bedroom and additional features include His and Hers walk-in closets, built-in vanity, and whirlpool bath. Two bedrooms, each with private bath and double walk-in closets, are located on the second floor. A bonus guest or hobby room is located on the first floor. The lovely rear terrace features double sets of stairs to the rear yard and each of the main wings has a grand fan-shaped window with multi-panes that overlooks the view.

Popular History House Series

Design V12133

First Floor: 3,024 square feet
Second Floor: 826 square feet
Total: 3,850 square feet

L **D**

● A country-estate home which will command all the attention it truly deserves. The projecting pediment gable supported by the finely proportioned columns lends an aura of elegance. The window treatment, the front door detailing, the massive, capped, chimney, the cupola, the brick veneer exterior and the varying roof planes complete the characterization of this impressive home. Inside, there are 3,024 square feet on the first floor. In addition, there is a two bedroom second floor should its development be necessary. However, whether called upon to function as a one, or 1½ story home it will provide a lifetime of gracious living. Don't overlook the compartment baths, the laundry and the many built-ins available.

Design V12693

Square Footage: 3,462

● This elegant Georgian manor is reminiscent of historic Rose Hill, built 1818 in Lexington, Kentucky. It is typical of the classic manors with Greek Revival features built in Kentucky as the 19th Century dawned. Note the classical portico of four Ionic columns plus the fine proportions. Also noteworthy is the updated interior, highlighted by a large country kitchen with fireplace and an efficient work center that includes an island cooktop. The country kitchen leads directly into a front formal dining room, just off the foyer. On the other side of the foyer is a front living room. A large library is located in the back of the house. It features built-in bookcases plus a fireplace, one of four fireplaces.

The exterior detailing of this design recalls 18th-Century New England architecture. Enter by way of the centered front door and you are greeted into the foyer. Directly to the right is the study or optional bedroom or to the left is the living room. This large formal room features sliding glass doors to the sun-drenched solarium. The beauty of the solarium will be appreciated from the master bedroom and the dining room along with the living room.

Design V12615

First Floor: 2,563 square feet
Second Floor: 552 square feet
Total: 3,115 square feet

L D

Design V11787

First Floor: 2,656 square feet
Second Floor: 744 square feet
Total: 3,400 square feet

D

● Can't you picture this dramatic home sitting on your property? The curving front drive is impressive as it passes the walks to the front door and the service entrance. The roof masses, the centered masonry chimney, the window symmetry and the 108 foot expanse across the front are among the features that make this a distinctive home. Of interest are the living and family rooms — both similar in size and each having its own fireplace.

● Organized zoning by room functions makes this Traditional design a comfortable home for living, as well as classic in its styling. A central foyer facilitates flexible traffic patterns. Quiet areas of the house include a media room and luxurious master bedroom suite with fitness area, spacious closet space and bath, as well as a lounge or writing area. Informal living areas of the house include a sun room, large country kitchen, and efficient kitchen with an island. Service areas include a room just off the garage for laundry, sewing, or hobbies. The second floor garage can double as a practical shop. Formal living areas include a living area and formal dining room. The second floor holds two bedrooms that would make a wonderful children's suite, with a study or TV area also upstairs.

Design V12921
First Floor: 3,215 square feet
Sun Room: 296 square feet
Second Floor: 711 square feet
Total: 4,222 square feet

L **D**

BEDROOM 13⁸x14⁰

BEDROOM 13⁸x14⁰

BATH

BALCONY

RAILING

UPPER FOYER

● This contemporary design also has a great deal to offer. Study the living areas. A fireplace opens up to both the living room and country kitchen. Privacy is the key word when describing the sleeping areas. the first floor master bedroom is away from the traffic of the house and features a dressing/exercise room, whirlpool tub and shower and a spacious walk-in closet. Two more bedrooms and a full bath are on the second floor. The three car garage is arranged so that the owners have use of a double-garage with an attached single on reserve for guests. The cheerful sun room adds 296 sq. ft. to the total.

SUN RM. 20⁰x14⁰

SLOPED CEILING

TERRACE

LIVING RM. 21⁰x14⁰

MEDIA RM. 15⁰x11⁸

MASTER BEDROOM 16⁰x22⁰

WHIRLPOOL SKYLIGHT ABOVE

BATH

COUNTRY KITCHEN 18⁰x30⁰

OPEN THRU FIREPLACE

DRESSING/ EXERCISE RM. 16⁸x12⁴

SKYLIGHT ABOVE

DINING RM. 14⁰x12⁰

BALCONY OVER

RAILING OPEN

WALK-IN CLOSET

SNACK BAR

FOYER POWDER RM.

COVERED PORCH

WASH RM.

PANTRY

CHINA SHELVES

SHELVES WORK BENCH

FREEZER

COVERED PORCH

COVERED PORCH

CLUTTER RM. 17⁸x14⁴

WORK ISLAND

2 CAR GARAGE 22⁸x22⁸

1 CAR GARAGE 20⁸x11⁰

Design V12920
First Floor: 3,067 square feet
Second Floor: 648 square feet
Total: 3,715 square feet

L **D**

97'-0"

Design V11928
Square Footage: 3,272

● You'll find this contemporary home is worthy of your consideration if you're looking for a house of distinction. The dramatic exterior is a sure-fire stopper. Even the most casual passer-by will take a second look. Interesting roof surfaces, massive brick chimney wall, recessed entrance, raised planters and garden wall are among the features that spell design distinction. And yet, the exterior is only part of the story this home has to tell. Its interior is no less unique. Consider the sunken living room, sloping, beamed ceiling of the family room, wonderful kitchen/laundry area, four-bedroom sleeping area with all those closets, bath facilities and sliding doors.

Design V12938
First Floor: 4,518 square feet
Second Floor: 882 square feet
Total: 5,400 square feet

● A semi-circular fanlight and sidelights grace the entrance of this striking contemporary. The lofty foyer, with balcony above, leads to an elegant, two-story living room with fireplace. The family room, housing a second fireplace, leads to a glorious sunroom; both have dramatic sloped ceilings.

The kitchen and breakfast room are conveniently located for access to the informal family room or to the formal dining room via the butler's pantry. The large adjoining clutter room with work island offers limitless possibilities for the seamstress, hobbyist, or indoor gardener. An executive-sized, first-

floor master suite offers privacy and relaxation; the bath with whirlpool tub and dressing area with twin walk-in closets open to a study that could double as an exercise room. Two second-floor bedrooms with private baths and walk-in closets round out the livability in this gracious home.

Design V12791
Square Footage: 3,809

● The use of vertical paned windows and the hipped roof highlight the exterior of this unique design. Upon entrance one will view a charming sunken atrium with skylight above plus a skylight in the dining room and one in the lounge. Formal living

will be graciously accommodated in the living room. It features a raised hearth fireplace, two sets of sliding glass doors to the rear terrace plus two more sliding doors, one to an outdoor dining terrace and the other to an outdoor lounge. Informal living

will be enjoyed in the family room with snack bar and in the large library. All will praise the fine planning of the master suite. It features a bay window, "his" and "her" dressing room with private baths and an abundance of closet space.

Design V12710
Square Footage: 3,296

● Artful design! In the skylight foyer, a balcony overlooks the lower level conversation pit. The gathering room features sloped ceilings, a raised hearth fireplace and triple sliding glass doors leading to the terrace. A drawing room and activities room (an additional 1,135 sq. ft. of livability on lower level) provide even more living space. Check out the kitchen carefully! Its size alone is unusual but there's also a built-in desk, island range and walk-in pantry. A luxury master suite with four closets, a dressing room, private bath and entry to the terrace. Two more large bedrooms. This is a glamourous home. Its unique design makes you proud when guests arrive. And its spacious qualities make family life a joy. The storage facilities in this plan are particularly noteworthy.

Design V12765
Square Footage: 3,365

D

● This three (optional four) bedroom contemporary is a most appealing design. It
offers living patterns that will add new
dimensions to your everyday routine. The
sloped ceilings in the family room, dining
room and living room add much spaciousness to this home. The efficient kitchen has
many fine features including the island
snack bar and work center, built-in desk,
china cabinet and wet bar. Adjacent to the
kitchen is a laundry room, washroom and
stairs to the basement. Formal and informal
living will each have its own area. A raised
hearth fireplace and sliding glass doors to
the rear terrace in the informal family
room. Another fireplace in the front formal
living room. You will enjoy all that natural
light in the garden room from the skylights
in the sloped ceiling.

Design V12747
Square Footage: 3,211

● This home will provide its occupants with a glorious adventure in contemporary living. Its impressive exterior seems to foretell that great things
are in store for even the most casual
visitor. A study of the plan reveals a
careful zoning for both the younger
and older family members. The quiet
area consists of the exceptional master
bedroom suite with private terrace, the
study and the isolated living room. For
the younger generation, there is a zone
with two bedrooms, family room and
nearby pool. The kitchen is handy and
serves the nook and family rooms with
ease. Be sure not to miss the sloping
ceilings, the dramatic planter and the
functional terrace.

Design V12343

Square Footage: 3,110

● If yours is a growing active family the chances are good that they will want their new home to relate to the outdoors. This distinctive design puts a premium on private outdoor living. And you don't have to install a swimming pool to get the most enjoyment from this home. Developing this area as a garden court will provide the indoor living areas with a breathtaking awareness of nature's beauty. Notice the fine zoning of the plan and how each area has its sliding glass doors to provide an unrestricted view. Three bedrooms plus study are serviced by three baths. The family and gathering rooms provide two great living areas. The kitchen is most efficient.

Design V12720
Square Footage: 3,130

● A raised hearth fireplace lights up the sunken gathering room which is exceptionally large and located at the very center of this home! For more living space, a well-located study and formal dining room each having a direct entrance to the gathering room. Plus a kitchen with all the right features . . . an island range, pantry, built-in desk and separate breakfast nook. There's an extended terrace, too . . . accessible from every room! And a master suite with double closets, dressing room and private bath. Plus two family bedrooms, a first-floor laundry and lots of storage space. A basement too, for additional space. This is a liveable home! You can entertain easily or you can hide-out with a good book. Study this plan with your family and pick out your favorite features. Don't miss the dramatic front entry planting areas, or the extra curb area in the garage.

Design V12534
Square Footage: 3,262

L

● The angular wings of this ranch home surely contribute to the unique character of the exterior. These wings effectively balance what is truly a dramatic and inviting front entrance. Massive masonry walls support the wide overhanging roof with its exposed wood beams. The patterned double front doors are surrounded by delightful expanses of glass. The raised planters and the masses of quarried stone (make it brick if you prefer) enhance the exterior appeal. Inside, a distinctive and practical floor plan stands ready to shape and serve the living patterns of the active family. The spacious entrance hall highlights sloped ceiling and an attractive open stairway to the lower level recreation area. An impressive fireplace and an abundance of glass are features of the big gathering room. Interestingly shaped dining room and study flank this main living area. The large kitchen offers many of the charming aspects of the family-kitchen of yesteryear. The bedroom wing has a sunken master suite.

175

Design V11711
First Floor: 2,580 square feet
Second Floor: 938 square feet
Total: 3,518 square feet

● If the gracious charm of the Colonial South appeals to you, this may be just the house you've been waiting for. There is something solid and dependable in its well-balanced facade and wide, pillared front porch. Much of the interest generated by this design comes from its interesting expanses of roof and angular projection of its kitchen and garage. The feeling of elegance is further experienced upon stepping inside, through double doors, to the spacious entrance hall where there is the separate coat room. Adjacent to this is the powder room, also convenient to the living areas. The work area of the kitchen and laundry room is truly outstanding. Designed as a five bedroom house, each is large. Storage and bath facilities are excellent.

TRADITIONAL DESIGNS UNDER 1500 Sq. Ft. . . .

as featured in the following pages, capture the warmth and charm of an early period in our history. Here we see appealing examples of the one-story house reflecting the beauty that results from effective and prudent use of early American design features. These include, double-hung, muntined windows, panelled doors with sidelights, shutters, cupolas, flower boxes, carriage lamps, wood siding with corner boards, covered front entrances, etc. And above all, pleasing proportion is a prime requisite for achieving that delightful exterior appeal that assures a lasting value for, perhaps, life's biggest single investment. Here are houses for the modest budget.

Design V12707

Square Footage: 1,267

L D

● Here is a charming Early American adaptation that will serve as a picturesque and practical retirement home. Also, it will serve admirably those with a small family in search of an efficient, economically built home. The living area, highlighted by the raised hearth fireplace, is spacious. The kitchen features eating space and easy access to the garage and basement. The dining room is adjacent to the kitchen and views the rear yard. Then, there is the basement for recreation and hobby pursuits. The bedroom wing offers three bedrooms and two full baths. Don't miss the sliding doors to the terrace from the living room and the master bedroom. Storage units are plentiful including a pantry cabinet in the eating area of the kitchen. This plan will be efficient and livable.

Design V11173
Square Footage: 1,500

● A picturesque, L-shaped traditional one-story with an attractive, covered porch. This floor plan is wonderfully zoned. All the major areas are but a few steps from the front entry hall. The living room with its bay window enables one to have a delightful view of the rear yard. It will lend itself to fine furniture arrangements and be free of cross-room traffic, too. Three bedrooms in the sleeping area plus a full bath. The homemaker will love the efficient kitchen as well as the separate laundry area. The extra washroom, through the laundry, is handy from the outdoors. The favorite spot will be the large family room. This multi-purpose area functions well with the kitchen. Built-in china cabinets are located in the two front corners of this area. Certainly a delightful feature. Two storage areas are in the garage. Note that the garage can be built to accommodate either one or two cars.

Design V11193
Square Footage: 1,396

● This L-shaped, one-story with its attached two-car garage incorporates many of the time-tested features of older New England. The attractive cut-up windows, the shutters, the panelled door, the fence and the wood siding contribute to the charm of the exterior. The floor plan is outstanding by virtue of such proven features as the separate dining room, the family-kitchen, the quiet living room with its bay window and the privacy of the bedroom area. The U-shaped work center will be easy to work in.

Design V11327
Square Footage: 1,392

● A design to overcome the restrictions of a relatively narrow building site. This home has one of the best one-story plans you'll ever see. Its four bedrooms and two baths form what amounts to a separate wing. The fourth bedroom is located next to the living room so it may serve as a study, if needed. The traffic plan pivoting in the front entry, is excellent. And the kitchen is in just the right place - next to the dining and family rooms, close to the front and side doors and near the laundry. Another fine quality of the kitchen is its snack bar pass-thru to the family room. Formal living will take place in the rear living/dining room. This area can open up to the rear terrace by two sets of sliding glass doors (another set is in the family room). An optional basement plan is included with the purchase of this design.

OPTIONAL BASEMENT PLAN

Design V11316
Square Footage: 1,488

● As picturesque as they come. Within 1,488 square feet, there are the fine sleeping facilities, two full baths, family room, a formal dining area, a big living room, an excellent kitchen and plenty of closets. Other noteworthy features include the fireplace, sliding glass doors to the rear terrace, a fine basement, a pass-thru to family room from kitchen, an attached garage and an appealing front porch.

OPTIONAL
NON - BASEMENT

Design V11939
Square Footage: 1,387

L **D**

● A finely proportioned house with more than its full share of charm. The brick veneer exterior contrasts pleasingly with the narrow horizontal siding of the oversized attached two-car garage. Perhaps the focal point of the exterior is the recessed front entrance with its double Colonial styled doors. The secondary service entrance through the garage to the kitchen area is a handy feature. Study the plan. It features three bedrooms, two full baths, living room with fireplace, front kitchen with an eating area, formal dining room, plenty of storage potential plus a basement for additional storage or perhaps to be developed as a recreational area.

Design V11190
Square Footage: 1,232

● Build this L-shaped house on your lot with the garage door facing the street, or with the front entry door facing the street. Whichever orientation you choose, and you should take into consideration lot restriction and any particular view you might want to enjoy from the living areas, you will find the floor plan a very fine one. The center entrance hall features twin coat closets, a slate floor and an attractive six foot high room divider. This built-in unit has a planter on top with storage space below which is accessible from the living room.

Design V11107
Square Footage: 1,416

L **D**

● A smart looking traditional adaptation which, because of its perfectly rectangular shape, will be most economical to build. The low-pitched roof has a wide overhang which accentuates its low-slung qualities. The attached two-car garage is oversized to permit the location of extra bulk storage space. Further, its access to the house is through the handy separate laundry area. This house will function as either a four bedroom home, or as one that has three bedrooms, plus a quiet study. Features include a fireplace in the living room, built-in china cabinet in the breakfast room, sizable vanity in the main baths and more.

Design V11803
Square Footage: 1,434

● The texture of brick enhances the beauty of this pleasing traditional home. The center entrance with its double doors is protected by the covered porch. The end living room will be free of annoying cross-room traffic. A centered fireplace wall with end book shelves is an outstanding feature of this area. The separate dining room is ideally located between the living room and kitchen which allows for its maximum use.

Design V11374
Square Footage: 1,248

● A low-pitched, overhanging roof that hugs the ground and gives an impression that belies the actual dimensions of the home is a feature of this design. Board and batten siding, stone veneer, muntined windows and paneled shutters are all earmarks of Early American styling. Planning is open and pleasant; the living area leads to the dining space and through sliding glass doors to the outdoor terrace; the in-line kitchen leads to the all-purpose family room.

OPTIONAL NO BASEMENT PLAN

Design V11367
Square Footage: 1,432

● Brick veneer, a projecting two-car garage with a gabled end, wood shutters, attractive window treatment, paneled front door and a wood fence with lamp post are among the features that make the exterior of this traditional house so charming. The formal living room with all that blank wall space for effective furniture placement, is just the right size for quiet conversation. The family room will be the hub of the informal activities with a snack bar and pass-thru to the kitchen. Adjacent to the kitchen is a room which may function as a study, sewing room, TV room or formal dining room. Note the two full baths and stall shower.

Design V11944
Square Footage: 1,474

● Imagine, four bedrooms and two full baths in a home under 1,500 square feet. As if this wasn't enough to make this a home of distinction, there is an abundance of livability in the other half of the floor plan. Here, there is an excellent living room which looks out upon the rear terrace, a large family dining area and an efficient U-shaped kitchen. It will be difficult to find a better investment.

Design V11189
Square Footage: 1,240

● When you obtain the blueprints for this picturesque frame home you will receive details for both basement and non-basement construction. Whatever your choice of construction your family will love the basic livability provided by the arrangement of the three bedrooms, two full baths, the formal living room, the family-dining room and the efficient U-shaped kitchen. The single car garage may be readily adapted to accommodate two cars. Note the three garage storage closets.

Design V11147
Square Footage: 1,264

● "Who could ask for anything more" is an appropriate theme for this house. It is easy on the budget with only 1,264 square feet, but it includes big-house features, such as four bedrooms, one-and-one-half baths, a fireplace, a family room and an over-sized garage, plus the convenience of more closets than the normal family would require. Don't miss the built-in chest, china cupboard and the kitchen cooking equipment.

Design V11074
Square Footage: 1,356

● There is much to consider when deciding upon the selection of this house as your new home. First of all, the exterior leaves nothing to be desired. It has exceptional eye appeal and will surely retain its charm for generations to come. The projecting bedroom wing, the attached two-car garage and the large covered front porch are major features which help set the character of the exterior. Then, the floor plan with its L-shaped zoning could hardly be improved upon.

Design V13211
Square Footage: 1,344

● This is a captivating version of the three bedroom, two-bath L-shaped home. Notice that spacious living-dining area with the many windows to the side plus a view of the rear terrace from the dining room. The living room also has a fireplace for added appeal. The breakfast room also will enjoy the rear terrace and includes such features as a pantry, china cabinet and storage closet. The kitchen is an efficient work center with nearby adjacent basement stairs. The basement could be developed into an informal recreation area.

Design V11188
Square Footage: 1,326

● A charming, traditionally styled, L-shaped home which can be built most economically. Constructed on a concrete slab, the house itself forms a perfect rectangle, thus assuring the most efficient use of materials. The center entrance routes traffic to the various areas of this plan most conveniently. Compact, yet spacious. The three bedrooms are sizable and enjoy their privacy. The entire breadth of the rear experiences the delightful feeling of openness.

Design V12122
Square Footage: 1,248

● An ideal home for a family of modest size with a modest budget. This charming frame house can be built most economically. The main portion of the house is a perfect 52 x 24 foot rectangle. The projecting two-car garage with its cupola and traditionally sloped roof, adds immeasurably to the exterior appeal. The double front doors are sheltered by the covered porch. Inside, there is a wealth of livability. Two full baths, located back-to-back for plumbing economy, service the three bedrooms.

OPTIONAL BASEMENT PLAN

Design V11025 Square Footage: 1,426

● A real charmer. At the front of the house, parents have a private master suite with a full bath and generous closet space. Opposite the master bedroom is a secluded living room, without any through-traffic, and a center fireplace that provides a focus of interest for arranging furniture. Recreational facilities may be developed in the full basement. This area also lends itself to developing additional storage.

● This traditional one-story home with its attached two-car garage virtually overflows with livability. There is not a foot of wasted space incorporated in this plan. Seldom is such good use made of a nominal amount of space. This home can be called upon to function as either a three or a four bedroom home. If the former, then the extra room may be utilized as a family room or study. There are two eating areas.

Design V13204 Square Footage: 1,250

Design V11024
Square Footage: 1,252

● "Charming", is but one of the many words that could be chosen to describe this traditional home. While essentially a frame house, the front exterior features natural quarried stone. Below the overhanging roof, the windows and door treatment is most pleasing. The board fence with its lamp post completes a delightful picture. Highlighting the interior is the living room with its raised hearth fireplace.

● With the kitchen in this strategic location, the homemaker does not have to go through half of the house in order to get to the front door. The second bath with its stall shower is convenient to the third bedroom, the family area and the outdoor terrace. The main bath has a delightful built-in vanity. And how about the living room which has a large picture window and an attractive fireplace? Note storage closet.

Design V11197
Square Footage: 1,232

Design V11075
Square Footage: 1,232

● This picturesque traditional one-story home has much to offer the young family. Because of its rectangular shape and its predominantly frame exterior, construction costs will be economical. Passing through the front entrance, visitors will be surprised to find so much livability in only 1,232 square feet. Consider these features: spacious formal living and dining area; two full baths; efficient kitchen; and large, rear family room. In addition there is the full basement for further recreational facilities and bulk storage. The attached garage is extra long to accommodate the storage of garden equipment, lawn furniture, bicycles, etc.

Design V11366
Square Footage: 1,280

● The extension of the main roof, along with the use of ornamental iron, vertical siding and glass side lites flanking the paneled door, all contribute to a delightful and inviting front entrance to this L-shaped design. There is much to recommend this design—from the attached two-car garage to the walk-in closet of the master bedroom. Don't overlook the compartmented master bath with its stall shower and powder room; the built-in china cabinet with an attractive planter above or the two closets right in the center of the house.

Design V11191
Square Footage: 1,232

L **D**

● A careful study of the floor plan for this cozy appearing traditional home reveals a fine combination of features which add tremendously to convenient living. For instance, observe the wardrobe and storage facilities of the bedroom area. A built-in chest in the one bedroom and also one in the family room. Then, notice the economical plumbing of the two full back-to-back baths. Postively a great money saving feature for today and in the future. Further, don't overlook the location of the washer and dryer which have cupboards above the units themselves. Observe storage facilities. Optional two-car garage is available if necessary.

Design V13208
Square Footage: 1,152

● This appealing traditional, L-shaped home has much to offer those in search of a moderately sized home which can be built within the confines of a relatively small budget. First of all, consider the charm of the exterior. Surely this will be one of the most appealing houses on the street. And little wonder. Its proportion and architectural detailing are excellent. The shutters, the window treatment, the roof lines, the planter and the fence and lamp post are all captivating features.

Design V11373
Square Footage: 1,200

D

● A traditional L-shaped home with an attractive recessed front entrance which leads into a floor plan where traffic patterns are most efficient. It is possible to go from one room to any other without needlessly walking through a third room. The daily household chores will be easily dispatched. The U-shaped kitchen has an abundance of cupboard and counter space, plus a pass-thru to the snack bar in the family room. The washer and dryer location is handy.

Design V11058
Square Footage: 1,200

● When you build this charming L-shaped traditionally designed home don't leave out the wood fence and lamp post. These are just the features needed to complete the picture. A porch shelters the front door which leads to the centered entry flanked by the formal living room and the informal family room. The kitchen is but a step from the separate dining room. The laundry equipment, the extra wash room and heater location are all grouped together.

Design V12570
Square Footage: 1,176

L **D**

● This attractive Tudor offers a study which could double ideally as a guest room, sewing room or even serve as the TV room. The living area is a spacious L-shaped zone for formal living and dining. The efficient kitchen is handy to the front door and overlooks the front yard. It features a convenient breakfast nook for those informal meals. Handy to the entry from the garage and the yard are the stairs to the basement. Don't overlook the attractive front porch.

Design V11279
Square Footage: 1,200

● This cozy traditional ranch house is ideal for a retired couple. Its small size and one-story plan make it easy for them to enjoy and maintain. Its low cost also makes it feasible for young married couples, who, as their families and income expand, can add bedrooms to the front or side of the bedroom wing. The house provides good circulation to living, sleeping and utility zones so that no room has the interruption of cross traffic.

Design V12607
Square Footage: 1,208

[L] [D]

● Here is an English Tudor retirement cottage with two sizable bedrooms, a full bath, plus an extra wash room. The living and dining areas are spacious and overlook both front and rear yards. Sliding glass doors in both these areas lead to the outdoor terrace. Note the fireplace in the living room. In addition to the formal dining area with its built-in china cabinet, there is a delightful breakfast eating alcove in the kitchen. The U-shaped work area is wonderfully efficient. The laundry is around the corner. Blueprints include optional basement details.

OPTIONAL BASEMENT

● Picturesque and practical are two words to aptly describe the merits of this fine L-shaped traditional home. The delightful proportion and the appealing details help create the charming image. The floor plan is a particularly well-planned one. In less than 1,500 square feet there are three bedrooms, 2½ baths, a family room, a 25 foot formal living and dining area, a strategically located kitchen, a first floor laundry and a basement. Other noteworthy features include the two fireplaces, the wood box, sliding glass doors to side terrace and excellent storage facilities throughout.

Design V11094
Square Footage: 1,484

Design V11297
Square Footage: 1,034

● The U-shape of this appealing home qualifies it for a narrow building site. The efficiency of the floor plan recommends it for convenient living during the retirement years. The charm of the exterior surely makes it a prize-winner. The attractive wood fence and its lamp post complete the enclosure of the flower court—a delightful setting for the walk to the covered front entrance. The work area is outstanding. There is the laundry with closet space, an extra wash room and a fine kitchen with eating space.

Design V11309
Square Footage: 1,100

● Here is a real low-cost charmer. Delightful proportion and an effective use of materials characterize this Colonial version. Vertical boards and battens, a touch of stone and pleasing window treatment catch the eye. The compact, economical plan offers spacious formal living and dining areas plus a family room. The kitchen is strategically located—it overlooks the rear yard and is but a few steps from the outdoor terrace. The attached garage has a large storage and utility area to the rear.

Design V11364
Square Footage: 1,142

D

● The family working within the confines of a restricted building budget will find this eye-catching traditional ranch home the solution to its housing needs. The brick exterior with its recessed front entrance, wood shutters, bowed window, attached garage and wood fence is charming, indeed. The living room is free of cross-room traffic and lends itself to effective and flexible furniture placement. The master bedroom has its own private bath with stall shower, while the main bath features a built-in vanity and adjacent linen storage.

Design V13213
Square Footage: 1,060

● It would be difficult to find a design with more livability built into its 1,060 square feet. There are features galore. Make a list.

Design V11399
Square Footage: 1,040

● A real winner which will surely satisfy the restricted building budget, while returning a tremendous amount in the way of convenient living and pride of ownership.

Design V12198
Square Footage: 1,193

56'-0"

TERRACE

MASTER BED RM. 10⁰ x 12⁸

BED RM. 8⁴ x 11⁰

KITCHEN FAMILY RM. 17⁰ x 13⁶

W.R.

BATH

CL.

CL.

GARAGE 13⁸ x 23⁴

32'-5"

BED RM. 10⁰ x 10⁰

BED RM. 10⁰ x 10⁰

LIN.

CL.

RAISED HEARTH

LIVING RM. 18⁴ x 13⁶

WOOD FENCE

LAMP POST

BASEMENT PLAN

56'-0"

TERRACE

MASTER BED RM. 10⁰ x 12⁸

BED RM. 8⁴ x 11⁰

KITCHEN FAMILY RM. 17⁰ x 13⁶

W.R.

BATH

AIR COND.

GARAGE 13⁸ x 23⁴

32'-5"

BED RM. 10⁰ x 10⁰

BED RM. 10⁰ x 10⁰

LIN.

CL.

RAISED HEARTH

LIVING RM. 18⁴ x 13⁶

WOOD FENCE

LAMP POST

NON BASEMENT PLAN

● Can't you just picture this delightfully proportioned traditional home sitting on your property? Surely it is an exciting thought to contemplate. And the appeal isn't just restricted to the outside, either! The floor plan is an extremely simple one. Yet it features four bedrooms, excellent storage facilities, a private wash room for the master bedroom, an in-line kitchen with a long bank of wall cupboards, a generous all-purpose family area and a raised hearth fireplace. Blueprints for this design include both basement and nonbasement details for construction.

Design V11311 Square Footage: 1,050

L D

● Delightful design and effective, flexible planning comes in little packages, too. This fine traditional exterior with its covered front entrance features an alternate basement plan. Note how the non-basement layout provides a family room and mud room, while the basement option shows kitchen eating and dining room. Sensible planning.

OPTIONAL BASEMENT PLAN

Design V11531
Square Footage: 936

● This is but another example of delightful custom design applied to a small home. The detailing of the windows and the door, plus the effective use of siding and brick contribute to the charm. The attached garage helps make the house appear even bigger than it really is. The front-to-rear living/dining area opens onto the rear terrace through sliding glass doors. The washer and dryer with wall cabinets above complete the efficient work center area. Observe the extra kitchen closet.

Design V11522
Square Footage: 960

● Certainly a home to make its occupants proud. The front exterior is all brick veneer, while the remainder of the house and garage is horizontal siding. The slightly overhanging roof, the wood shutters and the carriage lights flanking the front door are among the features that will surely catch the eyes of the passer-by. The living room has excellent wall space for furniture placement. The family room, the full basement and the attached garage are other features. Don't miss the sliding glass doors.

Design V12153
Square Footage: 960

D

● If you can't make up your mind as to which of the delightful traditional exteriors you like best on the opposing page, you need not decide now. The blueprints you receive show details for the construction of all three front exteriors. However, before you order, decide whether you wish your next home to have a basement or not. If you prefer the basement plan order Design V12153 above. Should your preference be for a non-basement plan you should order blueprints for Design V12154 below. Whatever your choice, you'll forever love the charm of its exterior and the comfort and convenience of the interior. The three bedrooms will serve your family ideally.

Design V12154
Square Footage: 960

D

Design V12163 Square Footage: 864

● Traditional charm is an apt description of this low-cost one story. Every foot of space makes its vital contribution to total livability. There is a full basement.

● A hip-roofed contemporary with an attached carport. Both kitchen and dining room accessible to rear terrace. List the many storage units. Don't miss linen closets.

Design V12166 Square Footage: 864

Design V13223 Square Footage: 1,032

● The master bedroom and kitchen of this efficient plan have direct access to the washroom. A full bath is convenient to all three bedrooms. The kitchen is but a few steps from the rear yard.

Design V12165 Square Footage: 880

● Whether called upon to function as a two or a three bedroom home, this attractive design will serve its occupants ideally for many years. There are two eating areas.

Design V12159 Square Footage: 1,077

● A perfect rectangle which will be easy and economical to build. There is a family kitchen, three bedrooms, full bath plus powder room and bulk storage area in the garage.

Design V11187
Square Footage: 1,120

● A lovely ranch with everything for a growing family. The large front living room is highlighted by a corridor kitchen and family room to the rear. Note the closet space in the master bedroom and both children's rooms. A rear terrace with family room access adds outdoor livability.

● A cozy plan, but just right for a small family or empty nesters. An ample living room/dining room area leads the way to a rear kitchen overlooking a terrace. Two full baths serve three bedrooms — one a master bedroom. Multi-paned windows with quaint shutters add a touch of charm to the design.

Design V11113
Square Footage: 1,008

L **D**

● Here are three optional front exteriors which can be built with either the basement plan, V12160, or the non-basement plan, V12161. Whichever number you order, the blueprints will include details for all three optional front elevations. It is interesting to observe the variations in the two floor plans. Don't miss the extra storage facilities. Notice the location of the stacked washer and dryer in the non-basement plan.

Design V12160
Square Footage: 960

Design V12161
Square Footage: 960

TERRACE

MASTER BEDROOM
11⁰ x 13⁰

GATHERING RM.
14⁰ x 13¹⁰

DINING RM.
11⁰ x 10⁰

BATH

DRESSING RM.

KITCHEN
11⁴ x 12⁸

NICHE

TERRACE

BEDROOM
11⁰ x 12⁰

BATH

FOYER

COVERED PORCH

46'-4"

GARAGE
21⁰ x 22⁰

50'-0"

GATHERING RM.
14⁰ x 13¹⁰

DINING RM.
11⁰ x 10⁰

TERRACE

KITCHEN
10⁸ x 12⁸

OVENS

FOYER

GARAGE

ALTERNATE KITCHEN PLAN

Design V12911
Square Footage: 1,233

● A low budget retirement house can be a neighborhood showplace, too. Exquisite proportion, fine detailing, projecting wings, and interesting roof lines help provide the appeal of this modest one-story. Each of the bedrooms has excellent wall space and wardrobe storage potential. The master bath features a vanity, twin lavatories, stall shower, plus a whirlpool. Another full bath is strategically located to service the second bedroom as well as other areas of the house. Open planning results in a spacious living-dining area with fireplace and access to the outdoor terraces. This design offers a choice between two kitchen layouts. Which do you prefer? The one which functions informally with the gathering room, or its more formal counterpart? Each layout has all the amenities to assure a pleasant and efficient workday. Don't miss the basement for the development of additional livability.

CONTEMPORARY DESIGNS UNDER 2000 Sq. Ft. . . .

offer a refreshing and exciting break from the many other so-called "high-styled" traditional exteriors. Their simple, straightforward, uncluttered appearance makes contemporary exteriors a favorite of many. The houses in this section exemplify the fact that distinctive, yet practical, contemporary design can come in modest packages. Whether simple rectangles, modified L-shapes, or irregular configurations, their floor plans can deliver interesting and convenient living patterns. Whether their exteriors have a low, ground-hugging profile, a geometric shape, or an angular appearance they can capture the eye of the most casual passer-by in a most pleasing fashion.

● This is most certainly an outstanding contemporary design. Study the exterior carefully before your journey to inspect the floor plan. The vertical lines are carried from the siding to the paned windows to the garage door. The front entry is recessed so the overhanging roof creates a covered porch.

Note the planter court with privacy wall. The floor plan is just as outstanding. The rear gathering room has a sloped ceiling, raised hearth fireplace, sliding glass doors to the terrace and a snack bar with pass-thru to the kitchen. In addition to the gathering room, there is the living room/study. This

room could be utilized in a variety of ways depending on your family's choice. The formal dining room is convenient to the U-shaped kitchen. Three bedrooms and two closely located baths are in the sleeping wing. This plan includes details for the construction of an optional basement.

Design V12818
Square Footage: 1,566

L D

Design V12703
Square Footage: 1,445

D

● This modified, hip-roofed contemporary design will be the answer for those who want something both practical, yet different, inside and out. The covered front walk sets the stage for entering a modest sized home with tremendous livability. The focal point will be the pleasant conversation lounge. It is sunken, partially open to the other living areas and shares the enjoyment of the thru-fireplace with the living room. There are two bedrooms, two full baths and a study. The kitchen is outstanding.

Design V12753
Square Footage: 1,539

D

● In this day and age of expensive building sites, projecting the attached garage from the front line of the house makes a lot of economic sense. It also lends itself to interesting roof lines and plan configurations. Here, a pleasing covered walkway to the front door results. A privacy wall adds an extra measure of design appeal and provides a sheltered terrace for the study/bedroom. You'll seldom find more livability in 1,539 square feet. Imagine, three bedrooms, two baths, a spacious living/dining area and a family room.

Design V12744
Square Footage: 1,381

● Here is a practical and an attractive contemporary home for that narrow building site. It is designed for efficiency with the small family or retired couple in mind. Sloping ceilings foster an extra measure of spaciousness. In addition to the master bedroom, there is the study that can also serve as the second bedroom or as an occasional guest room. The single bath is compartmented and its dual access allows it to serve living and sleeping areas more than adequately. Note raised hearth fireplace, snack bar, U-shaped kitchen, laundry, two terraces, etc.

Design V12892

Square Footage: 1,623

D

● What a striking contemporary! It houses an efficient floor plan with many outstanding features. The foyer has a sloped ceiling and an open staircase to the basement. To the right of the foyer is the work center. Note the snack bar, laundry and covered dining porch, along with the step-saving kitchen. Both the gathering and dining rooms overlook the backyard. Each of the three bedrooms has access to an outdoor area. Now, just think of the potential use of the second floor loft. Its 160 square feet of livability could be used as a den, sewing room, lounge or any of many other activities. It overlooks the gathering room and front foyer and has two large skylights.

Design V12809

Square Footage: 1,551

● One-story living can be very rewarding and this contemporary home will be just that. Study the indoor-outdoor living relationships which are offered in the back of the plan. Sliding glass doors are in each of the rear rooms leading to the terrace. The formal dining room has a second set of doors to the porch. Many enjoyable hours will be spent here in the hot tub. A sloped ceiling with skylights is above the hot tub area. Back to the interior, there is a large gathering room. It, too, has a sloped ceiling which will add to its spacious appearance. The interior kitchen is conveniently located between the formal and informal dining areas. Two, or optional three, bedrooms are ready to serve the small family.

TERRACE

TERRACE

49'-8"

50'-0"

FORMAL DINING

GATHERING RM.
23⁶x11⁰-14⁸

STUDY/
BEDROOM
9²x11⁰

MASTER
BEDROOM
13⁶x11⁰

SLOPED
CEILING

SLOPED
CEILING

SLOPED
CEILING

BRKFST. RM.
8⁸x10⁴

SNACK BAR

BAR

LIN

OPEN OVER CLOSET

CL

CL

DESK

KITCHEN
12⁰x9⁰

RANGE

REF'G

DRESSING RM.

LAUNDRY

FOYER

BATH

CL

BATH

SKY-
LIGHT

TUB

BEDROOM
10⁰x10⁰

SKY-
LIGHT

TUB

CURB

COVERED
PORCH

ENTRANCE COURT

GARAGE
19⁴x21⁸

Design V12864

Square Footage: 1,387

L **D**

● Projecting the garage to the front of a house is very economical in two ways. One, it reduces the required lot size for building (in this case the overall width is under 50 feet). And, two, it will protect the interior from street noise and unfavorable winds. Many other characteristics about this design deserve mention, too. The entrance court and covered porch are a delightful way to enter this home. Upon entering, the foyer will take you to the various areas. The interior kitchen has an adjacent breakfast room and a snack bar on the gathering room side. Here, one will enjoy a sloped ceiling and a fireplace. A study with a wet bar is adjacent. If need be, adjust the plan and make the study the third bedroom. Sliding glass doors in the study and master bedroom open to the terrace.

213

Design V12330
Square Footage: 1,854

● The masonry masses of this home's exterior are pleasing. While the blueprints call for the use of stone, you may wish to substitute brick veneer. Sloping ceiling and plenty of glass will assure the living area of a fine feeling of spaciousness. The covered porches enhance the enjoyment of outdoor living. Two baths serve the three bedroom sleeping area.

Design V13163
Square Footage: 1,552

OPTIONAL BASEMENT

● Four bedrooms and two full baths will very adequately serve the growing family occupying this appealing contemporary. Its perfectly rectangular shape means economical construction. Note the attractive built-in planter adjacent to the front door. The large storage area behind the carport will solve any storage problems. Laundry and wash room are strategically located to serve the family.

Design V11021
Square Footage: 1,432

OPTIONAL BASEMENT PLAN

● Behind the double front doors of this straight-forward, contemporary design there is a heap of living to be enjoyed. The large living room with its dramatic glass wall and attractive fireplace will never fail to elicit comments of delight. The master bedroom has a whole wall of wardrobe closets and a private bath. Another two bedrooms and a bath easily serve the family.

Design V12182
Square Footage: 1,558

● What a great new dimension in living is represented by this unique contemporary design! Each of the major zones comprise a separate unit which, along with the garage, clusters around the atrium. High sloped ceilings and plenty of glass areas assure a feeling of spaciousness. The quiet living room will enjoy its privacy, while activities in the informal family room will be great fun functioning with the kitchen. A snack bar opens the kitchen to the atrium. The view, above right, shows portions of snack bar and the front entry looking through the glass wall. There are two full baths strategically located to service all areas conveniently. Storage facilities are excellent, indeed. Don't miss the storage potential found in the garage. There is a work bench and storage balcony above.

Design V12702

Square Footage: 1,636

● A rear living room with a
sloping ceiling, built-in bookcases, a raised hearth fireplace
and sliding glass doors to the
rear living terrace highlight this
design. If desired, bi-fold doors
permit this room to function
with the adjacent study. An
open railing next to the stairs to
the basement recreation area
fosters additional spaciousness.
The kitchen has plenty of cabinet and cupboard space. It features informal eating space and
is but a step or two from the
separate dining room. Note side
dining terrace. Each of the
three rooms in the sleeping
wing has direct access to outdoor living. The master bedroom highlights a huge walk-in
wardrobe closet, dressing room
with built-in vanity and private
bath with large towel storage
closet. Projecting the two-car
garage with its twin doors to the
front not only contributes to an
interesting exterior, but reduces
the size of the building site required for this home.

TERRACE   TERRACE

TERRACE

DINING RM.
12⁰ x 10⁰

GATHERING RM.
16⁰ x 16⁴

STUDY
10⁰ x 10⁰

MASTER BEDROOM
12⁰ x 13⁴

WALK-IN CLOSET

BRKFST RM.
12⁰ x 8⁰

SLOPED CEILING

DESK

BAR

CL.

DRESS. RM.

VANITY

COOK TOP

LINEN

BATH

KITCHEN
14⁰ x 10⁸

PNTRY

DN. RAILING

SLOPED CEILING

FOYER

CL.

BATH

CL.

S

OVENS

B.C.

REF'G

D.W

W.R.

MUD RM.

CL.

PORCH

BEDROOM
12⁰ x 11⁰

TERRACE

62'-4"

GARAGE
21⁴ x 21⁴

CURB   SLOPED   CEILING

66'-0"

Design V12918
Square Footage: 1,693

● Alternating use of stone and wood gives a textured look to this striking Contemporary home with wide overhanging roof lines and built-in planter box. The design is just as exciting on the inside with two bedrooms, including a master suite, a study (or optional third bedroom), rear gathering room with fireplace and sloped ceiling, rear dining room, and efficient U-shaped kitchen with pass-thru to an adjoining breakfast room. A mud room and washroom are located between kitchen and spacious two-car garage. Includes plans for optional basement.

Design V11917
Square Footage: 1,728

● Imagine your family living in this appealing one-story home. Think of how your living habits will adjust to the delightful patterns offered here. Flexibility is the byword; for there are two living areas — the front, formal living room and the rear, informal family room. There are two dining areas — the dining room overlooking the front yard and the breakfast room looking out upon the rear yard. There are outstanding bath facilities — a full bath for the master bedroom and one that will be handy to the living areas as a powder room. Then there is the extra wash room just where you need it — handy to the kitchen, the basement and the outdoors.

Design V11891
Square Footage: 1,986

● There is much more to a house than just its exterior. And while the appeal of this home would be difficult to beat, it is the living potential of the interior that gives this design such a high ranking. The sunken living room with its adjacent dining room is highlighted by the attractive fireplace, the raised planter and the distinctive glass panels.
A raised hearth fireplace, snack bar and sliding glass doors which open to the outdoor deck are features of the family room. The work center area is efficient. It has plenty of storage space and a laundry area.

Design V11396
Square Footage: 1,664

● Three bedrooms, 2½ baths, a formal dining area, a fine family room and an attached two-car garage are among the highlights of this frame home. The living-dining area is delightfully spacious with the fireplace wall, having book shelves at each end, functioning as a practical area divider. The many storage units found in this home will be a topic of conversion. The cabinets above the strategically located washer and dryer, the family room storage wall and walk-in closet and the garage facilities are particularly noteworthy. Blueprints show how to build this house with and without a basement.

Design V12902

Square Footage: 1,632

L

● A sun space highlights this passive solar design. It has access from the kitchen, dining room and garage. It will be a great place to enjoy meals because of its location. Three skylights highlight the interior - one in the kitchen, laundrey and master bath. An air-locked vestibule helps this design's energy efficiency. Interior livability is excellent. The living/dining room has a sloping ceiling, fireplace and two sets of sliding glass doors to the terrace. This area will cater to numerous family activities. Additional activities can take place in the basement. Note its open staircase. Three bedrooms are in the sleeping wing. The square footage of the sun space is 216 and is not included in the above figure.

Design V12886
Square Footage: 1,733

● This one-story house is attractive with its contemporary exterior. It has many excellent features to keep you and your family happy for many years. For example, notice the spacious gathering room with sliding glass doors that allow easy access to the greenhouse. Another exciting feature of this room is that you will receive an abundance of sunshine through the clerestory windows. Also, this plan offers you two nice sized bedrooms. The master suite is not only roomy but also unique because through both the bedroom and the bath you can enter a greenhouse with a hot tub. The hot tub will be greatly appreciated after a long, hard day at work. Don't forget to note the breakfast room with access to the terrace. You will enjoy the efficient kitchen that will make preparing meals a breeze. A greenhouse window here is charming. An appealing, open staircase leads to the basement. The square footages of the greenhouses are 394 and are not included in the above figure.

TERRACE

TERRACE

70'-0"

51'-8"

BRKFST. RM.
11⁰ x 10⁰ + BAY

DINING RM.
10⁴ x 12⁴

GATHERING RM.
17⁰ x 20⁴

BEDROOM
11⁴ x 10⁸

MASTER
BEDROOM
12⁰ x 16⁴

SLOPED
CEILING

8'-0" FLAT CEILING

SNACK BAR

PASS

OVENS

KITCHEN
11⁰ x 11⁰

CURIOS

RAILING

LIN.

CL.

CL.

WALK IN
CLOSET

DRSG
RM.

LAUND
8⁰ x 5⁰

CL.

FOYER

SLOPED
CEILING

DN.

BATH

COOK
TOP

REF'G

LS

SLOPED
CEILING

BATH

CURB

COVERED
PORCH

MEDIA RM.
14⁸ x 11⁰

T.V. STEREO / VCR, SPKR
SPEAKERS, ETC.

WHIRLPOOL

SLOPED
CEILING

SLOPED
CEILING

GARAGE
21⁴ x 21⁸ + STORAGE

SLOPED
CEILING

STORAGE

Design V12913
Square Footage: 1,835

D

● This smart design features multi-gabled ends, varied roof lines, and vertical windows. It also offers efficient zoning by room functions and plenty of modern comforts for Contemporary family lifestyle. A covered porch leads through a foyer to a large central gathering room with fireplace, sloped ceiling, and its own special view of a rear terrace. A modern kitchen with snack bar has a pass-thru to a breakfast room with view of the terrace. There's also an adjacent dining room. A media room isolated along with bedrooms from the rest of the house offers a quiet private area for listening to stereos or VCRs. A master bedroom suite includes its own whirlpool. A large garage includes extra storage.

Design V12917
Square Footage: 1,813

● Here's an attractive design with many of today's most-asked-for features: gathering room with fireplace, separate formal dining room, roomy kitchen with equally spacious breakfast area, and three bedrooms, including a master suite with huge walk-in closet and two private vanities. One other plus: a great-to-stretch-out-on terrace leading to the backyard.

Design V12795
Square Footage: 1,952

● This three-bedroom design leaves no room for improvement. Any size family will find it difficult to surpass the fine qualities that this home offers. Begin with the exterior. This fine contemporary design has open trellis work above the front, covered private court. This area is sheltered by a privacy wall extending from the projecting garage. Inside, the floor plan will be just as breathtaking. Begin at the foyer and choose a direction. To the right is the sleeping wing equipped with three bedrooms and two baths. Straight ahead from the foyer is the gathering room with thru-fireplace to the dining room. To the right is the work center. This area includes a breakfast room, a U-shaped kitchen and laundry.

Design V12754
Square Footage: 1,844

● This really is a most dramatic and refreshing contemporary home. The slope of its wide overhanging roofs is carried right indoors to provide an extra measure of spaciousness. The U-shaped privacy wall of the front entrance area provides an appealing outdoor living spot accessible from the front bedroom. The rectangular floor plan will be economical to build. Notice the efficient use of space and how it all makes its contribution to outstanding livability. The small family will find its living patterns delightful, indeed. Two bedrooms and two full baths comprise the sleeping zone. The open planning of the L-shaped living and dining rooms is most desirable. The through-fireplace is just a great room divider. The kitchen and breakfast nook function well together. There is laundry and mechanical room nearby.

Design V12796
Square Footage: 1,828

● This home features a front living room with sloped ceiling and sliding glass doors which lead to a front private court. What a delightful way to introduce this design. This bi-nuclear design has a great deal to offer. First — the children's and parent's sleeping quarters are on opposite ends of this house to assure the utmost in privacy. Each area has its own full bath. The interior kitchen is a great idea. It frees up valuable wall space for the living areas exclusive use. There is a snack bar in the kitchen/family room for those very informal meals. Also, a planning desk is in the family room. The dining room is conveniently located near the kitchen plus it has a built-in china cabinet. The laundry area has plenty of storage closets plus the stairs to the basement. This home will surely be a welcome addition to any setting.

225

Design V12591
Square Footage: 1,428

● Good times and easy work! There's an efficient kitchen with lots of work space and a large storage pantry. Plus a separate breakfast nook to make casual meals convenient and pleasant. This home creates its own peaceful enviroment! It's especially pleasing to people who love the outdoors.

Design V12797
Square Footage: 1,791

● The exterior appeal of this delightful one-story is sure to catch the attention of all who pass by. The overhanging roof adds an extra measure of shading along with the privacy wall which shelters the front court and entry. The floor plan also will be outstanding to include both leisure and formal activities. The gathering room has a sloped ceiling, sliding glass door to rear terrace and a thru-fireplace to the family room. This room also has access to the terrace and it includes the informal eating area. A pass-thru from the U-shaped kitchen to the eating area makes serving a breeze. Formal dining can be done in the front dining room. The laundry area is adjacent to the kitchen and garage and houses a washroom. Peace and quiet can be achieved in the study. The sleeping zone consists of three bedrooms and two full back-to-back baths. Additional space will be found in the basement.

Design V12792
Square Footage: 1,944

● Indoor-outdoor living hardly could be improved upon in this contemporary design. All of the rear rooms have sliding glass doors to the large terrace. Divide the terrace in three parts and the nook and dining room have access to a dining terrace, the gathering room to a living terrace and two bedrooms to a lounging terrace. A delightful way to bring the outdoor view inside. Other fine features include the efficient kitchen which has plenty of storage space and an island range, a first floor laundry with stairs to the basement and a powder room adjacent to the front door.

TERRACE

| BED RM. 13⁰ x 11⁰ | FAMILY RM. 20⁰ x 13⁰ | | MASTER BED RM. 17⁰ x 13⁰ |

56'-10"

48'-10"

BATH

LIN.

DINING RM. 9⁸ x 10⁸

KITCHEN 4 8 10 x 8

D.W. S.

REF'G RANGE OVENS

SCREEN

PNTRY

STOR.

BATH

LINEN

AIR COND.

WASH DRY

UTILITY RM. 17⁰ x 7⁰

ENTRY

DN.

BED RM. 11⁰ x 13⁰

LIVING RM. 18⁰ x 13⁰

PORCH

GARAGE 19⁴ x 21⁴

Design V12351
Square Footage: 1,862

D

● The extension of the wide over-hanging roof of this distinctive home provides shelter for the walkway to the front door. A raised brick planter adds appeal to the outstanding exterior de-sign. The living patterns offered by this plan are delightfully different, yet ex-tremely practical. Notice the separation of the master bedroom from the other two bedrooms. While assuring an extra measure of quiet privacy for the par-ents, this master bedroom location may be ideal for a live-in-relative. Locating the kitchen in the middle of the plan frees up valuable outside wall space and leads to interesting planning. The front living room is sunken for dramat-ic appeal and need not have any cross-room traffic. The utility room houses the laundry and the heating and cool-ing equipment.

Design V12363
Square Footage: 1,978

● You will have a lot of fun deciding what you like best about this home with its eye-catching glass-gabled living room and wrap-around raised planter. A covered porch shelters the double front doors. Projecting to the rear is a family room identical in size with the formal living room. Between these two rooms there are features galore. There is the efficient kitchen with pass-thru and informal eating space. Then, there is the laundry with a closet, pantry and the basement stairs nearby. Also, a full bath featuring a stall shower. The dining room has a sloped ceiling and an appealing, open vertical divider which acts as screening from the entry. The three bedroom, two bath sleeping zone is sunken. The raised hearth fireplace in the living room has an adjacent wood box.

Design V11884
Square Footage: 1,925

● If you are searching for something with an air of distinction both inside and out then search no more. You could hardly improve upon what this home has to offer. You will forever be proud of the impressive hip-roof, angular facade. Its interest will give it an identity all its own. As for the interior, your everyday living patterns will be a delight, indeed. And little wonder, clever zoning and a fine feeling of spaciousness set the stage. As you stand in the entrance hall, you look across the tip of a four foot high planter into the sunken living room. Having an expanse of floor space, the wall of windows and the raised hearth fireplace, the view will be dramatic. Notice covered porch, play terrace and quiet terrace which will provide great outdoor enjoyment.

● Here is a relatively low-cost home with a majority of the features found in today's high priced homes. The three-bed-room sleeping area highlights two full baths. The living area is a huge room of approximate-ly 25 feet in depth zoned for both formal living and dining activities. The kitchen is ex-tremely well-planned and in-cludes a built-in desk and pan-try. The family room has a snack bar and sliding glass doors to the terrace. Blueprints include optional basement details.

Design V11357
Square Footage: 1,258

OPTIONAL BASEMENT PLAN

Design V11129
Square Footage: 1,904

● Study this floor plan with care, for there is much to recommend it to the large family. The living room and separate dining area look out upon the rear yard. Sliding glass doors per-mit the dining area to function with the terrace — a delightful indoor-out-door living feature. An appealing two-way fireplace may be enjoyed from both the living and dining areas. The efficient U-shaped kitchen over-looks the front yard and is but a few steps from the entry hall as well as the service entrance and garage.

Design V12298
Square Footage: 2,489 (Excluding Atrium)

● If you've ever wanted to enjoy outdoor living indoors, this distinctive and refreshing design comes close to providing that opportunity. All the tremendous livability offered in the basic rectangular plan is wrapped in around a breathtaking 24 x 16 foot atrium which is open to the sky. Sliding glass doors provide direct access to this unique area from the family room, the dining and the master bedroom. Also noteworthy is the functioning of other areas such as: the living and dining rooms; the kitchen and laundry; the master bedroom and its dressing/bath area. The two front bedrooms are serviced by a second full bath. That's a four foot, six inch high planter with storage below separating the living and dining rooms. This will be just a great area for formal entertaining.

Design V11283
Square Footage: 1,904 (Excluding Atrium)

● Here is a unique home whose livable area is basically a perfect square. Completely adaptable to a narrow building site, the presence of the atrium permits the enjoyment of private outdoor living "indoors". Sliding glass doors open onto this delightful atrium with its attractive planting areas.

Design V12383
Square Footage: 1,984

● Design your home around an atrium and you will enjoy living patterns unlike any you have experienced in the past. This interior area is assured complete outdoor privacy. Five sets of sliding glass doors enhance the accessibility of this unique area. With the two-car garage projecting from the front of the house, this design will not require a large piece of property. Worthy of particular note is the separation of the master bedroom from the other three bedrooms - a fine feature to assure peace and quiet. Side-by-side are the formal and informal living rooms. Both function with the rear terrace. Separating the two rooms is the thru-fireplace and double access wood box.

Design V13203
Square Footage: 1,291

● The degree to which your family's living patterns will be efficient will depend upon the soundness of the basic floor plan. Here is an exceptionally practical arrangment for a medium sized home. Traffic patterns will be most flexible. The work area is strategically located close to the front door and it will function ideally with both the indoor and outdoor informal living areas. The master bath will serve the living room and the sleeping area. The second bath will serve the work area, the family room and third bedroom. Note stall shower.

Design V13212
Square Footage: 1,493

● Imagine ushering your first visitors through the front door of your new home. After you have placed their coats in the big closet in the front entry, you will show them your three sizable bedrooms and the two full baths. Next, you will take them through the separate dining area, the efficient kitchen and into the large family room with its wall of built-in storage units. Your visitors will comment about the sliding glass doors which open onto the terrace from the family room.

Design V11072
Square Footage: 1,232

● Low-pitched overhanging roof, vertical siding and patterned masonry screen wall create a charming exterior for this house. A fireplace divides the living room from the entry hall. Seven-foot high cabinets separate the kitchen from the living/dining area. The dining area opens through sliding glass doors to a private covered porch and the rear terrace. The informal area is enhanced by a wall of windows overlooking the terrace and a three-foot high built-in planter. For recreation and bulk storage there is a full basement.

235

Design V11281
Square Footage: 1,190

● Whatever you call it, contemporary or traditional, or even transitional, the prudent incorporation of newer with old design features results in a pleasant facade. The window and door detailing is obviously from an early era; while the low-pitched roof and the carport are features of relatively more recent vintage. Inside, there is an efficient plan which lends itself to the activities of the small family. As a home for a retired couple, or a young newlywed couple, this will be a fine investment. Certainly it will not require a big, expensive piece of property. The plan offers two full baths, three bedrooms, an excellent L-shaped kitchen, 23-foot living and dining area and a basement. Note side terrace.

Design V13195
Square Footage: 1,120

● This 28 x 40 foot rectangle is a fine example of how delightful and refreshing contemporary design can become. Though simple in basic construction and floor planning, this home has an abundance of exterior appeal and interior livability. Observe the low-pitched, wide overhanging roof, the attached 24 foot square covered porch/carport, the effective glass area and vertical siding, plus the raised planter. The center entrance is flanked by the formal living room and the informal, all-purpose family room. A snack bar is accessible from the kitchen. Sliding glass doors lead to the outdoor living area. In addition to the main bath there is an extra wash room handy to both the master bedroom and the kitchen.

Design V12755
Square Footage: 1,200

● Here is truly an outstanding, low-cost design created to return all the pride of ownership and livability a small family or retired couple would ask of a new home. The living/dining area measures a spacious 23 feet. It has a fireplace and two sets of sliding glass doors leading to the large rear terrace. The two bedrooms also have access to this terrace. The kitchen is a real step-saver and has a pantry nearby. The study, which has sliding glass doors to the front porch, will function as that extra all-purpose room. Use it for sewing, guests, writing or reading or just plain napping. The basement offers the possibility for the development of additional recreation space. Note the storage area at the side of the garage. Many years of enjoyable living will surely be obtained in this home designed in the contemporary fashion.

FAMILY DINING 9⁰ x 11⁶

KIT. 11⁰ x 8⁰

W. R.

W. D.

CL.

RANGE

DN

CL.

BATH

Design V13196
Square Footage: 992

● Here is another low-cost home which will return big dividends. Its basic rect-angular shape, simple (yet attractive) overhanging roof, frame exterior and non-basement plan all add up to con-struction economies.

60'-0"

8'-0" 12'-0" 40'-0"

TERRACE

GARAGE 19⁴ x 23⁴

GARAGE 11⁴ x 23⁴

FAMILY DINING 9⁰ x 11⁶

KIT. 11⁰ x 8⁰

RANGE

WALK-IN CL.

CL.

BATH

CL.

MASTER BED RM. 11⁸ x 11⁶

W. P.

24'-0" 26'-0"

LIVING RM. 17⁴ x 11⁶

BED RM. 9⁰ x 10⁰

LIN.

BED RM. 10⁴ x 11⁶

56'-0"

TERRACE

STORAGE

STORAGE

KIT. 8⁰ x 11⁶

FAMILY RM. 13⁰ x 11⁶

BATH

BED RM. 10⁰ x 11⁶

PANTRY

REF'S

STOR.

LIN.

CL.

32'-0"

CARPORT 12⁰ x 19⁸

LIVING RM. 18⁰ x 11⁶

BED RM. 9⁰ x 11⁶

BED RM. 13⁴ x 11⁶

Design V12158
Square Footage: 1,058

● A fine contemporary with a low-pitched, wide overhanging roof. Note the outdoor planters, attached carport (make it a garage, if you wish) and the two storage areas.

Design V12199
Square Footage: 1,185

BASEMENT PLAN

NON BASEMENT PLAN

● Here is a smart, contemporary version of the design featured on the opposite page. It has all the amenities for large family livability at modest cost. While the parents have their master bedroom with private wash room, the kids have three bedrooms and are served by the main bath. In addition to the living room, there is extra livability to be enjoyed in the spacious family area which has access to the rear terrace. Don't miss all those closets or the bulk storage room of the carport. Blueprints include optional basement and non-basement details.

Design V12167
Square Footage: 864

● This 36' x 24' contemporary rectangle will be economical to build whether you construct the basement design at left, V12167, or the non-basement version below, V12168.

Design V12168
Square Footage: 864

● This non-basement design features a storage room and a laundry area with cupboards above the washer and dryer. Notice the kitchen eating space.

Design V12194
Square Footage: 882

36'-0"

24'-5"

BED RM.
10⁰ x 12⁰

BED RM.
10⁰ x 8⁸

BED RM.
10⁴ x 8⁸

CL.

CL.

CL.

CL.

LIN.

BATH

AIR COND

D.

W.

STOR.

REF G.

S.

RANGE

STOR.

KIT.
12⁴ x 8⁸

STOR.

LIVING RM.
16⁰ x 11⁰

CL.

SLIDING DOOR

● Here is a basic 36 x 24 foot rectangle that can be built with either the contemporary or traditional exterior. What's your preference? Observe the grouping of plumbing facilities. This is a positive economy factor. The kitchen is sizable and has plenty of space for eating. There will be no lack of space to put things with all the closet and storage areas. The living room has space for effective furniture placement. The washer and dryer are strategically situated at the source of most soiled linen. There is a recessed sliding door between the kitchen and the vestibule.

Design V12822
First Floor: 1,363 square feet
Second Floor: 351 square feet
Total: 1,714 square feet

L

● Here is a truly unique house whose interior was designed with the current decade's economies, lifestyles and demographics in mind. While functioning as a one-story home, the second floor provides an extra measure of livability when required. Note the two optional layouts. The second floor may serve as a lounge, studio or hobby area overlooking the great room. Or, it may be built to function as a complete private guest room. It would be a great place for the visiting grandchildren. Don't miss the outdoor balcony. In addition, this two-story section adds to the dramatic appeal of both the exterior and the interior. Within only 1,363 square feet, this contemporary delivers refreshing and outstanding living patterns for those who are buying their first home, those who have raised their family and are looking for a smaller home and those in search of a retirement home. The center entrance routes traffic effectively to the great room. The adjacent covered porch will provide an ideal spot for warm weather, outdoor dining. The sleeping area may consist of one bedroom and a study, or two bedrooms. Each room functions with the sheltered wood deck - a perfect location for a hot tub.

Floor plan labels

TERRACE

54'-8"

COVERED DECK

STUDY/BEDROOM 11⁰ x 11⁰

GREAT RM. 16⁰ x 14²

COVERED PORCH

LOUNGE ABOVE

MASTER BEDROOM 12⁰ x 14⁶

DINING RM. 14⁰ x 9⁴

PANTRY

BATH

LINEN

UP DN

FOYER

MUD RM.

KITCHEN 13⁰ x 8⁰

54'-0"

WALK-IN CLOSET

DRESSING RM.

COVERED PORCH

SEAT

CURB

GARAGE 21⁴ x 21⁸

UPPER GREAT RM.

RAILING

LOUNGE / HOBBIES 16⁰ x 9²

STOR.

UPPER FOYER

BATH

RAILING

BALCONY

LOUNGE / GUEST RM. / GRANDCHILDREN'S RM. 16⁰ x 19²

BATH

UPPER FOYER

RAILING

ALTERNATE SECOND FLOOR

Design V12821
First Floor: 1,363 square feet
Second Floor: 351 square feet
Total: 1,714 square feet

L

Design V12871

Living Area: 1,824 square feet
Greenhouse Area: 81 square feet
Total: 1,905 square feet

D

● A greenhouse area off the dining room and living room provides a cheerful focal point for this comfortable three-bedroom Trend home. The spacious living room features a cozy fireplace and sloped ceiling. In addition to the dining room, there's a less formal breakfast room just off the modern kitchen. Both kitchen and breakfast areas look out into a front terrace. Stairs just off the foyer lead down to a recreation room. Master bedroom suite opens to a terrace. A mud room and washroom off the garage allow rear entry to the house during inclement weather.

Design V13330

First Floor: 1,394 square feet
Second Floor: 320 square feet
Total: 1,714 square feet

● Outdoor living and open floor planning are highlights of this moderately sized plan. Amenities include a private hot tub on a wooden deck that is accessible via sliding glass doors in both bedrooms, and a two-story gathering room. An optional second-floor plan allows for a full 503 square feet of space with a balcony.

CONTEMPORARY DESIGNS OVER 2000 Sq. Ft. . . .

can offer a delightful change of pace for your new home planning program. The unique individuality of many contemporary exteriors is re-freshing, indeed. The clean, simple lines of the contemporary house offer a break from the past. The lack of adornment is preferred by many. Interesting new shapes not only lead to dramatic exteriors, but to unusual floor plans which deliver exciting living patterns. Open planning, sunken living areas, open stairwells, sloping ceilings, skylights, large and prudently placed glass areas and indoor planting areas all make significant contributions to the enjoyment of contemporary living. And, of course new materials and equipment make their contribution, too.

Design V12756
Square Footage: 2,652

L **D**

● This one-story, contemporary design is bound to serve your family well. It will assure the best in contemporary living with its many fine features. No-tice the bath with tub and stall shower, dressing room and walk-in closet fea-tured with the master bedroom. Two more family bedrooms are adjacent. The sunken gathering room/dining room is highlighted by the sloped ceil-ing and sliding glass doors to the large, rear terrace. This formal area is a full 32' x 16'. Imagine the great furniture placement that can be done in this area. In addition to the gathering room, there is an informal family room with a fireplace. You will enjoy the efficient kitchen and get much use out of the work island, pantry and built-in desk. Note the service entrance with wash-room and laundry.

Clutter Room, Media Room To The Fore

● Something new? Something new, indeed!! Here is the introduction of two rooms which will make a wonderful contribution to family living. The clutter room is strategically placed between the kitchen and garage. It is the nerve center of the work area. It houses the laundry, provides space for sewing, has a large sorting table, and even plenty of space for the family's tool bench. A handy potting area is next to the laundry tray. Adjacent to the clutter room, and a significant part of the planning of this whole zone, are the pantry and freezer with their nearby counter space. These facilities surely will expedite the unloading of groceries from the car and their convenient storing. Wardrobe and broom closets, plus washroom complete the outstanding utility of this area. The location of the clutter room with all its fine cabinet and counter space means that the often numerous family projects can be on-going. This room is ideally isolated from the family's daily living patterns. The media room may be thought of as the family's entertainment center. While this is the room for the large or small TV, the home movies, the stereo and VCR equipment, it will serve as the library or study. It would be ideal as the family's home office with its computer equipment. Your family will decide just how it will utilize this outstanding area.

Design V12915 Square Footage: 2,758

L **D**

● The features of this appealing contemporary design go far beyond the clutter and media rooms. The country kitchen is spacious and caters to the family's informal living and dining activities. While it overlooks the rear yard it is just a step from the delightful greenhouse. Many happy hours will be spent here enjoying to the fullest the outdoors from within. The size of the greenhouse is 8'x18' and contains 149 sq. ft. not included in the square footage quoted above. The formal living and dining areas feature spacious open planning. Sloping ceiling in the living room, plus the sliding glass doors to the outdoor terrace enhance the cheerfulness of this area. The foyer is large and routes traffic efficiently to all areas. Guest coat closets and a powder room are handy. The sleeping zone is well-planned. Two children's bedrooms have fine wall space, good wardrobe facilities and a full bath. The master bedroom is exceptional. It is large enough to accommodate a sitting area and has access to the terrace. Two walk-in closets, a vanity area with lavatory and a compartmented bath are noteworthy features. Observe the stall shower in addition to the dramatic whirlpool installation. The floor plan below is identical with that on the opposite page and shows one of many possible ways to arrange furniture.

FURNITURE LAYOUT

Design V12857

Square Footage: 2,982

L

● Imagine yourself occupying this home! Study the outstanding master bedroom. You will be forever pleased by its many features. It has "his" and "her" baths each with a large walk-in closet, sliding glass doors to a private, side terrace (a great place to enjoy a morning cup of coffee) and an adjacent study. Notice that the two family bedrooms are separated from the master bedroom. This allows for total privacy both for the parents and the children. Continue to observe this plan. You will have no problem at all entertaining in the gathering room. Your party can flow to the adjacent balcony on a warm summer evening. The work center has been designed in an orderly fashion. The U-shaped kitchen utilizes the triangular work pattern, said to be the most efficient. Only a few steps away, you will be in the breakfast room, formal dining room, laundry or washroom. Take your time and study every last detail in this home plan.

COVERED PORCH

TERRACE

GATHERING RM.
21⁰x21⁶

DINING RM.
14²x11¹⁰

STUDY
11⁸x13⁴

MASTER
BED RM.
13⁰x18⁸

SHLVS   SHLVS

WALK-IN CLOSET

THRU FIREPLACE

DRESSING/BATH

BREAKFAST
14²x11

DESK   BAR

DN

BOOKS   CABINET

POWDER RM.

TUB   VANITY

SEAT

BATH

SHELVES

PATIO

LINEN   WALK-IN CLOSET

S

PANTRY   OVEN

FOYER

BATH

KITCHEN
13⁰x10⁰

RANGE

DN   DN

BED RM.
11⁰x12⁰

S

BED RM.
11⁶x12⁰

REF'G.

DN

CL.

STEP-UP

DN   DN

COVERED PORCH

TUB   SLOPED CEILING

72'-4"

CURB

GARAGE
31⁴x21⁸

85'-10"

Design V12789 Square Footage: 2,732

L D

● An attached three car garage! What a fantastic feature of this three bedroom contemporary design. And there's more. As one walks up the steps to the covered porch and through the double front doors the charm of this design will be overwhelming. Inside, a large foyer greets all visitors and leads them to each of the three areas, each down a few steps. The living area has a large gathering room with fireplace and a study adjacent on one side and the formal dining room on the other. The work center has an efficient kitchen with island range, breakfast room, laundry and built-in desk and bar. Then there is the sleeping area. Note the raised tub with sloped ceiling.

84'-0"

56'-4"

TERRACE

TERRACE

TERRACE

7° HIGH FLAT CEILING

LIVING RM.
13⁸ x 19⁶

FAMILY RM.
13⁸ x 19⁶

SLOPED CEILING

SLOPED CEILING

THRU-FIREPLACE

RAISED HEARTH

WALK-IN CLOSET

MASTER BED RM.
17⁶ x 13⁶

NOOK
12⁰ x 13⁰

SNACK BAR

L.S.

D.W.

DRESSING RM.

KITCHEN
11⁰ x 13⁰

OVENS

RANGE

SEAT

BATH

S

CL.

7° HIGH FLAT CEILING

DESK

REF'G.

LEDGE

STORAGE

8° HIGH FLAT CEILING

BUTLER'S PANTRY

L.T.

WASH.

DRY.

BATH

LINEN

SKYLIGHT ABOVE

LAUNDRY

CL.

CL.

STUDY-BED RM.
14⁰ x 12⁰

ENTRY

DINING RM.
15⁴ x 12⁰

WASH RM.

SERV. ENTRANCE

DN.

B.CL.

CL.

CL.

CL.

CL.

PORCH

CURB

BED RM.
11⁶ x 16⁸

BED RM.
11⁶ x 13⁴

ENTRY COURT

GARAGE
23⁴ x 22⁰

GATES

Design V12764
Square Footage: 2,946

● If uniqueness is what you're looking for in your new home, then this three (optional four) bedroom design will be ideal. Notice the large, gated-in entry court, vertical paned windows and contrasting exterior materials. All of these features compose an attractive design suitable for any location. Within but a second after entering this home one will be confronted with features galore. The entry/dining area has a focal point of a built-in planter with a skylight above. The living and family rooms both have an attractive sloped ceiling. They share a raised hearth, thru-fireplace and both have access to the large wrap-around terrace. The kitchen-nook area also has access to the terrace and has the features of a snack bar, built-in desk and large butler's pantry.

Labels within floor plan:
TERRACE
FAMILY RM. 21⁴x14⁸
DINING
COVERED PORCH
SKYLIGHT SKYLIGHT SKYLIGHT
SLOPED CEILING
MASTER BED RM. 13⁰x14⁸
SHELVES
WALK-IN CLOSET
DRESSING
BATH
SNACK BAR
PANTRY
KITCHEN 17⁰x9⁴
LIVING RM. 22⁰x15⁰
SLOPED CEILING
BED RM. 12⁰x11⁰
LINEN
OVEN
REF'G RANGE
LAUNDRY
POWDER RM.
FOYER
SLOPED CEILING
GRILLE
BOOKS
CL
CL
SRM CL
ON
CL
ON
CL
BATH
BED RM. 12⁰x11⁰
CURB
GARAGE 21⁴x21⁸
PORCH
56'-4"
66'-0"

Design V12790
Square Footage: 2,075

● Enter this comtemporary hip-roofed home through the double front doors and immediately view the sloped-ceilinged living room with fireplace. This room will be a sheer delight when it comes to formal entertaining. It has easy access to the kitchen and also a powder room nearby. The work area will be convenient. The kitchen has an island work center with snack bar. The laundry is adjacent to the service entrance and stairs leading to the basement. This area is planned to be a real "step saver". The sleeping wing consists of two family bedrooms, bath and master bedroom suite. Maybe the most attractive feature of this design is the rear covered porch with skylights above. It is accessible by way of sliding glass doors in the family/dining area, living room and master bedroom.

251

Design V12866

Square Footage: 2,371

● An extra living unit has been built into the design of this home. It would make an excellent "mother-in-law" suite. Should you choose not to develop this area as indicated, maybe you might use it as two more bedrooms, a guest suite or even as hobby and game rooms. Whatever its final use, it will complement the rest of this home. The main house also deserves mention. The focal point will be the large gathering room. Its features include a skylight, sloped ceiling, centered fireplace flanked on both sides by sliding glass doors and adjacent is a dining room on one side, study on the other. The work center is clustered together. Three bedrooms and two baths make up the private area. Note the outdoor areas: court with privacy wall, two covered porches and a large terrace.

Design V12819

Square Footage: 2,459

 D

● Indoor-outdoor living will be enjoyed to the fullest in this rambling one-story contemporary plan. Each of the rear rooms in this design, excluding the study, has access to a terrace or porch. Even the front breakfast room has access to a private dining patio. The covered porch off the living areas, family, dining and living rooms, has a sloped ceiling and skylights. A built-in barbecue unit and a storage room will be found on the second covered porch.

Inside, the plan offers exceptional living patterns for various activities. Notice the thru-fireplace that the living room shares with the study. A built-in etagere is nearby. The three-car garage has an extra storage area.

Design V12730
Square Footage: 2,490

D

● Here is a basic one-story home that is really loaded with livability on the first floor and has a bonus of an extra 1,086 sq. ft. of planned livability on a lower level. What makes this so livable is that the first floor adjacent to the stairs leading below is open and forms a balcony looking down into a dramatic planting area. The first floor traffic patterns flow around this impressive and distinctive feature. In addition to the gathering room, study and family room, there is the lounge and activity room. Notice the second balcony open to the activity room below. The master bedroom is outstanding with two baths and two walk-in closets. The attached three-car garage has a bulk storage area and is accessible through the service area.

Floor plan labels:

87'-8"

TERRACE

GATHERING RM.
17⁴ x 20²

OPEN TO
LOWER LEVEL

SKYLIGHT

DINING RM.
12² x 13⁰

TERRACE

KITCHEN
10⁵ x 19⁰

EATING

PANTRY

GARDEN, BOAT,
STOR. GARAGE
11⁴ x 21⁰

WALK IN
CLOSET

MASTER
BED RM.
12² x 16⁰

VANITY

DRESSING
RM.

BATH

TUB

WALK IN
CLOSET

RAISED HEARTH

DN.

DN.

OPEN

HALLWAY

FAMILY RM.
13⁴ x 19⁰

SHELVES

SHELVES

DESK

COUNTER

BATH

LINEN

DN.

CL.

LAUNDRY

WASH DRY

SERV.
ENT.

ENTRY

RAIL.

OPEN

PORCH

STUDY
11⁸ x 12¹⁰

CURB

BATH

LINEN

CL.

BED RM.
11⁶ x 13⁸

BED RM.
11⁶ x 13⁸

GARAGE
23⁴ x 23⁸

BASEMENT

WOOD
BOX

RAISED HEARTH

OPEN TO
GATHERING RM.
ABOVE

FAMILY RM.
27² x 19⁸

CRAWL SPACE

DN.

DN.

UP

GAMES
19⁰ x 12⁸ - 16⁸

UNEX.

UNEX.

Design V12721
Square Footage: 2,667

● Visually exciting! A sunken gathering room with a sloped ceiling, raised hearth fireplace, corner balcony and skylight . . . the last two features shared by the formal dining room. There's more. Two family rooms . . . one on the lower level (1,153 sq. ft.) with a raised hearth fireplace, another adjacent to the kitchen with a snack bar! Plus a study and game room. A lavish master suite and two large bedrooms. A first floor laundry and reams of storage space, including a special garage for a boat, sports equipment, garden tools etc. There's plenty of space for family activities in this home. From chic dinner parties for friends to birthday gatherings for kids, there's always the right setting . . . and so much room that adults and children can entertain at the same time.

Design V12255
Square Footage: 2,356

● Convenient living could hardly ask for anything more. Study this design inside and out. It is positively outstanding from every angle.

Design V12256
Square Footage: 2,632

● A dream home for those with young ideas. A refreshing, contemporary exterior with a unique, highly individualized interior. What are your favorite features.

GARAGE
23⁴ x 23⁴

CURB

WASH RM.
COUNTER
LAUNDRY
DRY. WASH LT.
L.S. REFG.
KITCHEN
13⁰ x 10⁰
DW
RANGE

TERRACE

PANTRY
OVEN
B.C.
CL.

LIVING RM.
16⁰ x 20¹⁰

SLOPED CEILING

STUDY
10⁶ x 14⁴

SLOPED CEILING

MASTER BED RM.
17⁴ x 13⁴

WALK-IN CLOSET

VANITY

LINEN

BATH

BATH

TERRACE

DESK

DN.

BOOKS

VANITY

BATH

LINEN

CL.

CL.

NOOK
13⁰ x 10⁰

TERRACE

ENTRY

CL.

CL.

BED RM.
13⁶ x 12⁰

BED RM.
13⁴ x 15⁸

TERRACE

DINING RM.
17⁰ x 12⁰

PORCH

70'-4"

70'-0"

Design V12537
Square Footage: 2,602

● A low-pitched, wide overhanging roof and masses of quarried stone (make it some other material of your choice if you wish) set the character of this contemporary design. The recessed front entrance with its patterned door and glass panels is, indeed, dramatic.

An attractive wrought iron gate opens to the private, side eating terrace. Sloping ceilings and raised hearth through-fireplace highlight the living room/study area. Spaciousness is further enhanced by the open stairwell to the recreation area which may be devel-

oped below. The kitchen, with its island cooking range and plenty of counter and cupboard space will be a joy in which to function. The area between kitchen and garage is well-planned. The separate laundry has extra counter space.

Design V12304

Square Footage: 2,313

● What an appealing home! And what a list of reasons why it is so eye-catching. First of all, there is the irregular shape and the low-pitched, wide-over-hanging roof. Then, there is the interesting use of exterior materials, including vertical glass window treatment. Further, there are the raised planters flanking the porch of the recessed entrance. Inside, the traffic patterns are excellent. Among the focal points is the 33 foot, beam ceilinged living area. This will surely be fun to plan and furnish for the family's living and dining pursuits. Among other highlights is the layout of the laundry-kitchen-nook area. The extra washroom is strategically located. The sleeping wing has much to offer with its privacy, its convenient bath facilities, and its fine storage.

TERRACE

GATHERING RM.
19⁴ x 19⁶

MASTER
BED RM.
12⁰ x 15⁶

CL.   SEAT

DRESSING RM.

VANITY   CL.

BATH

SLOPED CEILING

RAISED HEARTH

FAMILY RM.
13⁰ x 15⁶

LAUNDRY

KITCHEN
10⁰ x 12⁰

EATING

WASH. DRY.

WASH. RM.

D.W.

LS

REFG.

OVEN

RANGE

DESK

DN.

CL.

BATH

CL.   CL.

LINEN

CL.

CL.   CL.

RAIL

SLOPED CEILING

DN.

ENTRY

PANTRY

DN.

SERVICE ENTRANCE

P.

BED RM.
12⁰ x 11¹⁰

CL.

BED RM.
12⁰ x 13⁶

PORCH

DINING RM.
13⁰ x 17⁰

CURB

DN.

DN.

GARAGE
21⁴ x 23⁸

76'-8"

48'-8"

Design V12717
Square Footage: 2,310

● Great for family life! There's a spacious family room for casual activities.
And a "work efficient" kitchen that
features a built-in desk and appliances,
a large pantry plus a pass-through to
the family room for added convenience. A first floor laundry, too, with
adjacent washroom and stairs to the
basement. Want glamour? There's a
sloped ceiling in the entry hall plus a
delightful "over the railing" view of
the sunken gathering room. And the
gathering room itself! More than 19' by
19' . . . with a sloped ceiling, raised
hearth fireplace and sliding glass doors
to the rear terrace. A 13' by 17' formal
dining room, too. The curb area in the
garage is convenient.

Design V12930
Square Footage: 2,032

● The clean lines of this L-shaped contemporary are enhanced by the interesting, wide overhanging roof planes. Horizontal and vertical siding compliment one another. The low privacy fence adds interest as it forms a delightful front courtyard adjacent to the covered walkway to the front door.

Here's a floor plan made to order for the active small family or empty-nesters. Sloping ceilings and fine glass areas foster a spacious interior. The master bedroom has an outstanding dressing room and bath layout. The guest room has its own full bath. Note how this bath can function as a handy

powder room. A favorite room will be the study with its fireplace and two sets of sliding glass doors. Don't miss the open-planned gathering and dining rooms, or the kitchen/laundry area. The breakfast room has its own terrace. Notice the rear covered porch. Fine indoor-outdoor relationships.

Design V12595
Square Footage: 2,653

● A winged design puts everything in the right place! At the center, formal living and dining rooms with sloped ceiling share one fireplace for added charm. Sliding glass doors in both rooms open onto the main terrace. In the right wing, there is a spacious family room with another raised hearth fireplace, built-in desk, dining area and adjoining smaller terrace. Also, a first floor laundry with pantry and half bath. A study, the master suite and family bedrooms (all bedrooms having access to a third terrace) plus baths are in the left wing. This home has a floor plan that helps you organize your life. Notice the open staircase leading to the basement.

Design V12745
Square Footage: 2,890

● Just imagine the fun everyone will have living in this contemporary home with its frame exterior and accents of stone veneer (make it brick, if you prefer). The living areas revolve around the dramatic atrium-type planting area flooded with natural light from the skylight above. The formal living room is sunken and has a thru-fireplace to the dining room. Also a large gathering room with a second raised hearth fireplace, sloped ceiling, sliding glass doors to a rear terrace and informal eating area. Observe the sloping ceilings, the laundry with pantry, the wash room and the study. Master bedroom has a stall shower, a tub with seat, a vanity and two lavatories.

Design V12329
Square Footage: 2,268

● Brick privacy walls create for this design an inviting entrance court. Such an area provides a pleasing view from the kitchen and the nook. Front porch sitting will have its privacy as well as an appealing atmosphere. The center entrance is but a few steps from the main areas of the plan. Four bedrooms and two baths will serve the growing family well. Note that two of the bedrooms have direct access to the terrace. Closet space is outstanding. The living and dining rooms encompass a large area with the living room well-defined by being sunken one step. The sloped ceiling family room with its commanding fireplace is off by itself. The laundry and washroom are well situated.

Design V12529
Square Footage: 2,326

● The front entrance court with its plant areas and surrounding accents of colorful quarried stone (make it brick, if you prefer), provides a delightful introduction to this interesting contemporary home. The spacious entry hall leads directly to a generous L-shaped living and dining area. Sliding glass doors provide direct access to the outdoor terrace. An efficient, interior kitchen will be fun in which to work. It could hardly be more strategically located — merely a step or two from the formal dining area, the breakfast nook, and the family room. Although this home has a basement, there is a convenient first floor laundry and an extra washroom. The four bedroom sleeping wing has two full baths. Two of the rooms have access to the outdoor terraces. Notice garage storage.

Design V12532
Square Footage: 2,112

● Here is a refreshing, modified U-shaped contemporary that is long on both looks and livability. The board and batten exterior creates simple lines which are complimented by the low-pitched roof with its wide overhang and exposed rafters. The appeal of the front court is enhanced by the massive stone columns at the edge of the covered porch. A study of the floor plan reveals interestingly different and practical living patterns. The location of the entry hall represents a fine conservation of space for the living areas. The L-shaped formal living-dining zone has access to both front and rear yards. The informal living area is a true family kitchen. Its open planning produces a spacious and cheerful area. Note sloping, beamed ceiling, raised hearth fireplace and sliding glass doors.

Design V12793
Square Footage: 2,065

• Privacy will be enjoyed in this home both inside and out. The indoor-outdoor living relationships offered in this plan are outstanding. A covered porch at the entrance. A privacy court off the master bedroom divided from the front yard with a privacy wall. A covered porch serving both the living and dining rooms through sliding glass doors. Also utilizing a privacy wall. Another covered porch off the kitchen eating area. This one is the largest and has skylights above. Also a large rear ter-race. The kitchen is efficient with eating space available, an island range and built-in desk. Storage space is abundant. Note storage area in the garage and its overall size. Three front bedrooms. Raised hearth fireplace in the living room.

Design V12303
Square Footage: 2,330

● This hip-roof ranch home has a basic floor plan that is the favorite of many. The reasons for its popularity are, of course, easy to detect. The simple rectangular shape means relatively economical construction. The living areas are large and are located to the rear to function through sliding glass doors with the terrace. The front kitchen is popular because of its view of approaching callers and its proximity to the front entry. The big utility room serves as a practical buffer between the garage and the kitchen.

Worthy of particular note is the efficiency of the kitchen, the stylish living room fireplace, the beamed ceiling, the sunken family room with its wall of built-ins (make that a music wall if you wish). Observe the snack bar and the fine master bath.

Design V12523
Square Footage: 2,055

● For those who like refreshing contemporary lines, this design will rate at the top. The wide overhanging roof, the brick masses, the glass areas, the raised planters, and the covered front entrance highlight the facade. As for the interior, all the elements are present to assure fine living patterns. Consider the room relationships and how they function with one another. Note how they relate to the outdoors.

Design V11820
Square Footage: 2,730

● Whatever the location, snugly tucked in among the hills or impressively oriented on the flatlands - this trim hip-roof ranch home will be fun to own. Here is a gracious exterior whose floor plan has "everything". Traffic patterns are excellent. The zoning of the sleeping wing, as well as the formal and informal living areas, is outstanding. Indoor-outdoor living relationships are most practical and convenient.

Design V12359
Square Footage: 2,078

● The low-pitched, wide-overhanging roof with its exposed beams, acts as a visor for the projecting living room. This will be an exceedingly pleasant room with its sunken floor, sloped ceiling, large glass area, and raised hearth fireplace. At the rear of this living rectangle is the family room. Between these two living areas is the efficient kitchen with its adjacent eating area. The utility room and its laundry equipment is nearby, as is the powder room. A separate dining room acts as the connecting link to the bedroom zone. Note the master bedroom with its dressing room, twin lavatories and two closets.

Design V12506
Square Footage: 2,851

● Here is a home that is sure to add an extra measure of fun to your family's living patterns. The exterior is extremely pleasing with the use of paned glass windows, the hipped roof and the double front doors. The initial impact of the interior begins dramatically in the large foyer. The ceiling is sloped, while straight ahead one views the sunken living room. Impressive are the masonry columns with a railing between each. The stairwell to the partial basement is open and has a view of the outdoor planter. The sleeping area consists of three bedrooms, baths and a study (or fourth bedroom if you prefer). Two raised hearth fireplaces, pantry, washroom and more. List your favorite features.

TERRACE

66'-0"

MASTER BEDROOM
15⁰ x 15⁴
SLOPED CEILING

LIVING RM.
23⁰ x 15⁴
SLOPED CEILING

RAISED HEARTH

DINING RM.
12⁴ x 15⁴
SLOPED CEILING

CL

BATH

LINEN CL

BEDROOM
15⁰ x 10⁸
SLOPED CEILING

BEDROOM
11⁶ x 10⁸
SLOPED CEILING

CL

LINEN STOR

STOR

BATH

BEDROOM
11⁶ x 13⁴
SLOPED CEILING

FOYER

COVERED WALK

TRELLIS

HIGH GLASS WALL ABOVE

ATRIUM
17⁰ x 16⁰

FAMILY RM.
17⁸ x 13⁴
HIGH GLASS WALL ABOVE

SLOPED CEILING

RAISED HEARTH

WOOD BOX

REF'G

KITCHEN
11⁴ x 10⁸
SLOPED CEILING

OVEN

D.W.

BRKFST. RM.
11⁴ x 9⁰
SLOPED CEILING

TERRACE

PANTRY

AIR COND.

W D

LAUNDRY

CL

WASH RM.

DN

CURB

STORAGE AREA OVER

SLOPED CEILING

GARAGE
23⁴ x 21⁸

STORAGE
11⁴ x 15⁴

72'-0"

BRKFST. RM.

FAM. RM.

PANTRY

W D

LAUNDRY

WOOD BOX

DN

DN

W.R.

GARAGE

CURB

OPTIONAL PARTIAL BASEMENT

Design V12135
Square Footage: 2,495 (Excluding Atrium)

● For those seeking a new experience in home ownership. The proud occupants of this contemporary home will forever be thrilled at their choice of such a distinguished exterior and such a practical and exciting floor plan. The variety of shed roof planes contrast dramatically with the simplicity of the vertical siding. Inside, there is a feeling of spaciousness resulting from the sloping ceilings. The uniqueness of this design is further enhanced by the atrium. Open to the sky, this outdoor area, indoors, can be enjoyed from all parts of the house. The sleeping zone has four bedrooms, two baths and plenty of closets. The informal living zone has a fine kitchen and breakfast room. The formal zone consists of a large living-dining area with fireplace.

270

SOLAR ORIENTED DESIGNS . . .

exist in almost limitless sizes, shapes and types. Most houses can be made more, or less, solar oriented by proper planning of room locations in relation to the siting of the structure on a piece of property. Selection of a floor plan with an array of windows that will face the north in the winter can hardly be recommended. Better to choose either a different plan or site. However, the designs in this section offer a study of the many alternatives to planning a more solar oriented house. Note the atriums, greenhouses, sunspaces, garden rooms, underground and berm houses and even the solar panels that are presented for your consideration.

Design V12832

Square Footage: 2,805 (Excluding Atrium)

D

● The advantage of passive solar heating is a significant highlight of this contemporary design. The huge skylight over the atrium provides shelter during inclement weather, while permitting the enjoyment of plenty of natural light to the atrium below and surrounding areas. Whether open to the sky, or sheltered by a glass or translucent covering, the atrium becomes a cheerful spot and provides an abundance of natural light to its adjacent rooms. The stone floor will absorb an abundance of heat from the sun during the day and permit circulation of warm air to other areas at night. During the summer, shades afford protection from the sun without sacrificing the abundance of natural light and the feeling of spaciousness. Sloping ceilings highlight each of the major rooms, three bedrooms, formal living and dining and study. The conversation area between the two formal areas will really be something to talk about. The broad expanses of roof can accommodate solar panels should an active system be desired to supplement the passive features of this design.

A Sunspace Spa Highlights this Trend House

● Contemporary in exterior styling, this house is energy oriented. It calls for 2 x 6 exterior wall construction with placement on a north facing lot. Traffic flows through the interior of this plan by way of the foyer. Not only is the foyer useful, but it is dramatic with its sloped ceiling and second floor balcony and skylight above. Excellent living areas are throughout. A spacious, sunken living room is to the left of the foyer. It shares a thru-fireplace, faced with fieldstone, with the study. Sloped ceilings are in both of these rooms. Informal activities can take place in the family room. It, too, has a fireplace and is adjacent to the work center. Two of the bedrooms are on the second floor with a lounge overlooking the gathering room below. The master bedroom is on the first floor. A generous amount of closet space with mirrored doors will enhance its appearance. Study the spacious master bath with all of its many features. Its direct access to the sunspace spa. will be appreciated.

Design V12900

First Floor: 2,332 square feet
Second Floor: 953 square feet
Total: 3,285 square feet

● Passive solar benefits will be acquired from the spa. It transmits light and heat to the other parts of the house. Heat stored during the day, by the stone floor, will be circulated at night by mechanical means. Shades may be used to control the amount of heat gain. This spa provides a large area where various activities can be done at the same time. Note the bar, whirlpool and exercise area. It will be a cheerful and spacious family recreation area. There are 551 square feet in the sunspace spa which are not included in the above totals.

Design V12858
Square Footage: 2,231

● This sun oriented design was created to face the south. By doing so, it has minimal northern exposure. It has been designed primarily for the more temperate U.S. latitudes using 2 x 6 wall construction. The morning sun will brighten the living and dining rooms, along with the adjacent terrace. Sun enters the garden room by way of the glass roof and walls. In the winter, the solar heat gain from the garden room should provide relief from high energy bills. Solar shades allow you to adjust the amount of light that you want to enter in the warmer months. Interior planning deserves mention, too. The work center is efficient. The kitchen has a snack bar on the garden room side and a serving counter to the dining room. The breakfast room with laundry area is also convenient to the kitchen. Three bedrooms are on the northern wall. The master bedroom has a large tub and a separate shower with a four foot square skylight above. When this design is oriented toward the sun, it should prove to be energy efficient and a joy to live in.

Floor plan labels:
- WHIRLPOOL
- BATH
- SAUNA
- DRESSING RM.
- VANITY
- MASTER BEDROOM 17⁰x12⁰ +BAY
- WALK-IN CLOSET
- LINEN
- BATH
- CL
- EXERCISE/GARDEN RM. 18⁰x11⁰
- TERRACE
- RAISED HEARTH
- GATHERING RM. 18⁶x18⁰
- SLOPED CEILING
- DINING RM. 11⁸x11⁸
- BRKFST RM. 11⁶x12⁰
- GLASS
- PASS THRU
- BAR/BUTLER'S PANTRY
- COOK TOP
- D.W.
- KITCHEN 11⁶x12⁰
- PANTRY
- REF'S.
- BEDROOM 11⁴x11⁰
- BEDROOM 11⁴x11⁰
- FOYER
- RAILING
- DN
- UP
- PDR. RM.
- STOR.
- W. D.
- LAV.
- LAUNDRY
- COVERED PORCH
- GARAGE 23⁴x22⁸

Dimensions: 64'-8" (width), 75'-0" (depth)

Design V12873
Square Footage: 2,838

● This modern three-bedroom home incorporates many of the Contemporary features so popular today. A large gathering room with cozy raised-hearth fireplace and sloped ceiling is central focus and centrally located. Adjacent to the gathering room is a dining room that adjoins a bar or butler's pantry. This handy service area also has pass-thru entry to the central gathering room. Just off the pantry is a large modern kitchen with central cook-top island and adjoining breakfast room. The master bedroom suite is especially luxurious with its own sauna, whirlpool, dressing room, bay window, and adjoining exercise room. This adjacent exercise room could double as a lovely garden room. It's located just off the back terrace. There's even a powder room for guests in front, and a covered porch to keep visitors dry. A laundry is conveniently located off the spacious two-car garage. Note the large view glass off the rear exercise/garden room. This is a comfortable and modern home, indeed.

Design V12882

Square Footage: 2,832

● This contemporary, one-story design should be oriented on a west-facing site if it is built in the northern regions of the country. The result will be minimal exposure to the cold northern winds during the winter. Study the north side of this plan. There is only one small window and it will be protected by the privacy wall. This means that the rooms on the opposite side of the house will have the desirable southern exposure. A westerly exposure for the living room will be most beneficial in many areas of the country. This plan reflects interesting living patterns and excellent indoor/outdoor relationships. Wide overhanging roofs, skylights, glass gables, vented walkways, wind-buffering privacy fences and 2x6 construction are among this design's energy oriented features.

Design V12881
Square Footage: 2,770

● Energy-efficiency will be obtained in this unique, contemporary design. This plan has been designed for a south facing lot in the temperate zones. There is minimal window exposure on the north side of the house so the interior will be protected. The eastern side of the plan, on the other hand, will allow the morning sunlight to enter. As

the sun travels from east to west, the various rooms will have light through windows, sliding glass doors or skylights. The garage acts as a buffer against the hot afternoon sun. The living areas are oriented to the front of the plan. They will benefit from the southern exposure during the cooler months. During the summer months,

this area will be shielded from the high, hot summer sun by the overhanging roof. If you plan to build in the south, this house would be ideal for a north facing site. This results in a minimum amount of hot sun for the living areas and a maximum amount of protection from the sun on the rear, southern side of the house.

48'-10"

75'-5"

ROOF
SKYLIGHTS
SLOPED CEILING
LEDGES — SOLARIUM
RAILING
BALCONY

MASTER BEDROOM
13⁰ x 17⁶

LIVING RM.
26⁰ x 13⁰

DRESSING RM.

POWDER RM.

DINING RM.
12⁰ x 12⁰

EXERCISE

BATH

FOYER

TUB

PORCH

EATING

SKYLIGHT ABOVE

KITCHEN
13'⁴ x 12⁰

RANGE

OVEN

CURB

SLOPED CEILING

SLOPED CEILING

GARAGE
21⁸ x 21⁸

STORAGE

SOLARIUM
46⁶ x 13⁸

WHIRLPOOL SPA

EQUIP STORAGE

FLAGSTONE FLOOR

BEDROOM
12⁸ x 12⁰

FAMILY RM.
20⁴ x 25⁰

BEDROOM
13⁰ x 11⁰

BATH

BATH

LINEN

BAR

AIR COND.

LAUNDRY

BASE CABINETS
WALL CABINETS

WINE CELLAR

MECHANICAL RM./
STORAGE

SOLAR STORAGE TANK

Design V12835 Main Level: 1,626 square feet
Lower Level: 2,038 square feet; Total: 3,664 square feet

● Passive solar techniques with the help of an active solar component - they can work together or the active solar component can act as a back-up system - heat and cool this striking contemporary design. The lower level solarium is the primary passive element. It admits sunlight during the day for direct-gain heating. The warmth, which was absorbed into the thermal floor, is then radiated into the structure at night. The earth berms on the three sides of the lower level help keep out the winter cold and summer heat. The active system uses collector panels to gather the sun's heat. The heat is transferred via a water pipe system to the lower level storage tank where it is circulated throughout the house by a heat exchanger. Note that where active solar collectors are a design OPTION, which they are in all of our active/passive designs, they must be contracted locally. The collector area must be tailored to the climate and sun angles that characterize your building location.

Design V12830 Main Level: 1,795 square feet; Lower Level: 1,546 square feet; Total: 3,341 square feet

● Outstanding contemporary design! This home has been created with the advantages of passive solar heating in mind. For optimum energy savings, this delightful design combines passive solar devices, the solarium, with optional active collectors. Included with the purchase of this design are four plot plans to assure that the solar collectors will face the south. The garage in each plan acts as a buffer against cold northern winds. Schematic details for solar application also are included. Along with being energy-efficient, this design has excellent living patterns. Three bedrooms, the master bedroom on the main level and two others on the lower level at each side of the solarium. The living area of the main level will be able to enjoy the delightful view of the solarium and sunken garden.

Design V12827

Upper Level: 1,618 square feet
Lower Level: 1,458 square feet
Total: 3,076 square feet

● The two-story solarium with skylights above is the key to energy savings to this bi-level design. Study the efficiency of this floor plan. The conversation lounge on the lower level is a unique focal point.

Design V12884 First Floor: 1,855 square feet
Second Floor: 837 square feet; Total: 2,692 square feet

● The greenhouse in this design enhances its energy-efficiency and allows for spacious and interesting living patterns. Being a one-and-a-half story design, the second floor could be developed at a later date when the space is needed. The greenhouses add an additional 418 sq. ft. to the above quoted figures.

● Earth shelters the interior of this house from both the cold of the winter and the heat of the summer. This three bedroom design has passive solar capabilities. The sun room, south facing for light, has a stone floor which will absorb heat. When needed, the heat will be circulated to the interior by opening the sliding glass doors or by mechanical means. Entrance to this home will be obtained through the vestibule or the garage. Both have a western exposure. A large, centrally located, skylight creates an open feeling and lights up the interior of this plan where the formal and informal living areas are located. The sun room contains 425 sq. ft. not included in total to the right.

Design V12862
Square Footage: 2,808

Design V12903
Square Footage: 2,555

● Earth berms on the sides of this house help it achieve energy-efficiency. The maximum amount of light enters this home by way of the many glass areas on the southern exposure. Every room in this plan, except the study, has the benefit of the southern sun. A garden room, tucked between the family and dining rooms, can be used for passive solar capabilities. A front privacy wall and the entrance court will shield the interior from the harsh northern winds. The air-locked vestibule also will be an energy saver. Summer heat gain will be reduced by the wide overhanging roof. The occupants of this home will appreciate the excellent interior planning. Garden room contains 144 sq. ft. not included in above total.

Design V12860

Square Footage: 2,240

● Here is truly a unique home to satisfy your family's desires for something appealing and refreshing. This three bedroom home is also, the very embodiment of what's new and efficient in planning and technology. This is an excellent example of outstanding coordination of house structure, site, interior livability and the sun. Orienting this earth sheltered house toward the south assures a warm, bright and cheerful interior. Major contributions to energy-efficiency result from the earth covered roof, the absence of northern wall exposure and the lack of windows on either end of the house. This means a retention of heat in the winter and cool air in the summer. An effective use of skylights provide the important extra measure of natural light to the interior. Sliding glass doors in the living and dining rooms also help bring the light to the indoors. This earth sheltered house makes no sacrifice of good planning and excellent, all 'round livability. The section is cut through the living room and the skylit hall looking toward the bedrooms.

Design V12838
Square Footage: 2,309

96'-0"

42'-0"

STUDY BEDROOM 10⁴ x 11⁰

FAMILY RM. 18⁶ x 11⁰

KITCHEN 12⁰ x 14⁰

PANTRY

MECHANICAL ROOM

SOLAR WATER STORAGE

WALK-IN CLOSET

DRSG. RM.

BATH

BATH

CL.

SKYLIGHT ABOVE

LAUND.

MASTER BEDROOM 12⁰ x 17⁰

BEDROOM 10⁴ x 11⁰

LIVING RM. 30⁰ x 23⁰

DINING

VESTIBULE (AIR LOCK)

POR. RM.

GARAGE 22¹⁰ x 23⁰

TERRACE

TERRACE

● Here is a dramatic earth sheltered home which will function well with the sun. The spaciousness of the living area in this design is enhanced by the central location of the dramatic skylight. In addition to the passive solar heating gain for the living and bedroom areas, the impressively designed "mansard" roof effect lends itself to the installation of active solar heating panels. The illustration above shows panels only on the garage wing. Consultation with local solar heating experts will determine the effectiveness in your area of additional panels. A special room adjacent to the garage will accommodate mechanical equipment.

SKYLIGHT

PARAPET

EARTH COVER

GRAVEL

WATERPROOFING

PLYWOOD ON RIGID INSULATION

2" CONCRETE SLAB OVER PRECAST CONCRETE PLANKS

MIRRORS

FAMILY ROOM

SLDG GLASS DOOR

LIVING/ DINING ROOM

INSULATION

DRYWALL

WATERPROOFING

INSULATION

12" REINFORCED MASONRY WALL

Design V12861
Square Footage: 2,499

● Berming the earth against the walls of a structure prove to be very energy efficient. The earth protects the interior from the cold of the winter and the heat of the summer. Interior lighting will come from the large skylight over the garden room. Every room will benefit from this exposed area. The garden room will function as a multi-purpose area for the entire family. The living/dining room will receive light from two areas, the garden room and the wall of sliding glass doors to the outside. Family living will be served by the efficient floor plan. Three bedrooms and two full baths are clustered together. The kitchen is adjacent to the air-locked vestibule where the laundry and utility rooms are housed. The section is cut through the dining, garden and master bedroom facing the kitchen.

● Earth berms are banked against all four exterior walls of this design to effectively reduce heating and cooling demands. The berming is cost-efficient during both hot and cold seasons. In the winter, berming reduces heat loss through the exterior walls and shields the structure from cold winds. It helps keep warm air out during the summer. The two most dramatic interior highlights are the atrium and thru-fireplace. Topped with a large skylight, the atrium floods the interior with natural light. Shades are used to cover the atrium in the summer to prevent solar heat gain. Three bedrooms are featured in this plan and they each open via sliding glass doors to the atrium. This would eliminate any feeling of being closed in. An island with range and oven is featured in the kitchen. Informal dining will be enjoyed at the snack bar. The family/dining room can house those more formal dining occasions. The section at the right is cut through the study, atrium and rear bedroom looking toward master bedroom.

Design V12833
Square Footage: 2,386

Design V12863

Square Footage: 2,955

● Livability is outstanding in this earth-shelter design. Each of the three bedrooms has access to the terrace, along with the gathering and dining rooms. All of the sliding glass doors, along with the atrium, will brighten the interior nicely. The atrium will be enjoyed from the lounge, kitchen and gathering/dining rooms. Efficient work space will be found in the kitchen. It has easy access to the atrium and dining room.

OPTIONAL EXTERIORS & PLANS . . . *as highlighted*

in this section offer a fine study in the interchangeability of varying exterior styles on a given floor plan. Occasionally one's enthusiasm for a favorite floor plan may not be matched by a similar feeling about that plan's exterior styling. Further, within one's family, members may differ about their style preferences. Here are a variety of floor plans which offer an excellent opportunity to observe how (with minor modifications) that particular plan can have differently styled exteriors. As you study these plans which range in size from 1344-1880 sq. ft. note the fine proportion and detailing of the Traditional, Contemporary, Tudor and French exteriors.

● Here is a unique series of designs with three charming exterior adaptations — Southern Colonial, Western Ranch, French Provincial - and two distinctive floor plans. Each plan has a different design number and is less than 1,600 square feet.

● If yours is a preference for the floor plan featuring the 26 foot keeping room, you should order blueprints for Design V12611. Of course, the details for each of the three delightful exteriors will be included. On the other hand, should the plan with the living,-dining and family rooms be your favorite, order blueprints for Design V12612 and get details for all three exteriors.

There are many points of similarity in the two designs. Each has a fireplace, 2½ baths, sliding glass doors to the rear terrace, master bedroom with walk-in closet and private bath with stall shower and a basement. It is interesting to note that two of the exteriors have covered porches. Don't miss the beamed ceilings, the various storage facilities and the stall showers.

Design V12611
Square Footage: 1,557

L **D**

Design V12612
Square Footage: 1,571

L **D**

Design V12802
Square Footage: 1,729

L **D**

● The three exteriors shown at the left house the same, efficiently planned one-story floor plan shown below. Be sure to notice the design variations in the window placement and roof pitch. The Tudor design to the left is delightful. Half-timbered stucco and brick comprise the facade of this English Tudor variation of the plan. Note authentic bay window in the front bedroom.

Design V12803
Square Footage: 1,679

L **D**

● Housed in varying facades, this floor plan is very efficient. The front foyer leads to each of the living areas. The sleeping area of two, or optional three, bedrooms is ready to serve the family. Then there is the gathering room. This room is highlighted by its size, 16 x 20 feet. A contemporary mix of fieldstone and vertical wood siding characterizes this exterior. The absence of columns or posts gives a modern look to the covered porch.

Design V12804
Square Footage: 1,674

L **D**

● Stuccoed arches, multi-paned windows and a gracefully sloped roof accent the exterior of this Spanish-inspired design. Like the other two designs, the interior kitchen will efficiently serve the dining room, covered dining porch and breakfast room with great ease. Blueprints for all three designs include details for an optional non-basement plan.

OPTIONAL NON-BASEMENT

Design V12805

Square Footage: 1,547

● Three completely different exterior facades share one compact, practical and economical floor plan. The major design variations are roof pitch, window placement and garage openings. Each design will hold its own when comparing the three exteriors. The design to the right is a romantic stone-and-shingle cottage design. This design, along with the other two designs presented here, is outstanding.

Design V12806

Square Footage: 1,584

● Even though these exteriors are different in their styling and have a few design variations, their floor plans are identical. Each will provide the family with a livable plan. In this brick and half-timbered stucco Tudor version, the living-dining room expands across the rear of the plan and has direct access to the covered porch. Notice the built-in planter adjacent to the open staircase leading to the basement.

Design V12807

Square Footage: 1,576

● Along with the living-dining areas of the other two plans, this sleek contemporary styled home's breakfast room also will have a view of the covered porch. A desk, snack bar and mud room housing the laundry facilities are near the U-shaped kitchen. Clustering these work areas together is very convenient. The master bedroom has a private bath.

OPTIONAL NON-BASEMENT

Design V12565
Square Footage: 1,540

L **D**

● This modest sized floor plan has much to offer in the way of livability. It may function as either a two or three bedroom home. The living room is huge and features a fine, raised hearth fireplace. The open stairway to the basement is handy and will lead to what may be developed as the recreation area. In addition to the two full baths, there is an extra wash room. Adjacent is the laundry room and the service entrance from the garage. The blueprints you order for this design will show details for each of the three delightful elevations above. Which is your favorite? The Tudor, the Colonial or the Contemporary?

61'-8"

44'-0"

TERRACE

KITCHEN
8'² x 12'

NOOK
7'⁰ x 10'⁰

DINING

MASTER
BED RM.
12'² x 12'²

RAISED HEARTH

LIVING RM.
24'⁰ x 15'⁶

REFR. PANTRY

BATH

WASH
RM.

LAUNDRY

ENTRY

BATH

STUDY-
BED RM.
12'² x 11'⁶

PORCH

BED RM.
12'⁰ x 11'⁶

GARAGE
21'⁴ x 21'⁴

Design V12505
Square Footage: 1,366

L **D**

● This design offers you a choice of three distinctively different exteriors. Which is your favorite? Blueprints show details for all three optional elevations. A study of the floor plan reveals a fine measure of livability. In less than 1,400 square feet there are features galore. An excellent return on your construction dollar. In addition to the two eating areas and the open planning of the gathering room, the indoor-outdoor relationships are of great interest. The basement may be developed for recreational activities. Be sure to note the storage potential, particularly the linen closet, the pantry, the china cabinet and the broom closet.

Design V11305
Square Footage: 1,382

D

● Order blueprints for any one of the three exteriors shown on these two pages and you will receive details for building this outstanding floor plan at the right. You'll find the appeal of these exteriors difficult to beat. As for the plan, in less than 1,400 square feet there are three bedrooms, two full baths, a separate dining room, a formal living room, a fine kitchen overlooking the rear yard and an informal family room. In addition, there is the attached two-car garage. Note the location of the stairs when this plan is built with a basement. Each of the exteriors is predominantly brick - the front of Design V11305 (above) features both stone and vertical boards and battens with brick on the other three sides. Observe the double front doors of the French design, V11382 (below) and the Contemporary design, V11383 (bottom). Study the window treatment.

Design V11382
Square Footage: 1,382

D

Design V11383
Square Footage: 1,382

D

Design V11307
Square Footage: 1,357

L **D**

● These three stylish exteriors have the same practical, L-shaped floor plan. Design V11307 (above) features a low-pitched, wide-overhanging roof, a pleasing use of horizontal siding and brick and an enclosed front flower court. Design V11380 (below) has its charm characterized by the pediment gables, the effective window treatment and the masses of brick. Design V11381 (bottom) is captivating because of its hip-roof, its dentils, panelled shutters and lamp post. Each of these three designs has a covered front porch. Inside, there is an abundance of livability. The formal living and dining area is spacious, and the U-shaped kitchen is efficient. There is informal eating space, a separate laundry and a fine family room. Note the sliding glass doors to the terrace. The blueprints include details for building either with or without a basement. Observe the pantry of the non-basement plan.

Design V11380
Square Footage: 1,399

L **D**

Design V11381
Square Footage: 1,399

L **D**

Design V11938
Square Footage: 1,428

● An efficient plan designed to fit each of the three delightful exteriors above. You can reserve your choice of exterior until you receive the blueprints. Each set you order contains the details for the construction of all three. Note the differences in exterior materials, window treatment, car storage facilities and roof lines. Observe the beamed ceiling, all purpose family room and the kitchen eating space. There is a lot of living in 1,428 square feet.

Design V11323

Square Footage: 1,344

L **D**

● Incorporated in the set of blueprints for this design are details for building each of the three charming, traditional exteriors. Each of the three alternate exteriors has a distinction all its own. A study of the floor plan reveals fine livability. There are two full baths, a fine family room, an efficient work center, a formal dining area, bulk storage facilities and sliding glass doors to the quiet and living terraces. Laundry is strategically located near the kitchen.

Three Distinctively Styled Exteriors . . .

Design V12705
Square Footage: 1,746

L

Design V12706
Square Footage: 1,746

L **D**

. . . One Practical, Efficient Floor Plan

● Three different exteriors! But inside it's all the same livable house. Begin with the impressive entry hall . . . more than 19' long and offering double entry to the gathering room. Now the gathering room which is notable for its size and design. Notice how the fireplace is flanked by sliding glass doors leading to the terrace! That's unusual.

There's a formal dining room, too! The right spot for special birthday dinners as well as supper parties for friends. And an efficient kitchen that makes meal preparation easy whatever the occasion. Look for a built-in range and oven here . . . plus a bright dining nook with sliding doors to a second terrace. Three large bedrooms! All

located to give family members the utmost privacy. Including a master suite with a private dressing room, bath and a sliding glass door opening onto the main terrace. For blueprints of the hip-roof French adaptation on the opposite page order V12705. For the Contemporary version order V12706. The Colonial order V12704.

Design V12704
Square Footage: 1,746

L **D**

Design V11389

Square Footage: 1,488

D

● Your choice of exterior goes with this outstanding floor plan. If your tastes include a liking for French Provincial, Design V11389, above, will provide a lifetime of satisfaction. On the other hand, should you prefer the simple straightforward lines of comtemporary design, the exterior for Design V11387, below, will be your favorite. For those who enjoy the warmth of Colonial adaptations, the charming exterior for Design V11388, bottom, will be perfect. Of interest, is a comparison of these three exteriors. Observe the varying design treatment of the windows, the double front doors, the garage doors and the roof lines. Don't miss other architectural details. Study each exterior and the floor plan carefully. Three charming designs you won't want to miss.

Design V11387

Square Footage: 1,488

D

Design V11388

Square Footage: 1,488

D

Design V11864
Square Footage: 1,598

D

● What's your favorite exterior? The one above which has a distinctive colonial appearance, or that below with its sleek contemporary look? Maybe you prefer the more formal hip-roof exterior (bottom) with its French feeling. Whatever your choice, you'll know your next home will be one that is delightfully proportioned and is sure to be among the most attractive in the neighborhood. It is interesting to note that each exterior highlights an effective use of wood siding and stone (or brick, as in the case of Design V11866). The floor plan features three bedrooms, 2½ baths, a formal living and dining room, a snack bar and a mud room. The master bedroom of the contemporary design has its window located in the left side elevation wall.

Design V11865
Square Footage: 1,598

D

Design V11866
Square Footage: 1,598

D

Design V12810
Square Footage: 1,536

L D

Design V12814
Square Footage: 1,536

L D

OPTIONAL CRAWL SPACE PLAN

OPTIONAL FRONT ENTRANCE GARAGE

● 2 x 6 stud wall construction front and center! The designs on these two pages are particularly energy-efficient minded. All exterior walls employ the use of the larger size stud (in preference to the traditional 2 x 4 stud) to permit the installation of extra thick insulation. The high cornice design also allows for more ceiling insulation. In addition to the insulation factor, 2 x 6 studs are practical from an economic standpoint. According to many experts, the use of 2 x 6's spaced 24 inches O.C. results in the need for less lumber and saves construction time. However, the energy-efficient features of this series do not end with the basic framing members. Efficiency begins right at the front door where the vestibule acts as an airlock restricting the flow of cold air to the interior. The basic rectangular shape of the house spells efficiency. No complicated and costly construction here. Yet, there has been no sacrifice of delightful exterior appeal. Efficiency and economy are also embodied in such features as back-to-back plumbing, centrally located furnace, minimal window and door openings and, most important of all - size.

Design V12811
Square Footage: 1,581

L D

Design V12815
Square Footage: 1,581

L D

Design V12812
3-Bedroom Plan
Square Footage: 1,581

Design V12816
4-Bedroom Plan
Square Footage: 1,581

OPTIONAL CRAWL SPACE FLOOR PLAN

OPTIONAL FRONT ENTRANCE GARAGE

● Within 1,536 square feet there is outstanding livability and a huge variety of options from which to choose. For instance, of the four stylish exteriors, which is your favorite? The cozy, front porch Farmhouse adaptation; the pleasing Southern Colonial version, the French creation, or the rugged Western facade? Further, do you prefer a three or a four bedroom floor plan? With or without a basement? Front or side-opening garage? If you wish to order blueprints for the hip-roofed design with three bedrooms, specify Design V12812; for the four bedroom option specify V12816. To order blueprints for the three bedroom Southern Colonial, request Design V12811; for the four bedroom model, ask for Design V12815, etc. All blueprints include the optional non-basement and front opening garage details. Whatever the version you select, you and your family will enjoy the beamed ceiling of the family room, the efficient, U-shaped kitchen, the dining area, the traffic-free living room and the fine storage facilities. Truly a fine design series created to give each home buyer the maximum amount of choice and flexibility.

Design V12813
3-Bedroom Plan
Square Footage: 1,536

Design V12817
4-Bedroom Plan
Square Footage: 1,536

303

Design V12824
Square Footage: 1,550

● Low-maintenance and economy in building are the outstanding exterior features of this sharp one-story design. It is sheathed in long-lasting cedar siding and trimmed with stone for an eye-appealing facade. Entrance to this home takes you through a charming garden courtyard then a covered walk to the front porch. The garage extending from the front of the house serves two purposes; to reduce lot size and to buffer the interior of the house from street noise. Sliding glass doors are featured in each of the main rooms for easy access to the outdoors. A sun porch is tucked between the study and gathering rooms. Optional non-basement details are included with the purchase of this design.

TERRACE

51'-8"

TERRACE

TERRACE

SUN PORCH
SKYLITE ABOVE

GATHERING RM.
13⁴ x 16⁰

DINING RM.
11⁴ x 10⁰

STUDY
10⁰ x 10⁰

TERRACE

BRKFST.
11⁴ x 7⁴

MASTER
BEDROOM
11⁴ x 14⁰

KITCHEN
11⁴ x 10⁰

BATH

57'-4"

BEDROOM
11⁸ x 10⁸

FOYER

LAUNDRY

BATH

COVERED
PORCH

GARAGE
13⁴ x 21⁸

STOR.

Design V12825
Square Footage: 1,584

● With today's tight economy, this house will be a real bargain. It has all of the necessary features to insure gracious living yet keep costs down - generous living space, packed with amenities and constructed with durable materials. Locating the garage to the front of this design is practical because it makes the overall width only 51' so it will fit on a narrow lot and it will act as a buffer against street noise. The interior of this home will be interesting. Three sets of sliding glass doors at the rear of the plan will flood the interior with natural light. Since it is a modified open plan it will allow the sunlight to penetrate deep into the interior. The gathering room which seems expanded by the cathedral ceiling has a fireplace.

STUDY

M.B.R.

GATHERING RM.

AIR COND.

BRK.

KIT.

BATH

OPTIONAL NON-BASEMENT

Design V11322 Square Footage: 1,478

D

Design V11321
Square Footage: 1,478

D

Design V11320
Square Footage: 1,478

D

● Three totally different front elevations have the same basic floor plan layout. There is a separate set of blueprints for each attractive front exterior. The economically built plan, because of its simplicity, is outstanding.

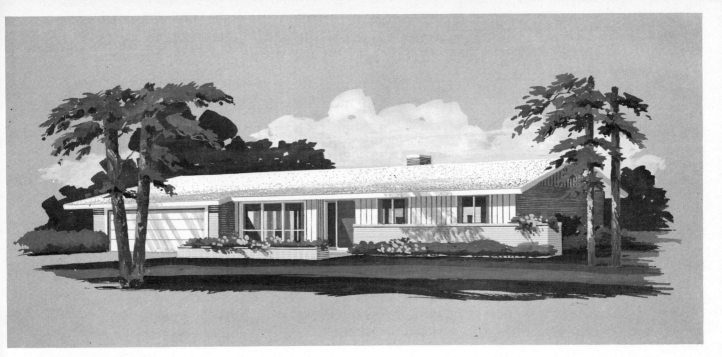

Design V11352 Square Footage: 1,592

Design V11351
Square Footage: 1,592

Design V11350
Square Footage: 1,592

60'-0"

TERRACE

FAMILY RM.
17⁸ x 13⁰

S. D.W.

KIT.
10⁰ x 10⁰

RANGE

REF'G PANTRY

DINING RM.
10⁰ x 13⁴

BATH

DN.

CL.

MASTER
BED RM.
11⁸ x 14⁰

34'-10"

32'-10"

CL.

BATH

LIN. CL.

GARAGE
19⁰ x 20⁰

LIVING RM.
12⁸ x 21⁰

ENTRY

CL.

CL.

CL.

CL.

BED RM.
10⁰ x 10⁰

BED RM.
10⁰ x 12⁴

DINING RM.
10⁰ x 12⁰

CL.

D.
W.

AIR
COND.

BATH

S

BATH

CL.

LIN. CL.

ENTRY

BED RM.
10⁰ x 10⁰

OPTIONAL NON-BASEMENT

● When you order blueprints for the exterior that appeals to you the most, you'll receive details for building with or without a basement. Note the family room and the arrangements of the two full baths.

Design V11946
Square Footage: 1,632

56' - 0"
54' - 0"

TERRACE

MASTER BED RM. 13⁰ x 11⁰

BED RM. 10⁰ x 13⁰

LIVING RM. 18⁰ x 12⁰

SLID. DR.

FAMILY RM. 11⁴ x 17⁰

BEAMED CEILING

SHOWER

BATH

CL.

CL.

STORAGE

AIR COND.

ENTRY

BATH

LIN.

DINING RM. 11⁸ x 11⁰

SNACKS

CL.

KIT. 11⁴ x 10⁴

RANGE

BED RM. 10⁸ x 10⁰

BED RM. 10⁰ x 10⁰

CL.

ENTRY COURT

PDR. RM.

WASH. DRY.

MUD RM. 8⁰ x 8⁰

CL. CL.

32' - 0"

60' - 0"

GARAGE 21⁴ x 23⁴

54' - 0"
52' - 0"

TERRACE

CL.

DRESS. RM.

LIVING RM. 18⁰ x 12⁰

SLDG. DR.

FAMILY RM. 11⁴ x 17⁰

SHOWER

BATH

MASTER BED RM. 13⁰ x 12⁰

BEAMED CEILING

BATH

CL.

AIR COND.

LIN.

CL.

ENTRY

DINING RM. 11⁸ x 11⁰

SNACKS

OPEN

KIT. 11⁴ x 10⁰

RANGE

BED RM. 11⁰ x 13⁴

STUDY BED RM. 10⁰ x 10⁰

ENTRY COURT

PDR. RM.

WASH. DRY.

MUD RM. 8⁰ x 8⁰

32' - 0"

60' - 0"

GARAGE 21⁴ x 23⁴

Design V11945
Square Footage: 1,568

● Here is a delightful one-story home with a most unusual, yet appealing shape. The projecting elements add that extra measure of appeal that contributes so much to individuality. Interestingly enough, this basic exterior may have two different floor plans. If you wish blueprints for the three bedroom home order Design V11945: for four bedroom blueprints, order Design V11946. Whichever you select, you will enjoy the efficiency of the remainder of the plan. There are formal living and dining rooms, an informal family room with a beamed ceiling, a U-shaped kitchen and a strategically placed mud room with an adjacent powder room for easy convenience.

Design V11947
Square Footage: 1,764

● When it comes to housing your family, if you are among the contemporary-minded, you'll want to give this L-shaped design a second, then even a third, or fourth, look. It is available as either a three or four bedroom home. If you desire the three bedroom, 58 foot wide design order blueprints for V11947; for the four bedroom, 62 foot wide design, order V11948. Inside, you will note a continuation of the contemporary theme with sloping ceilings, exposed beams and a practical 42 inch high storage divider between the living and dining rooms. Don't miss the mud rooms.

Design V11948
Square Footage: 1,876

Design V11331

Square Footage: 1,880

● Here is a heap of living which will fit within the confines of a relatively narrow building site. The front projecting two-car garage and the rear projecting master bedroom allow this outstanding home to be located on a much smaller, and often times less expensive, piece of property than as if the plan were a long rectangle. However, should you wish to build on a couple of acres, don't despair. The delightful exterior still will be a showplace, and the efficient floor plan will remain just as practical and livable. Blueprints for this design include details for both the optional basement and optional hip-roof elevation below. Which do you prefer?

Design V11747

First Floor: 1,690 square feet
Second Floor: 1,060 square feet
Total: 2,750 square feet

● Two very similar floor plans, each with its own distinctive exterior style and potential for one-floor livability. Plan V11747 is slightly larger and features a lovely bay window in the dining room. Plan V11906 makes use of second floor space in an expanded master suite. Both plans have excellent design, a thoughtful amount of built-ins, and true appeal.

Design V11906

First Floor: 1,514 square feet
Second Floor: 992 square feet
Total: 2,506 square feet

Design V12941
Square Footage: 1,842

D

● Here is a basic floor plan which goes with each of the differently styled exteriors. The Early American version above is charming, indeed. Horizontal siding, stone, window boxes, a dovecote, a picket fence and a garden court enhance its appeal. Note the covered entrance.

Design V12942
Square Footage: 1,834

D

● The Tudor exterior above will be the favorite of many. Stucco, simulated timber work and diamond-lite windows set its unique character. Each of the delightful exteriors features eye-catching roof lines. Inside, there is an outstanding plan to cater to the living patterns of the small family, empty nesters, or retirees.

Design V12943
Square Footage: 1,834

D

● The Contemporary optional exterior above features vertical siding and a wide-overhanging roof with exposed rafter ends. The foyer is spacious with sloped ceiling and a dramatic open staircase to the basement recreation area. Other ceilings in the house are also sloped. The breakfast, dining and media rooms are highlights, along with the laundry, the efficient kitchen, the snack bar and the master bath.

BONUS LIVABILITY . . .

for future expansion can result by allowing for the development of a second level of livability. Each of the following designs delivers complete one-story living and gives the appearance of being a one-story house. However, with the development of what would be unused attic space, additional sleeping facilities can be gained. These houses can be of minimal, or expanded, square footage on the first floor. Later as family size grows, or financial constraints lessen, the total livability can be considerably increased. Note the examples of how bonus space may be developed on a lower level. The basements of many one-story homes can be exposed to provide this bonus livability.

Design V12563
First Floor: 1,500 square feet
Second Floor: 690 square feet
Total: 2,190 square feet

L

● This charming Cape Cod definately will capture your heart with its warm appeal. This home offers you and your family a lot of livability. Upon entering this home, to your left, is a nice-sized living room with fireplace. Adjacent is a dining room. An efficient kitchen and a large, farm kitchen eating area with fireplace will be enjoyed by all. A unique feature on this floor is the master bedroom with a full bath and walk-in closet. Also take notice of the first floor laundry, the pantry and a study for all of your favorite books. Note the sliding glass doors in the farm kitchen and master bedroom. Upstairs you'll find two bedrooms, one with a walk-in closet. Also here, a sitting room and a full bath are available. Lastly, this design accommodates a three car garage.

Design V12699

First Floor: 2,188 square feet
Second Floor: 858 square feet
Total: 3,046 square feet

L

Second Floor

ROOF

BEDROOM 11⁰ x 15⁸

UPPER LIVING RM.

LOUNGE

BEDROOM 11⁰ x 12⁰

RAILING

VANITY

BATH

BATH

ACCESS PANEL

ATTIC

DN.

CL.

CL.

BALCONY

LINEN

CL.

UPPER FOYER

ROOF

ROOF

First Floor

TERRACE

TERRACE

WHIRLPOOL

MASTER BEDROOM 15⁴ x 18⁰

BATH.

LIVING RM. 18⁴ x 15⁰

LOUNGE ABOVE

36" HIGH CAB'T.

DINING RM. 12⁰ x 13⁰

EATING

CHINA

P.

DESK

GARAGE 21⁴ x 29⁴

VANITY

BALCONY ABOVE

B.C.

DN.

CL.

W.R.

MUD AREA

WALK-IN CLOSET

DN.

CL.

TV. VCR

COUNTRY KITCHEN 15⁸ x 21⁰

COOK TOP

REF'S.

LAUNDRY 11⁸ x 6⁰

W

D

FOYER

UP

PDR. RM.

MEDIA RM. 12⁰ x 10⁰

DW.

LOUNGE 12⁰ x 8⁸

PORCH

32'-0"

106'-8"

Design V12146

First Floor: 1,182 square feet
Second Floor: 708 square feet
Total: 1,890 square feet

L **D**

GARAGE
21⁴ x 21⁴

TERRACE

COVERED
PORCH
14⁰ x 12⁰

KITCHEN
9⁰ x 14⁰

FAMILY RM.
16⁰ x 11⁴

BATH

BED RM.
10⁰ x 11⁶

BEAMED CEILG.

FLOWER COURT

LIVING RM.
19⁰ x 13⁰

ENTRY HALL

BED RM.
13⁴ x 11⁶

80'-0"

35'-0"

MASTER BED RM.
16⁰ x 13⁰

PDR. RM.

BATH

CLIPPED CEILG.

STUDY BED RM.
13⁴ x 11⁴

WALK-IN CLOSET

DN.

ROOF

● Historically referred to as a "half house", this authentic adaptation has its roots in the heritage of New England. With completion of the second floor, the growing family doubles its sleeping capacity. Notice that both the family and living rooms have a fireplace. Don't overlook the many built-in units featured throughout the plan.

Design V11372

First Floor: 768 square feet
Second Floor: 432 square feet
Total: 1,200 square feet

● Low cost livability could hardly
ask for more. Here is an enchanting
Colonial exterior and a four bedroom
floor plan. Note stairs to basement
and carport.

Design V13189

First Floor: 884 square feet
Second Floor: 598 square feet
Total: 1,482 square feet

D

● Four bedrooms, two baths, a large kitchen/dining
area, plenty of closets, a full basement and an attached
two-car garage are among the highlights of this design.
Note the uniqueness of the second floor.

Design V11394

First Floor: 832 square feet
Second Floor: 512 square feet
Total: 1,344 square feet

L D

● The growing family with a restricted building budget will find this a great investment - a convenient living floor plan inside an attractively designed facade.

Design V12510

First Floor: 1,191 square feet
Second Floor: 533 square feet
Total: 1,724 square feet

L D

● The pleasant in-line kitchen is flanked by a separate dining room and a family room. The master bedroom is on the first floor with two more bedrooms upstairs.

● If symmetry means anything, this pleasant house has it. The projecting wings of the sleeping zone and the garage are virtually identical. However, the appeal of this charmer does not end with its symmetrical beauty. There is a world of livability to be fostered by this home.

Design V11964 First Floor: 2,150 square feet
Second Floor: 680 square feet; Total: 2,830 square feet

Design V11794 First Floor: 2,122 square feet
Second Floor: 802 square feet; Total: 2,924 square feet

● The inviting warmth of this delightful home catches the eye of even the most casual observer. Imagine, four big bedrooms! Formal and informal living can be enjoyed throughout this charming plan. A private, formal dining room is available for those very special occasions.

Design V11967

First Floor: 1,804 square feet
Second Floor: 496 square feet
Total: 2,300 square feet

● You'll always want that first impression your guests get of your new home to be a lasting one. There will be much that will linger in the memories of most of your visitors after their visit to this home. Of course, the impressive exterior will long be remembered. And little wonder with its distinctive projecting garage and bedroom wing, its recessed front porch, its horizontal siding and its interesting roof lines. Inside, there is much to behold. The presence of five bedrooms and three full baths will not be forgotten soon. Formal and informal areas will serve every family occasion.

Design V12780

First Floor: 2,006 square feet
Second Floor: 718 square feet
Total: 2,724 square feet

● This 1½-story contemporary has more fine features than one can imagine. The livability is outstanding and can be appreciated by the whole family. A two-story gathering room is reached from the entry foyer and has a sloped ceiling, raised hearth fireplace, and sliding glass doors to the rear terrace. The formal dining room, also with sloped ceiling, is located nicely between the gathering room and well-planned kitchen/nook. A master suite is complemented by a front study on this floor and two bedrooms and a full bath upstairs. Note the fine indoor-outdoor living relationships.

Design V12708

First Floor: 2,108 square feet
Second Floor: 824 square feet
Total: 2,932 square feet

D

● Here is a one-and-a-half
story home whose exterior is
distinctive. It has a contemporary feeling, yet it retains some
of the fine design features and
proportions of traditional
exteriors. Inside the appealing
double front doors there is liva-
ability galore. The sunken
rear living-dining area is delightfully spacious and is looked down into from the second
floor lounge. The open end
fireplace, with its raised hearth
and planter, is another focal
point. The master bedroom
features a fine compartmented
bath with both shower and tub.
The study is just a couple steps
away. The U-shaped kitchen is
outstanding. Notice the pantry
and laundry. Upstairs provides
children with their own sleeping, studying and TV quarters.
Absolutely a great design! Study
all the fine details closely with
your family.

Design V12502

Main Level: 2,606 square feet
Lower Level: 1,243 square feet
Total: 3,849 square feet

L

81'-8"

82'-8"

BALCONY

TERRACE

NOOK
11' x 9⁰

FAMILY RM.
13⁰ x 18⁴

DINING RM.
11' x 11⁶

LIVING RM.
18' x 15⁰

MASTER
BED. RM.
13⁰ x 17⁴

KITCHEN
11⁰ x 10⁰

RAISED HEARTH

RAISED HEARTH

SLOPED CEILING

BED RM.
13⁰ x 11⁴

PANTRY

ENTRANCE

STUDY
14⁰ x 11⁸

LINEN

DRESSING RM.

BATH

PORCH

PDR.
RM.

COURT

BATH

LT. WASH./DRY.

LAUNDRY
7⁸ x 8⁰

BED RM.
13⁰ x 11⁴

CURB

GARAGE
24' x 23³

TERRACE

CARD RM.
11⁰ x 10⁰

ACTIVITIES RM.
12' x 26⁴

BASEMENT

UNEX.

SNACK BAR

SUMMER KIT.
11' x 9⁰

AIR
COND.

W.R.

GAME RM.
23⁶ x 19⁰

● A home with two faces. From the street this design gives all the appearances of being a one-story, L-shaped home. One can only guess at the character of the rear elevation as dictated by the sloping terrain. A study of the interior reveals tremendous convenient living potential.

Design V12504

Main Level: 1,918 square feet
Lower Level: 1,910 square feet
Total: 3,828 square feet

● A front court area welcomes guests on their way to the double front doors. These doors, flanked by floor-to-ceiling glass panels, are sheltered by the porch. Adjacent to this area are the sliding glass doors of the breakfast nook which can enjoy to the fullest the beauty of the front yard. This design has taken advantage of the sloping site to open up the lower level. In this case, the lower level has virtually the same glass treatment as its corresponding room above.

● This hillside home gives all the appearances of being a one-story ranch home; and what a delightful one at that! Should the contours of your property slope to the rear, this plan permits the exposing of the lower level. This results in the activities room and bedroom/study gaining direct access to outdoor living. Certainly a most desirable aspect for active, outdoor family living. The large and growing family will be admirably served with five bedrooms and three baths. An extra washroom and separate laundry add to the convenient living potential.

Design V12549
Main Level: 2,260 square feet
Lower Level: 1,406 square feet
Total: 3,666 square feet

Design V12846 Main Level: 2,341 square feet; Lower Level: 1,380 square feet; Total: 3,721 square feet

Main Level floor plan labels:

66'-0"

DECK

FAMILY RM.
12⁰ x 17⁶

KITCHEN
11⁰ x 16⁰

DINING RM.
11⁴ x 14⁰

LIVING RM.
16⁰ x 17⁶

COVERED PORCH

MASTER BEDROOM
13⁸ x 15⁰

OVEN

RAISED HEARTH

66'-0"

BEDROOM
12⁰ x 11²

OPEN OVER PLANTER

PANTRY

FOYER

PDR RM.

LINEN

WALK-IN CLOSET

LINEN
TUB
BATH

COVERED PORCH

STUDY
12⁰ x 12⁰

BATH

BEDROOM
12⁰ x 11⁴

LAUNDRY

OPEN ABOVE

OPEN ABOVE

OPEN ABOVE

COURT

GARAGE
23⁴ x 22⁰

Lower Level floor plan labels:

COVERED TERRACE

LOUNGE
22⁶ x 17⁶

GUEST BEDROOM
11⁶ x 14⁰

BASEMENT

UNEXCAVATED

RAISED HEARTH

SNACK BAR

SUMMER KITCHEN
14⁸ x 9⁸

UP

LINEN

BATH

AIR COND.

STORAGE

UNEXCAVATED

HOBBIES / SHOP

GAMES RM.
21⁸ x 15⁰

● The street view of this Spanish design shows a beautifully designed one-story home, but now take a look at the rear elevation. This home has been designed to be built into a hill so the lower level can be opened to the sun. By so doing, the total livability is almost doubled. A unique feature of the lower level is the summer kitchen.

Design V12761

Main Level: 1,242 square feet
Lower Level: 1,242 square feet
Total: 2,484 square feet

L **D**

● Here is another one-story that doubles its livability by exposing the lowest level at the rear. Formal living on the main level and informal living, the activity room and study, on the lower level. Observe the wonderful outdoor living facilities. The deck acts as a cover for the terrace.

TERRACE

ACTIVITIES RM.
14⁰ x 17⁶

STUDY
15¹⁰ x 10⁰

BED RM.
10⁰ x 13¹⁰

BED RM.
11² x 12⁸

STORAGE

BATH

MECH. RM.

AIR COND.

VANITY

WALK IN CLOSET

UNEX.

UNEX.

DECK

50'-0"

LIVING RM.
14⁴ x 17⁶

DINING RM.
10⁰ x 10⁰

NOOK
8⁸ x 10⁰

BALCONY

MASTER BED RM.
11⁸ x 15⁰

KITCHEN
12⁰ x 13⁰

DN

UP

RAILING

BATH

WASH RM.

ENTRY

SERVICE ENTRANCE

OVEN

RANGE

WASH

DRY.

LAUNDRY

PORCH

CURB

52'-0"

GARAGE
21⁴ x 21⁸

STORAGE

Design V12781

First Floor: 2,132 square feet
Second Floor: 1,156 square feet
Total: 3,288 square feet

L **D**

● This beautifully designed two-story could be con-
sidered a dream house of a
lifetime. The exterior is
sure to catch the eye of
anyone who takes sight of
its unique construction.
The front kitchen features
an island range, adjacent
breakfast nook and pass-
thru to formal dining room.
The master bedroom suite
with its privacy and con-
venience on the first floor
has a spacious walk-in
closet and dressing room.
The side terrace is accessible through sliding glass
doors from the master bedroom, gathering room and
study. The second floor has
three bedrooms and storage
space galore. Also notice
the lounge which has a
sloped ceiling and a sky-
light above. This delightful
area looks down into the
gathering room. The out-
door balconies overlook the
wrap-around terrace. Surely an outstanding trend
house for decades to come.

Design V12488

First Floor: 1,113 square feet
Second Floor: 543 square feet
Total: 1,656 square feet

D

● A cozy cottage for the young at heart! Whether called upon to serve the young, active family as a leisure-time retreat at the lake, or the retired couple as a quiet haven in later years, this charming design will perform well. As a year round second home, the upstairs with its two sizable bedrooms, full bath and lounge area, looking down into the gathering room below, will ideally accommodate the younger generation.

Design V12927

First Floor: 1,425 square feet
Second Floor: 704 square feet
Total: 2,129 square feet

D

BONUS FEATURE — Some Of Our More Popular Plans With More Than One Story . . .

For those who may be as yet undecided on a one-story design and would like to explore other alternatives, we offer this collection. It represents some of our bestselling two-story and multi-level homes to whet the appetite. For an even greater selection, see our other books, Two-Story Homes or Multi-Level and Hillside Homes, which feature a vast array of designs in these categories.

Design V12283
First Floor: 1,559 square feet
Second Floor: 1,404 square feet
Total: 2,963 square feet

L D

● Reminiscent of the stately character of Federal architecture during an earlier period in our history, this two-story is replete with exquisite detailing. The cornice work, pediment gable, dentils, brick quoins at the corners, beautifully proportioned columns, front door detailing, window treatment and massive twin chimneys are among the features which make this design so unique and appealing.

Design V12683

First Floor: 2,126 square feet
Second Floor: 1,424 square feet
Total: 3,550 square feet

L **D**

● This historical Georgian home has its roots in the 18th-Century. Dignified symmetry is a hallmark of both front and rear elevations. The full two-story center section is delightfully complimented by the 1½-story wings. Interior livability has been planned to serve today's active family. The elegant gathering room, three steps down from the rest of the house, has ample space for entertaining on a grand scale. It fills an entire wing and is dead-ended so that traffic does not pass through it. Guests and family alike will enjoy the two rooms flanking the foyer, the study and formal dining room. Each of these rooms will have a fireplace as its highlight. The breakfast room, kitchen, powder room and laundry are arranged for maximum efficiency. This area will always have that desired light and airy atmosphere with the sliding glass door and the triple window over the kitchen sink. The second floor houses the family bedrooms. Take special note of the spacious master bedroom suite. It has a deluxe bath, fireplace and sunken lounge with dressing room and walk-in closet. Surely an area to be appreciated.

Design V12889

First Floor: 2,529 square feet
Second Floor: 1,872 square feet
Total: 4,401 square feet

L **D**

● This is truly classical, Georgian design at its best. Some of the exterior highlights of this two-story include the pediment gable with cornice work and dentils, the beautifully proportioned columns, the front door detailing and the window treatment. These are just some of the features which make this design so unique and appealing. Behind the facade of this design is an equally elegant interior. Imagine greeting your guests in the large receiving hall. It is graced by two curving staircases and opens to the formal living and dining rooms. Beyond the living room is the study. It has access to the rear terrace. Those large, informal occasions for family get-togethers or entertaining will be enjoyed in the spacious gathering room. It has a centered fireplace flanked by windows on each side, access to the terrace and a wet bar. Your appreciation for this room will be never-ending. The work center is efficient: the kitchen with island cook top, breakfast room, washroom, laundry and service entrance. The second floor also is outstanding. Three family bedrooms and two full baths are joined by the feature-filled master bedroom suite. Study this area carefully.

Design V12192

First Floor: 1,884 square feet
Second Floor: 1,521 square feet
Total: 3,405 square feet

L **D**

● This is surely a fine adaptation from the 18th-Century when formality and elegance were by-words. The authentic detailing of this design centers around the fine proportions, the dentils, the window symmetry, the front door and entranceway, the massive chimneys and the masonry work. The rear elevation retains all the grandeur exemplary of exquisite architecture. The appeal of this outstanding home does not end with its exterior elevations. Consider the formal living room with its corner fireplace. Also, the library with its wall of bookshelves and cabinets. Further, the dining room highlights corner china cabinets. Continue to study this elegant plan.

Design V12662

First Floor: 1,735 square feet
Second Floor: 1,075 square feet; Third Floor: 746 square feet
Total: 3,556 square feet

L

GARAGE
22⁸ x 22⁸

TERRACE

LAUNDRY

MUD RM.

COVERED PORCH

GATHERING RM.
20⁴ x 13²

KITCHEN
16⁴ x 13²

PANTRY

POWDER RM.

STUDY
10⁴ x 16⁸ BAY

PARLOR
14⁴ x 13²

FOYER

DINING RM.
14⁴ x 13²

BREAKFAST RM.
10⁴ x 16⁸ BAY

PORCH

64'-0"

BATH

BEDROOM
11¹⁰ x 14⁰

BEDROOM
11¹⁰ x 14⁰

ROOF

DRESSING RM.

BATH

BATH

LINEN

BEDROOM
13⁴ x 10⁶

MASTER BEDROOM
14⁴ x 17⁶

BEDROOM
14⁴ x 13⁶

ROOF

Design V12668 First Floor: 1,206 square feet
Second Floor: 1,254 square feet; Total: 2,460 square feet

L

● This elegant exterior houses a very livable plan. Every bit of space has been put to good use. The front country kitchen is a good place to begin. It is efficiently planned with its island cook top, built-ins and pass-thru to the dining room. The large great room will be the center of all family activities. Quiet times can be enjoyed in the front library. Study the second floor sleeping areas.

Design V12659 First Floor: 1,023 square feet; Second Floor: 1,008 square feet
Third Floor: 476 square feet; Total: 2,507 square feet

L **D**

● The facade of this three-storied, pitch-roofed house has a symmetrical placement of windows and a restrained but elegant central entrance. The central hall, or foyer, expands midway through the house to a family kitchen. Off the foyer are two rooms, a living room with fireplace and a study. The windowed third floor attic can be used as a study and studio. Three bedrooms are housed on the second floor.

Design V12733 First Floor: 1,177 square feet; Second Floor: 1,003 square feet; Total: 2,180 square feet

L D

● This is definitely a four bedroom Colonial with charm galore. The kitchen features an island range and other built-ins. All will enjoy the sunken family room with fireplace, which has sliding glass doors leading to the terrace. Also a basement for recreational activities with laundry remaining on first floor for extra convenience.

Design V12585 First Floor: 990 square feet; Second Floor: 1,011 square feet; Total: 2,001 square feet

L D

● An elegant Colonial! After entering through the front door one can either go directly to the formal area of the living room and dining room or to the informal area which is the front family room with fireplace. The U-shaped kitchen will serve the nook area and is just a step away from the washroom. Upstairs one will find all of the sleeping facilities.

Design V12622

First Floor: 624 square feet
Second Floor: 624 square feet
Total: 1,248 square feet

L D

● Appealing design can envelop little packages, too. Here is a charming, Early Colonial adaptation with an attached two-car garage to serve the young family with a modest building budget.

Design V11957 First Floor: 1,042 square feet; Second Floor: 780 square feet; Total: 1,822 square feet

L **D**

● When you order your blueprints for this design you will receive details for the construction of each of the three charming exteriors pictured above. Whichever the exterior you finally decide to build, the floor plan will be essentially the same except the location of the windows. This will be a fine home for the growing family. It will serve well for many years. There are four bedrooms and two full baths (one with a stall shower) upstairs.

Design V11956

First Floor: 990 square feet
Second Floor: 728 square feet
Total: 1,718 square feet

● The blueprints for this home include details for both the three bedroom and four bedroom options. The first floor livability does not change.

BEDROOM 9⁴ x 9⁴ · BATH · MASTER BEDROOM 10⁰ x 15⁰ · BATH · LINEN · DN · RAIL · BEDROOM 10⁰ x 10⁰ · BEDROOM 11⁴ x 10⁰

BATH · BATH · MASTER BEDROOM 14⁸ x 11⁸ · DN · RAIL · LINEN · BEDROOM 10⁰ x 10⁰ · BEDROOM 11⁴ x 13⁴

48'-0"

TERRACE

FAMILY RM. 19⁴ x 12⁰¹ · BRKFST. 7⁶ x 11² · KITCHEN 9⁶ x 11² · COOK TOP · DINING RM. 10⁰ x 11²

34'-10"

BOOKS · RAISED HEARTH · BOOKS · RAILING · DN · OVENS · REFG. · PTRY · CL · DN · PDR RM. · CL

GARAGE 19⁴ x 21⁰ · FOYER · UP · LIVING RM. 16⁰ x 13² · COVERED PORCH

Design V12694

First Floor: 2,026 square feet
Second Floor: 1,386 square feet
Total: 3,412 square feet

L

● This two-story design recalls the 18th-Century homestead of Sec. of Foreign Affairs John Jay in Katonah, N.Y. Downstairs features include a large country kitchen, clutter room, music alcove, and library wing. Upstairs are three sizable bedrooms, including a master suite with whirlpool.

ROOF

DN.

ATTIC 29⁴ x 26⁴
(HEADROOM 29⁴ x 10⁴)

ROOF

ROOF

BEDROOM /
STUDY
11⁰ x 13²

BATH DRESS. RM.

VANITY

MASTER
BEDROOM
13⁰ x 13²

CL.

CL.

BATH

CL.

DN.

CL.

LIN.

CL. CL.

UP TO
ATTIC

BEDROOM
10⁰ x 10⁶

CL.

BEDROOM
13⁰ x 10⁶

Design V12774

First Floor: 1,370 square feet
Second Floor: 969 square feet
Total: 2,339 square feet

L **D**

● Farmhouse adaptation with all the most up-to-date features expected in a new home. Beginning with the formal areas, this design offers pleasures for the entire family. There is the quiet corner living room which has an opening to the sizeable dining room. This room will enjoy plenty of natural light from the delightful bay window overlooking the rear yard. It is also conveniently located with the efficient U-shaped kitchen just a step away. The kitchen features many built-ins with pass-thru to the beamed ceiling nook. Sliding glass doors to the terrace are fine attractions in both the sunken family room and nook. The service entrance to the garage has a storage closet on each side, plus there is a secondary entrance through the laundry area. Recreational activities and hobbies can be pursued in the basement area. Four bedrooms, two baths upstairs.

59'-8"

TERRACE

44'-0"

RAISED HEARTH

FAMILY RM.
21⁴ x 13⁶

BREAKFAST RM.
14⁰ x 11⁶

KITCHEN
10⁰ x 11⁸

DINING RM.
13⁰ x 11⁶ + BAY

PASS
THRU

DN.

DESK B.RM. REF'G OVEN

LAUNDRY RM.
10⁰ x 7⁶

DN.

PDR.
RM.

CL.

DRY. WASH. LT

CL.

PANTRY

CURB

FOYER

LIVING RM.
17⁰ x 13⁶

GARAGE
21⁴ x 21⁸

COVERED PORCH

Design V12946

First Floor: 1,590 square feet
Second Floor: 1,344 square feet
Total: 2,934 square feet

L **D**

● Here's a traditional design that's made for down-home hospitality, the pleasures of casual conversation, and the good grace of pleasant company. The star attractions are the large covered porch and terrace, perfectly relaxing gathering points for family and friends. Inside, though, the design is truly a hard worker; separate living room and family room, each with its own fireplace; formal dining room; large kitchen and breakfast area with bay windows; separate study; workshop with plenty of room to maneuver; mud room; and four bedrooms up, including a master suite. Not to be overlooked are the curio niches, the powder room, the built-in bookshelves, the kitchen pass-thru, the pantry, the planning desk, the workbench, and the stairs to the basement.

BEDROOM 12⁰x13⁴

BEDROOM 12⁸x10⁰

ROOF

ATTIC

BATH

MASTER BEDROOM 18⁰x13⁴

DRESSING RM.

WALK-IN CLOSET

BATH

DN

LINEN

BEDROOM 14⁰x10⁸

ROOF

ROOF

Design V12908

First Floor: 1,427 square feet
Second Floor: 1,153 square feet
Total: 2,580 square feet

L **D**

● This Early American farmhouse offers plenty of modern comfort with its covered front porch with pillars and rails, double chimneys, building attachment, and four upstairs bedrooms. The first floor attachment includes a family room with bay window. It leads from the main house to a two-car garage. The family room certainly is central focus of this fine design, with its own fireplace and rear entrance to a laundry and sewing room behind the garage. Disappearing stairs in the building attachment lead to one bedroom over the garage. The upstairs also is accessible from stairs just off the front foyer. Included is a master bedroom suite. Downstairs one finds a modern kitchen with breakfast room, dining room, and front living room.

70'-0"

34'-0"

TERRACE

DINING RM. 12⁰x13⁴

KITCHEN 11⁰x13⁴

BRKFST RM. 9⁸x11⁰

LAUNDRY/SEWING 14⁴x8⁰

FREEZER

SEWING

DISAPPEARING STAIRS

PANTRY

PDR. RM.

FAMILY RM. 14⁰x17⁰+ BAY

LIVING RM. 18⁰x13⁴

FOYER

GARAGE 21⁴x21⁴

COVERED PORCH

Design V12520

First Floor: 1,419 square feet
Second Floor: 1,040 square feet
Total: 2,459 square feet

L **D**

● From Tidewater Virginia comes this historic adaptation, a positive reminder of the charm of Early American architecture. Note how the center entrance gives birth to fine traffic circulation. List the numerous features.

Design V12776
First Floor: 1,134 square feet
Second Floor: 874 square feet
Total: 2,008 square feet

L **D**

Design V12650
First Floor: 1,451 square feet
Second Floor: 1,091 square feet
Total: 2,542 square feet

L **D**

Expanding the Half-House

Design V12682
First Floor (Basic Plan): 976 square feet
First Floor (Expanded Plan): 1,230 square feet
Second Floor (Both Plans): 744 square feet
Total (Basic Plan): 1,720 square feet; Total (Expanded Plan): 1,974 square feet

L **D**

● Here is an expandable Colonial with a full measure of Cape Cod Charm. For those who wish to build the basic house, there is an abundance of low-budget livability. Twin fireplaces serve the formal living room and the informal country kitchen. Note the spaciousness of both areas. A dining room and powder room are also on the first floor of this basic plan. Upstairs three bedrooms and two full baths.

TERRACE

60'-0"

35'-0"

COVERED PORCH

DINING RM. 10⁸ x 12⁰

COUNTRY KITCHEN 20⁰ x 13⁰-15⁸

GARAGE 13⁸ x 20⁴

PDR. RM.

STUDY 13⁶ x 18⁰

FOYER

LIVING RM. 20⁰ x 13⁰

PORCH

BOOKS

ATTIC STORAGE (FUTURE ROOM)

ROOF

BEDROOM 12¹⁰ x 9⁸

BEDROOM 12¹⁰ x 9⁸

ROOF

LINEN

BATH

BATH

MASTER BEDROOM 11¹⁰ x 14⁰

ROOF

ROOF

● This expanded version of the basic house on the opposite page is equally as reminiscent of Cape Cod. Common in the 17th-Century was the addition of appendages to the main structure. This occurred as family size increased or finances improved. This version provides for the addition of wings to accommodate a large study and a garage. Utilizing the alcove behind the study results in a big, covered porch. Certainly a charming design whichever version you decide to build for your family.

Design V12657

First Floor: 1,217 square feet
Second Floor: 868 square feet
Total: 2,085 square feet

● Deriving its design from the traditional Cape Cod style, this facade features clapboard siding, small-paned windows and a transom-lit entrance flanked by carriage lamps. A central chimney services two fireplaces, one in the country-kitchen and the other in the formal living room which is removed from the disturbing flow of traffic. The master suite is located to the left of the upstairs landing. A full bathroom services two additional bedrooms on the second floor.

Design V12661

First Floor: 1,020 square feet
Second Floor: 777 square feet
Total: 1,797 square feet

L D

● Any other starter house or retirement home couldn't have more charm than this design. Its compact frame houses a very livable plan. An outstanding feature of the first floor is the large country kitchen. Its fine attractions include a beamed ceiling, raised hearth fireplace, built-in window seat and a door leading to the outdoors. A living room is in the front of the plan and has another fireplace which shares the single chimney. The rear dormered second floor houses the sleeping and bath facilities.

Design V12855

First Floor: 1,372 square feet
Second Floor: 1,245 square feet
Total: 2,617 square feet

L **D**

● This elegant Tudor house is perfect for the family who wants to move-up in living area, style and luxury. As you enter this home you will find a large living room with a fireplace on your right. Adjacent, the formal dining room has easy access to both the living room and the kitchen. The kitchen/breakfast room has an open plan and access to the rear terrace. Sunken a few steps, the spacious family room is highlighted with a fireplace and access to the rear, covered porch. Note the optional planning of the garage storage area. Plan this area according to the needs of your family. Upstairs, your family will enjoy three bedrooms and a full bath, along with a spacious master bedroom suite. Truly a house that will bring many years of pleasure to your family.

● This Tudor design has many fine features. The exterior is enhanced by front and side bay windows in the family and dining rooms. Along with an outstanding exterior, it also contains a modern and efficient floor plan within its modest proportions. Flanking the entrance foyer is a comfortable living room. The U-shaped kitchen is conveniently located between the dining and breakfast rooms.

Design V12800 First Floor: 999 square feet
Second Floor: 997 square feet; Total: 1,996 square feet

L **D**

● The charm of old England has been captured in this outstanding one-and-a-half story design. Interior livability will efficiently serve the various needs of all family members. The first floor offers both formal and informal areas along with the work centers. Features include: a wet-bar in the dining room, the kitchen's snack bar, first floor laundry and rear covered porch.

Design V12854 First Floor: 1,261 square feet
Second Floor: 950 square feet; Total: 2,211 square feet

L **D**

351

Design V12511

Main Level: 1,043 square feet
Upper Level: 703 square feet
Lower Level: 794 square feet
Total: 2,540 square feet

L **D**

Upper Level:

UPPER GATHERING RM.

BALCONY   BALCONY

BED RM.
11⁸ x 13⁸

BUNK RM.
11⁸ x 19⁰

BALCONY   RAILING

CL   CL
BATH

RAILING
UPPER FOYER   DN   CL   CL

Lower Level:

TERRACE

ACTIVITIES RM.
15⁴ x 18⁴

BASEMENT

BUNK RM. OPTIONAL
11⁴ x 15⁸

RAISED HEARTH

AIR COND.

BATH   UP

STORAGE CABINETS   CL   LT   WASH. DRY.

UNEX.

Main Level:

40'-4"

52'-0"

GATHERING RM.
15⁴ x 18⁴

DECK

BALCONY

STUDY-
BED RM.
11⁸ x 13⁸

DINING RM.
11⁸ x 11⁸

SNACK BAR

LINEN   CL

BATH   FOYER   KITCHEN
11⁸ x 9⁸

ON   UP

PANTRY REF. RANGE

PORCH

ENTRANCE COURT

OPEN TRELLIS

STORAGE

CARPORT
11⁸ x 20⁰

Design V12937
Main Level: 1,096 square feet
Upper Level: 1,115 square feet; Lower Level: 1,104 square feet
Total: 3,315 square feet

L

● This contemporary multi-level home features an extended rear balcony that covers a rear patio, plus a master bedroom suite, complete with whirlpool and raised-hearth pass-thru. Two other bedrooms and a second bath are on the upper level.

Design V12711

First Floor: 975 square feet
Second Floor: 1,024 square feet
Total: 1,999 square feet

L **D**

BALCONY

MASTER BED RM.
18⁰ x 13⁶

VANITY

DRESSING RM.

BATH

WALK-IN CLOSET

SHELVES

CL.

CL.

WALK-IN CLOSET

RAIL

DN.

LINEN

TWLS.

BATH

BED RM.
12⁰ x 11⁰

BED RM.
11⁰ x 17⁶

40'-4"

BALCONY ABOVE

TERRACE

GATHERING RM.
18⁰ x 13⁶

DINING RM.
13⁴ x 13⁶

RAISED HEARTH

STORAGE

UP

OVEN

SNACK BAR

COOK TOP

KITCHEN
13⁰ x 10⁰

DN.

PANTRY

REF'G.

DW.

CL.

STUDY
11⁰ x 9⁰ + BAY

FOYER

MUD RM.

WASH RM.

P

CL.

PORCH

CURB

GARAGE
21⁴ x 21⁸

52'-0"

● This stunning, contemporary, two-story house will captivate you with its many attractive features. Notice the projecting garage that will reduce the lot size as well as your cost. You will love the roomy kitchen with an adjacent snack bar. Take note of the spacious rear dining and gathering rooms. The fireplace and the view of the outdoors through the sliding glass doors will bring hours of pleasure to you and your family. A nice feature is the study with a handy storage closet. A few steps upstairs and you will be pleasantly surprised at what the master suite offers. Notice the spaciousness of the bedroom and walk-in closet. A dressing room and two vanities also can be found. An attractive feature is the sliding glass doors that lead to a balcony. Two other sizable bedrooms and a full bath are nearby. This home will be admired by all who view it.

● Tri-level living could hardly ask for more than this Rustic design has to offer. Not only can one enjoy the three levels but also there is a fourth basement level for bulk storage and perhaps, a shop area. The interior livability is outstanding. The main level has an L-shaped formal living/dining area with a fireplace in the living room and sliding glass doors in the dining room to the upper terrace, a U-shaped kitchen and an informal eating area. Down a few steps to the lower level is the family room with another fireplace and sliding doors to the lower terrace, a washroom and laundry. The upper level houses all of the sleeping facilities including three bedrooms, bath and master suite.

Design V12608

Main Level: 728 square feet
Upper Level: 874 square feet
Lower Level: 310 square feet
Total: 1,912 square feet

L D

Design V12905 First Floor: 1,342 square feet; Second Floor: 619 square feet; Total: 1,961 square feet

L **D**

● All of the livability in this plan is in the back! Each first floor room, except the kitchen, has access to the rear terrace via sliding glass doors. A great way to capture an excellent view. This plan is also ideal for a narrow lot seeing that its width is less than 50 feet. Two bedrooms and a lounge, overlooking the gathering room, are on the second floor.

Great Outdoor Projects

No house should go empty-landed for long. If you're searching for just the right structure to fill up those wide open spaces, we've got eight solid choices to show you. Among other exciting plans, you'll find a get-away-from-it-all gazebo that's big enough for small gatherings; a storage shed that does a number on clutter but looks great doing it; a two-dormer studio garage with all the comforts of home and a nice old-timey feel; and a gorgeous little crafts cottage with one very bright touch: an attached sunroom.

Plan V1-G108 is a good, solid gazebo; larger than most, it's better suited to entertaining alfresco. **Plan V1-G106** is no ordinary garage. In fact, it's a model building: room for two cars below and a complete studio apartment on top.

OUTDOOR PROJECTS INDEX & PRICE SCHEDULE

DESIGN		PAGE	PRICE	ADD'L SETS
V1-G106	Studio Garage	360	$40.00	$10.00
V1-G107	Storage Shed	361	$30.00	$10.00
V1-G108	Gazebo	365	$20.00	$10.00
V1-G109	Craft Cottage	362	$30.00	$10.00
V1-G110	Pool Cabana	358	$30.00	$10.00
V1-G111	Workshop Garage	359	$40.00	$10.00
V1-G112	Whirlpool Spa	364	$30.00	$10.00
V1-G113	Stable	363	$30.00	$10.00

TO ORDER, CALL TOLL FREE 1-800-521-6797, OR SEE PAGE 381.

24'-0"

12'-8"

BENCH SEAT

CHANGING RM.
5⁸ x 7⁶

SINK

SNACK AREA

OPTIONAL
COUNTER REF'G.

OPTIONAL
BUILT-IN
TABLE

EQUIPMENT RM.
7⁶ x 7⁶

FLOWER BOX

FLOWER BOX

LOUNGE AREA

Design V1G-110
Pool Cabana

Imagine this charming structure perched adjacent to your backyard swimming pool. Its exterior highlights such architectural features as hip and gable roofs, a decorative cupola, shuttered windows, flower boxes, and horizontal wood and shingle siding. Its plan offers a spacious sheltered party/lounge area with counter, sink, and refrigerator space. An optional built-in table could assure no rain-outs of those poolside snacks. Flanking this practical breezeway-type area are two rooms equal in size and utility. To the left is the changing room with a convenient bench. To the right is the equipment room for the handy storage of pool supplies and furniture. Surely a fine addition to the active family's backyard.

36'-0"

24'-0"

DISAPPEARING
STAIRS

LOFT ABOVE

SKYLIGHT

LADDER
LOFT OPENING

WORKSHOP
11⁸ x 19⁴

GARAGE
23⁰ x 23⁴

Design V1G-111
Workshop Garage

Here the appeal of Tudor exterior styling is applied to a free-standing workshop garage. Distinctive roof lines, simulated beamwork, stucco, and stone set the character. Three garage doors allow for flexible access to the vehicular and workshop areas. A skylight provides an extra measure of natural light for shop projects. Fine wall space provides plenty of area for handy tool placement above the U-shaped counter surfaces, which have storage potential below. For the storage of project lumber, there is an out-of-the-way loft. Around the corner from the shop is the folding stair unit in the garage. This provides access to another generous bulk storage area. The home craftsman will love this efficient above-ground workshop, storage unit.

ROOF

BATH | LINEN

BOOK SHELVES | BOOK SHELVES

STUDIO
23⁴ x 13² +DORMERS

RAILING

DN.

ROOF

P

W.H. | FURN.

GARAGE
23⁴ x 23⁴

24'-0"

UP

24'-0"

Design V1G-106
Studio Garage

Can you top this? Our two-car
garage has an artist's studio
nestled snugly on the second
floor. The Cape Cod-style
design, with three dormers,
large shutters, paneled doors,
and characteristic proportions
of roof to floor, makes a strong
visual statement that would
complement a large number of
traditional housing styles. An
exterior staircase, covered at
the top, leads to 300 square
feet of fully insulated studio
space; adjacent is a full
4x7-foot bath with shower
and linen storage.

COVERED PATIO
10⁰ x 10⁰

STORAGE AREA

WORKBENCH

12'-0"

12'-0"

Design V1G-107
Storage Shed
with Patio

Here's a hard-working storage shed with a number of bright touches. At 120 square feet, it's bigger than most. Cupola, birdhouse, shutters, and grooved plywood siding add up to a traditional look that complements many popular housing styles—from Cape Cods to Farmhouses. It's a flexible design, too, and could also be a potting shed, lath-house, or workshop. The nicest feature may well be the covered patio. After you cut the grass, just stash the lawn mower, take a seat, and survey your handiwork.

20'-0"

16'-0"

SUNROOM

DECK

WORK TABLE

UP

Design V1G-109
Craft Cottage

Great space for a cottage industry, this little building (250 square feet) is both functional and good looking. Ample counter space and shelving provide plenty of room to spread out materials and tools. Plus, a vaulted ceiling opens up the whole area. Next to the work space is a cozy sunroom (vaulted ceiling here, too). French doors and several windows, including a circle-head version above the doors, bathe the room in sunlight, while overhangs offer adequate shading. To get maximum sun, a south facing for the sunroom is best; it will also provide soft, even illumination for the north-facing work area.

24'-0"

HAY STORAGE
$14^2 \times 7^0$

TACK/FEED
$8^8 \times 7^0$

TACKING / GROOMING

32'-0"

24'-0"

STALL
$11^6 \times 9^2$

STALL
$11^6 \times 9^2$

8'-0"

COVERED PORCH

Design V1G-113
Country Stable

Charming, cross-hatched Dutch doors and a steepled roof are fitting country touches for this free-standing stable. Two horses and all their gear share plenty of room in two stalls, a tack and feed room, and a hay storage area. A long central corridor, with one wide and one regular entrance, contributes space for grooming your favorite mount or saddling up for a morning ride. The covered porch on the stall side acts as a weather buffer, keeping rain and hot sun away from precious animals. Shuttered windows are accented with window boxes. No horses? With some simple modifications, the stable becomes a writer's cottage or gardening workshop.

363

Design V1G-112
Soothing
Whirlpool/Sauna

A relaxing addition to back-yard space, this sauna and whirlpool spa combination promises respite from the hectic world. Joined to the house by wood decking and a sun-filtering trellis, the dry heat sauna has planked seating as well as a sink and shower and a bench seat in the dressing area. A small attached storage room neatly accommodates supplies and equipment. Just outside, raised planters flank the revitalizing whirlpool spa on two sides. The third side has a long bench seat. Additional bench seating borders the wood deck on two sides. Simple lines and open design allow this plan to blend perfectly with any style or type of house.

40'-0"

10'-10"   4'-0"   11'-2"   14'-0"

8'-0"

14'-5"

36'-0"

13'-7"

EQUIPMENT

TERRACE

PLANTINGS

SAUNA

WHIRLPOOL
SPA

SEAT

SEAT   STOR

SEAT

DN

UP

DN

DN

DN

TRELLIS ABOVE

DECK

HOUSE WALL

12'-0"

12'-0"

RAILING

RAILING

RAILING

OPEN
ABOVE

UP

Burnham

Design V1G-108
Neo-Classic
Gazebo

Our gazebo is a prime spot
for entertaining. At 200-plus
square feet of decking, it has
as much surface space as the
average family room. Plus, it's
just under 17½ feet tall, which
makes it the size of a typical
one-story house. As a result,
it's best suited for larger
lots—at least a half acre.
Boasting a number of
neo-classic features—perfect
proportions, columns,
bases—it's also a good match
with solid, traditional housing
styles: Capes, Georgians,
Farmhouses, and others. The
cupola is a homey touch that
lets light in to the decking
below. Cedar or redwood are
the building materials of
choice.

⬛ The Landscape Blueprint Package

For the home plans marked with an ⬛ in this book, Home Planners has created a front-yard landscape plan that matches or is complementary in design to the house plan. These comprehensive blueprint packages include all the necessary information you need to lay out and install a professional-looking front yard. Designed by an award-winning landscape architecture firm and prepared with attention to detail, these clear, easy-to-follow plans offer everything from a precise plot plan and regionalized plant and materials list to helpful sheets on installing your landscape and determining the mature size of your plants. These plans will help you achieve professional results, adding value and enjoyment to your property for years to come.

   Each set of blueprints is a full 18" x 24" in size with clear, complete instructions and easy-to-read type. Consisting of six detailed sheets, these plans show how all plants and materials are put together to form an exciting landscape for your home.

ELIZABETHAN TUDOR
Landscape Plan L219

Frontal Sheet. This artist's line sketch shows a typical house and all the elements of the finished front-yard landscape when plants are at or near maturity. This will give you a visual image or "picture" of the design and what you might expect your property to look like when fully landscaped.

Plan View. Drawn at 1/8" equals 1'-0", this is an aerial view of the property showing the exact placement of all landscape elements, including symbols and callouts for flowers, shrubs, ground covers, walkways, walls, gates, and other garden amenities. This sheet is the key to the design and shows you the contour, spacing, flow, and balance of all the elements in the design, as well as providing an exact "map" for laying out your property.

Regionalized Plant & Materials List. Keyed to the Plan View sheet, this page lists all of the plants and materials necessary to execute the design. It gives the quantity, botanical name, common name, flower color, season of bloom, and hardiness zone for each plant specified, as well as the amount and type of materials for all driveways, walks, walls, gates, and other structures. This becomes your "shopping list" for dealing with contractors or buying the plants and materials yourself. Most importantly, the plants shown on this page have been chosen by a team of professional horticulturalists for their adaptability, availability, and performance in your specific part of the country.

Planting and Maintaining Your Landscape. This valuable sheet gives handy information and illustrations on purchasing plant materials, preparing your site, and caring for your landscape after installation. Includes quick, helpful advice on planting trees, shrubs and ground covers, staking trees, establishing a lawn, watering, weed control, and pruning.

Zone Maps. These two informative maps offer detailed information to help you better select and judge the performance of your plants. Map One is a United States Department of Agriculture Hardiness Zone Map that shows the average low temperatures by zones in various part of the United States and Canada. The "Zone" listing for plants on Sheet 3 of your Plant and Materials List is keyed to this map. Map Two is a Regional Adaptation Map which takes into account other factors beyond low temperatures, such as rainfall, humidity, extremes of temperature, and soil acidity or alkalinity. This map is the key to plant adaptability and is used for the selection of plant lists in your plans.

Plant Size & Description Guide. Because people often have trouble visualizing plants, this handy regionalized guide provides a scale and silhouettes to determine the final height and shape of various trees and shrubs in your landscape plan. It also provides a quick means of choosing alternate plants in case you do not wish to install a certain tree or shrub or if you cannot find the plant at local nurseries.

To order, see page 369.

Landscape Plans Index

A complete Landscape Blueprint Package is available for each of the house plans listed below. See Regional Order Map below.

House Plan	Landscape Plan	Page	Price	Available For Regions:
V11075	V1-L225	190	X	1-3, 5, 6, 8
V11107	V1-L225	182	X	1-3, 5, 6, 8
V11113	V1-L202	206	X	1-3, 5, 6, 8
V11191	V1-L225	191	X	1-3, 5, 6, 8
V11228	V1-L217	58	Y	All
V11307	V1-L226	295	X	All
V11311	V1-L225	200	X	1-3, 5, 6, 8
V11323	V1-L225	297	X	1-3, 5, 6, 8
V11325	V1-L225	114	X	1-3, 5, 6, 8
V11343	V1-L226	94	X	All
V11380	V1-L226	295	X	All
V11381	V1-L226	295	X	All
V11394	V1-L202	317	X	1-3, 5, 6, 8
V11761	V1-L217	139	X	All
V11788	V1-L206	121	Z	1-6, 8
V11829	V1-L226	110	X	All
V11835	V1-L225	128	X	1-3, 5, 6, 8
V11892	V1-L225	51	X	1-3, 5, 6, 8
V11920	V1-L225	93	X	1-3, 5, 6, 8
V11939	V1-L225	180	X	1-3, 5, 6, 8
V11957	V1-L228	338	Y	All
V11989	V1-L220	24	Y	1-3, 5, 6, 8
V11993	V1-L213	60	Z	All
V12133	V1-L214	162	X	1-3, 5, 6, 8
V12146	V1-L203	315	Y	1-3, 5, 6, 8
V12170	V1-L221	26	X	1-3, 5, 6, 8
V12192	V1-L218	332	Z	1-6, 8
V12212	V1-L217	61	Y	All
V12220	V1-L217	47	Y	All
V12231	V1-L237	76	Y	7
V12283	V1-L206	329	Z	1-6, 8
V12316	V1-L225	120	X	1-3, 5, 6, 8
V12502	V1-L212	322	Z	All
V12505	V1-L226	293	X	All
V12510	V1-L200	317	X	1-3, 5, 6, 8
V12511	V1-L229	352	Y	All
V12520	V1-L201	344	Y	1-3, 5, 6, 8
V12534	V1-L227	175	Z	All
V12563	V1-L201	313	Y	1-3, 5, 6, 8
V12565	V1-L225	292	X	1-3, 5, 6, 8
V12570	V1-L225	194	X	1-3, 5, 6, 8
V12573	V1-L220	22	Y	1-3, 5, 6, 8
V12585	V1-L205	337	Y	1-3, 5, 6, 8
V12597	V1-L226	89	X	All
V12603	V1-L220	106	Y	1-3, 5, 6, 8
V12606	V1-L221	20	X	1-3, 5, 6, 8
V12607	V1-L220	195	Y	1-3, 5, 6, 8
V12608	V1-L228	355	Y	All
V12611	V1-L225	289	X	1-3, 5, 6, 8
V12612	V1-L226	289	X	All
V12615	V1-L211	164	Y	All
V12622	V1-L200	337	X	1-3, 5, 6, 8
V12650	V1-L201	345	Y	1-3, 5, 6, 8
V12657	V1-L200	348	X	1-3, 5, 6, 8
V12659	V1-L205	335	Y	1-3, 5, 6, 8
V12661	V1-L202	349	X	1-3, 5, 6, 8
V12662	V1-L216	333	Y	1-3, 5, 6, 8
V12668	V1-L214	334	X	1-3, 5, 6, 8
V12670	V1-L236	65	Z	3, 4, 7
V12671	V1-L234	82	Y	All
V12672	V1-L226	88	X	All
V12678	V1-L220	27	Y	1-3, 5, 6, 8
V12682	V1-L200	346	X	1-3, 5, 6, 8
V12683	V1-L214	330	X	1-3, 5, 6, 8
V12694	V1-L209	340	Y	1-6, 8
V12699	V1-L211	314	Y	All
V12704	V1-L225	299	X	1-3, 5, 6, 8
V12705	V1-L217	298	Y	All
V12706	V1-L225	299	X	1-3, 5, 6, 8
V12707	V1-L226	177	X	All
V12711	V1-L229	354	Y	All
V12728	V1-L221	28	X	1-3, 5, 6, 8
V12733	V1-L205	336	Y	1-3, 5, 6, 8
V12737	V1-L220	21	Y	1-3, 5, 6, 8
V12756	V1-L234	245	Y	All
V12761	V1-L229	326	Y	All
V12774	V1-L207	341	Z	1-6, 8
V12776	V1-L207	345	Z	1-6, 8
V12777	V1-L221	117	X	1-3, 5, 6, 8
V12779	V1-L217	49	Y	All
V12781	V1-L230	327	Z	All
V12789	V1-L228	249	Y	All
V12800	V1-L220	351	Y	1-3, 5, 6, 8
V12802	V1-L220	290	Y	1-3, 5, 6, 8
V12803	V1-L225	290	X	1-3, 5, 6, 8
V12804	V1-L232	290	Y	4, 7
V12805	V1-L220	291	Y	1-3, 5, 6, 8
V12806	V1-L220	291	Y	1-3, 5, 6, 8
V12807	V1-L220	291	Y	1-3, 5, 6, 8
V12810	V1-L204	302	Y	1-3, 5, 6, 8
V12811	V1-L204	302	Y	1-3, 5, 6, 8
V12812	V1-L204	303	Y	1-3, 5, 6, 8
V12813	V1-L204	303	Y	1-3, 5, 6, 8
V12814	V1-L204	302	Y	1-3, 5, 6, 8
V12815	V1-L204	302	Y	1-3, 5, 6, 8
V12816	V1-L204	303	Y	1-3, 5, 6, 8
V12817	V1-L204	303	Y	1-3, 5, 6, 8
V12818	V1-L234	209	Y	All
V12820	V1-L236	64	Z	3, 4, 7
V12821	V1-L229	242	Y	All
V12822	V1-L229	242	Y	All
V12827	V1-L229	280	Y	All
V12847	V1-L220	36	Y	1-3, 5, 6, 8
V12850	V1-L236	358	Z	3, 4, 7
V12851	V1-L217	50	Y	All
V12854	V1-L220	351	Y	1-3, 5, 6, 8
V12855	V1-L219	350	Z	1-3, 5, 6, 8
V12857	V1-L239	248	Z	All
V12864	V1-L225	213	X	1-3, 5, 6, 8
V12875	V1-L236	75	Z	3, 4, 7
V12878	V1-L200	87	X	1-3, 5, 6, 8
V12880	V1-L212	144	Z	All
V12888	V1-L211	149	Y	All
V12889	V1-L215	331	Z	1-6, 8
V12902	V1-L234	220	Y	All
V12905	V1-L229	356	Y	All
V12908	V1-L205	343	Y	1-3, 5, 6, 8
V12915	V1-L212	247	Z	All
V12920	V1-L212	167	Z	All
V12921	V1-L212	166	Z	All
V12937	V1-L229	353	Y	All
V12946	V1-L207	342	Z	1-6, 8
V12977	V1-L214	160	Z	1-3, 5, 6, 8

Regional Order Map

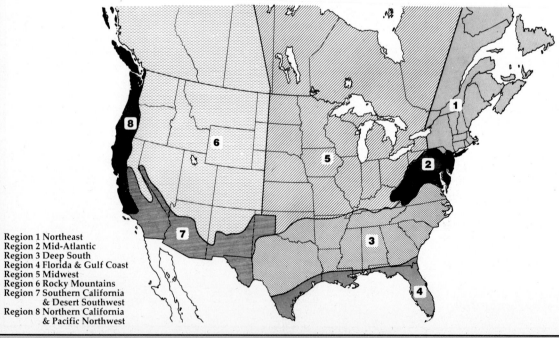

Region 1 Northeast
Region 2 Mid-Atlantic
Region 3 Deep South
Region 4 Florida & Gulf Coast
Region 5 Midwest
Region 6 Rocky Mountains
Region 7 Southern California & Desert Southwest
Region 8 Northern California & Pacific Northwest

L Landscape Blueprint Order Form

Landscape Plans Price Schedule			
Price Group	X	Y	Z
1 set	$35	$45	$55
3 sets	$50	$60	$70
6 sets	$65	$75	$85
Additional identical sets $10 each			
Reverse sets (mirror image) $10 each			

TO ORDER: Find the number of the House Plan in the Plans Index and note the corresponding Landscape Plan Number. Consult the Price Schedule (above) to determine the price of your plans, choosing the 1-, 3- or 6-set package and any additional or reverse sets you desire. To make sure your Plant and Materials List contains the best selection for your area, refer to the Regional Order Map (opposite) and specify the region in which you reside.

Complete the Order Coupon on this page and mail with your check or money order. If you prefer, you can also use a credit card or order C.O.D. (Sorry, no C.O.D. shipments to foreign countries including Canada.) Please include the correct postage and handling fees.

Our Exchange Policy
Because we produce and ship plans in response to individual orders, we cannot honor requests for refunds. However, you can exchange your entire order of blueprints, including a single set if you order just one, for a set of another landscape design. All exchanges carry an additional fee of $15.00, plus $5.00 for postage and handling if they're sent via surface mail; $7.00 for priority air mail.

About Reverse Blueprints
If you want to install your landscape in reverse of the plan as shown, we will include an extra set of blueprints with the Frontal Sheet and Plan View reversed for an additional fee of $10.00. Although callouts and lettering appear backwards, reverses will prove useful as a visual aid if you decide to flop the plan.

How Many Blueprints Do You Need?
To study your favorite landscape plan or make alterations of the plan to fit your site, one set of Landscape Blueprints may be sufficient. On the other hand, if you plan to install the landscape yourself using subcontractors or have a general contractor do the work for you, you will probably need more sets. Because you save money on 3-set or 6-set packages, you should consider ordering all the sets at one time. Use the checklist below to estimate the number you'll need:
Blueprint Checklist
_____ **Owner**
_____ **Landscape Contractor or Subcontractor**
_____ **Nursery or Plant Materials Supplier**
_____ **Building Materials Supplier**
_____ **Lender or Mortgage Source, if applicable**
_____ **Community Building Department for Permits (sometimes requires 2 sets)**
_____ **Subdivision Committee, if any**
_____ **Total Number of Sets**

Blueprint Hotline
Call Toll-Free 1-800-521-6797. We'll ship your order the following business day if you call us by 5:00 p.m. Eastern Time. When you order by phone, please be prepared to give us the Order Form Key Number shown in the box at the bottom of the Order Form.

CANADIAN CUSTOMERS: For faster, more economical service, Canadian customers should add 20% to all prices and mail in Canadian funds to:

Home Planners, Inc.
20 Cedar Street North
Kitchener, Ontario N2H 2WB
Phone (519) 743-4169

HOME PLANNERS, INC.
3275 WEST INA ROAD, SUITE 110
TUCSON, ARIZONA 85741

Please rush me the following Landscape Blueprints:

_____ Set(s) of Landscape Plan _____
(See Index and Price Schedule) $ _____

_____ Additional identical blueprints
in the same order @ $10.00 per set $ _____

_____ Reverse blueprints @ $10.00 per set $ _____

Please indicate the appropriate region of the country for Plant & Material List (See Map on opposite page):
[ ] Region 1 Northeast
[ ] Region 2 Mid-Atlantic
[ ] Region 3 Deep South
[ ] Region 4 Florida & Gulf Coast
[ ] Region 5 Midwest
[ ] Region 6 Rocky Mountains
[ ] Region 7 Southern California & Desert Southwest
[ ] Region 8 Northern California & Pacific Northwest
SUBTOTAL: (Arizona residents add 5% sales tax; Michigan residents add 4% sales tax) $ _____

POSTAGE AND HANDLING			
UPS DELIVERY-Must have street address — No P.O. Boxes			
•UPS Regular Service Allow 4-5 days delivery	☐ $5.00	$ _____	
•UPS 2nd Day Air Allow 2-3 days delivery	☐ $7.00	$ _____	
•UPS Next Day Air Allow 1-2 days delivery	☐ $16.00	$ _____	
POST OFFICE DELIVERY — If no street address			
•Priority Air Mail Allow 4-5 days delivery	☐ $7.00	$ _____	
C.O.D. (Pay mail carrier; Available in U.S. only)	☐		

TOTAL IN U.S. FUNDS $ _____
YOUR ADDRESS (please print)

Name _____

Street _____

City _____ State _____ Zip _____

Daytime telephone number (____) _____

CREDIT CARD ORDERS ONLY

Fill in the boxes below

☐☐☐☐☐☐☐☐☐☐☐☐☐☐☐
Credit card number

☐☐☐☐
Exp. Date: Month/Year

Check one   ☐ Visa   ☐ M/C

_____
Signature

Order Form Key
V1LP

369

D The Deck Blueprint Package

Many of the homes in this book can be enhanced with a professionally designed Home Planners' Deck Plan. Those home plans highlighted with a **D** have a matching or corresponding deck plan available which includes all the information you need in order to plan, lay out, and build a beautiful outdoor addition to the home. Our plans and details are carefully prepared in an easy-to-understand format that will guide you through every stage of your deck-building project. The Deck Blueprint Package contains four sheets outlining information pertinent to the specific Deck Plan you have chosen. A separate package — Deck Construction Details — provides the how-to data for building any deck, including instructions for adaptations and conversions.

In five information-packed sheets, these standard details provide all the general data necessary for building, adapting, and converting any deck. Included are layout examples, framing patterns, and foundation variations; details for ledgers, columns, and beams; schedules and charts; handrail, stair, and ramp details; and special options like spa platforms, planters, bars, benches and overhead trellises. This is a must-have package for the first-time deck builder and a useful addition to the custom deck plans shown on the next pages.

Custom Deck Plans

Each deck plan shown on pages 26 to 74 has been custom-designed by a professional architect. With each Custom Deck Plan, you receive the following:

Deck Plan Frontal Sheet. An artist's line drawing shows the deck as it connects to its matching or corresponding house. This drawing provides a visual image of what the deck will look like when completed, highlighting the livability factors.

Deck Framing and Floor Plans. In clear, easy-to-read drawings, this sheet shows all component parts of the deck from an aerial viewpoint with dimensions, notes, and references. Drawn at 1/4" = 1' - 0", the floor plan provides a finished overhead view of the deck including rails, stairs, benches, and ramps. The framing plan gives complete details on how the deck is to be built, including the position and spacing of footings, joists, beams, posts, and decking materials. Where necessary, the sheet also includes sections and closeups to further explain structural details.

Deck Elevations. Large-scale front and side elevations of the deck complete the visual picture of the deck. Drawn at 3/8" = 1' - 0", the elevations show the height of rails, balusters, stair risers, benches and other deck accessories.

Deck Materials List. This is a complete shopping list of all the materials needed (including sizes and amounts) to build your deck. The Materials List is complemented by section drawings showing placement of hardware such as thru-bolts, screws, nuts, washers, and nails and how these items are used to secure deck flooring, rails, posts, and joists. Scale is 3/4" = 1' - 0".

MATERIAL LIST		
QUANTITY	SIZE	DESCRIPTION
23	4"x4" – 4'	TREATED LUMBER
12	4"X4" – 5'	TREATED LUMBER
52 L.F.	2"x2"	TREATED BALUSTERS 30" LG.
300 L.F.	2"x4"	TREATED LUMBER
1850 L.F.	2"x6"	TREATED LUMBER
600 L.F.	2"x8"	TREATED LUMBER
10 L.F.	2"x10"	TREATED LUMBER
8 L.F.	2"x12"	TREATED LUMBER
70 L.F.		LANDSCAPE EDGE
550 S.F.		FILTER FABRIC
550 S.F.		2" DEEP PEA GRAVEL
60	3/8"ø x8" LG.	THRU-BOLTS W/ NUTS & WASHERS
30	3/8"ø x6" LG.	THRU-BOLTS W/ NUTS & WASHERS
4		1 1/2"x1 1/2"x1/8"–7" LG. STEEL ANGLES
16	3/16"ø x2"	LAG SCREWS
2 LBS.	8d	FOR RAILINGS
5 LBS.	16d	FOR POSTS & JOISTS
25 LBS.	10d	FOR DECKING
		NOTE: ALL NAILS TO BE HOT DIPPED GALVANIZED SCREW NAILS
		•QUANTITY OF NAILS MAY VARY DEPENDING ON TYPE OF CONNECTIONS USED.

TO ORDER, CALL TOLL FREE 1-800-521-6797, OR SEE PAGE 373.

Deck Plans Index

Deck Plans Price Schedule

PRICE GROUP	Q	R	S
1 set	$25.00	$30.00	$35.00
3 sets	$40.00	$45.00	$50.00
6 sets	$55.00	$60.00	$65.00

Additional identical sets: $10 each.
Reverse sets (mirror image): $10 each.

▪ Deck Blueprint Order Form

TO ORDER: Find the Deck Plan number in the Plans Index (opposite). Consult the Price Schedule (opposite) to determine the price of your plan, choosing the 1-, 3-, or 6-set package and any additional or reverse sets you desire. Complete the Order Coupon on this page and mail with your check or money order. If you prefer, you can also use a credit card or order C.O.D. (Sorry, no C.O.D shipments to foreign countries, including Canada.) Please include the correct postage and handling fees.

Our Service Policy
We try to process and ship every order from our office within 48 hours. For this reason, we won't send a formal notice acknowledging receipt of your order.

Our Exchange Policy
Because we produce and ship plans in response to individual orders, we cannot honor requests for refunds. However, you can exchange your entire order of blueprints, including a single set if you order just one, for a set of another deck design. All exchanges carry an additional fee of $15.00, plus $5.00 for postage and handling if they're sent via surface mail; $7.00 for priority air mail.

About Reverse Blueprints
If you want to install your deck in reverse of the plan as shown, we will include an extra set of blueprints with the Frontal Sheet, Framing and Floor Plans, and Elevations reversed for an additonal fee of $10.00. Although callouts and lettering appear backwards, reverses will prove useful as a visual aid if you decide to flop the plan.

How Many Blueprints Do You Need?
To study your favorite deck plan or make alterations of the plan to fit your home, one set of Deck Blueprints may be sufficient. On the other hand, if you plan to install the deck yourself using subcontractors or have a general contractor do the work for you, you will probably need more sets. Because you save money on 3-set or 6-set packages, you should consider ordering all the sets at one time. Use the checklist below to estimate the number you'll need:

Blueprint Checklist
_____ **Owner**
_____ **Deck Contractor or Subcontractor**
_____ **Building Materials Supplier**
_____ **Lender or Mortgage Source, if applicable**
_____ **Community Building Department for Permits**
_____ **(sometimes requires 2 sets)**
_____ **Subdivision Committee, if any**
_____ **Total Number of Sets**

Blueprint Hotline
Call Toll-Free 1-800-521-6797. We'll ship your order the following business day if you call us by 5:00 p.m. Eastern Time. When you order by phone, please be prepared to give us the Order Form Key Number shown in the box at the bottom of the Order Form.

CANADIAN CUSTOMERS: For faster, more economical service, Canadian customers should add 20% to all prices and mail in Canadian funds to:

Home Planners, Inc.
20 Cedar Street North
Kitchener, Ontario N2H 2W8
(519) 743-4169

HOME PLANNERS, INC.
3275 WEST INA ROAD, SUITE 110
TUCSON, ARIZONA 85741

Please rush me the following Deck Blueprints:

_____ Set(s) of Custom Deck Plan _____
(See Index and Price Schedule) $ _____

_____ Additional identical blueprints
in the same order @ $10.00 per set $ _____

_____ Reverse blueprints @ $10.00 per set $ _____

_____ Sets of Standard Deck
Details @ $14.95 per set $ _____

SUBTOTAL: (Arizona residents add 5% sales tax; Michigan residents add 4% sales tax) $ _____

POSTAGE AND HANDLING		
UPS DELIVERY—Must have street address — No PO Boxes		
•UPS Regular Service Allow 4-5 days delivery	☐ $5.00	$ _____
•UPS 2nd Day Air Allow 2-3 days delivery	☐ $7.00	$ _____
•UPS Next Dair Air Allow 1-2 days delivery	☐ $16.00	$ _____
POST OFFICE DELIVERY If no street address		
•Priority Air Mail Allow 4-5 days delivery	☐ $7.00	$ _____
C.O.D. (Pay mail carrier; Available in U.S. only)	☐	

TOTAL IN U.S. FUNDS $ _____

YOUR ADDRESS (please print)
Name _____

Street _____

City _____ State ____ Zip _____

Daytime telephone number (____) _____

CREDIT CARD ORDERS ONLY
Fill in the boxes below

☐☐☐☐☐☐☐☐☐☐☐☐☐☐
Credit card number

☐☐☐☐
Exp. Date: Month/Year

Check one ☐Visa ☐M/C

_____
Signature

Order Form Key
V1DP

373

When You're Ready To Order ...

Let Us Show You Our Blueprint Package.

Building a home? Planning a home? Our Blueprint Package contains nearly everything you need to get the job done right, whether you're working on your own or with help from an architect, designer, builder or subcontractors. Each Blueprint Package is the result of many hours of work by licensed architects or professional designers.

QUALITY

Hundreds of hours of painstaking effort have gone into the development of your blueprint set. Each home has been quality-checked by professionals to insure accuracy and buildability.

VALUE

Because we sell in volume, you can buy professional-quality blueprints at a fraction of their development cost. With our plans, your dream home design costs only a few hundred dollars, not the thousands of dollars that custom architects charge.

SERVICE

Once you've chosen your favorite home plan, you'll receive fast efficient service whether you choose to mail your order to us or call us toll free at 1-800-521-6797.

SATISFACTION

Our years of service to satisfied home plan buyers provide us the experience and knowledge that guarantee your satisfaction with our product and performance.

ORDER TOLL FREE 1-800-521-6797

After you've studied our Blueprint Package and Important Extras on the following pages, simply mail the accompanying order form on page 413 or call toll free on our Blueprint Hotline: 1-800-521-6797. We're ready and eager to serve you.

Each set of blueprints is an interrelated collection of floor plans, interior and exterior elevations, dimensions, cross-sections, diagrams and notations showing precisely how your house is to be constructed.

Here's what you get:

Frontal Sheet
This artist's sketch of the exterior of the house, done in two-point perspective, gives you an idea of how the house will look when built and landscaped. Large ink-line floor plans show all levels of the house and provide a quick overview of your new home's livability, as well as a handy reference for studying furniture placement.

Foundation Plan
Drawn to 1/4-inch scale, this sheet shows the complete foundation layout, including support

walls, excavated and unexcavated areas, if any and foundation notes. If slab construction rather than basement, the plan shows footings and details for a monolithic slab. This page, or another in the set, also includes a sample plot plan for locating your house on a building site.

Detailed Floor Plans

Complete in 1/4-inch scale, these plans show the layout of each floor of the house. All rooms and interior spaces are carefully dimensioned and keys are provided for cross-section details given later in the plans. The position of all electrical outlets and switches are clearly shown.

House Cross-Sections

Large-scale views, normally drawn at 3/8-inch equals 1 foot, show sections or cut-aways of the foundation, interior walls, exterior walls,

floors, stairways and roof details. Additional cross-sections are given to show important changes in floor, ceiling or roof heights or the relationship of one level to another. Extremely valuable for construction, these sections show exactly how the various parts of the house fit together.

Interior Elevations

These large-scale drawings show the design and placement of kitchen and bathroom cabinets, laundry areas, fireplaces, bookcases and other built-ins. Little "extras," such as mantelpiece and wainscoting drawings, plus moulding sections, provide details that give your home that custom touch.

Exterior Elevations

Drawings in 1/4-inch scale show the front, rear and sides of your house and give necessary notes on exterior materials and finishes. Particular attention is given to cornice detail, brick and stone accents or other finish items that make your home distinctive.

House Cross-Sections

Detailed Floor Plans

Exterior Elevations

Interior Elevations

Foundation Plans

Frontal Sheet

Important Extras To Do The Job Right!

Introducing six important planning and construction aids developed by our professionals to help you succeed in your home-building project.

To Order, Call Toll Free 1-800-521-6797

To add these important extras to your Blueprint Package, simply indicate your choices on the order form on page 381 or call us Toll Free 1-800-521-6797 and we'll tell you more about these exciting products.

MATERIALS LIST

For each design in our portfolio, we offer a customized materials take-off that is invaluable in planning and estimating the cost of your new home. This comprehensive list outlines the quantity, type and size of material needed to build your house (with the exception of mechanical system items). Included are:

- framing lumber
- roofing and sheet metal
- windows and doors
- exterior sheathing material and trim
- masonry, veneer and fireplace materials
- tile and flooring materials
- kitchen and bath cabinetry
- interior sheathing and trim
- rough and finish hardware
- many more items

This handy list helps you or your builder cost out materials and serves as a ready reference sheet when you're compiling bids. It also provides a cross-check against the materials specified by your builder and helps coordinate the substitution of items you may need to meet local codes.

(Note: Because of differing local codes, building methods, and availability of materials, our Materials Lists do not include mechanical materials. To obtain necessary take-offs and recommendations, consult heating, plumbing and electrical contractors. Materials Lists are not sold separately from the Blueprint Package.)

SPECIFICATION OUTLINE

This valuable 16-page document is critical to building your house correctly. Designed to be filled in by you or your builder, this booklet lists 166 stages or items crucial to the building process.

For the layman, it provides a comprehensive review of the construction process and helps in making the specific choices of materials, models and processes. For the builder, it serves as a guide to preparing a building quotation and forms the basis for the construction program.

Designed primarily as a reference for the homeowner, this Specification Outline can become a legally binding document. Once it is filled out and agreed upon by owner and builder, it becomes a complete Project Specification.

When combined with the blueprints, a signed contract and schedule, the Specification Outline becomes a legal document and record for the building of your home. Many home builders find it useful to order two of these outlines—one as a worksheet in formulating the specifications and another to be carefully completed as a legal document.

DETAIL SHEETS

Because local codes and requirements vary greatly, we recommend that you obtain drawings and bids from licensed contractors to do your mechanical plans. However, if you want to know more about techniques – and deal more confidently with subcontractors – we offer these remarkably useful detail sheets. Each is an excellent tool that will enhance your understanding of these technical subjects.

PLUMBING

The Blueprint Package includes locations for all the plumbing fixtures in your new house, including sinks, lavatories, tubs, showers, toilets, laundry trays and water heaters. However, if you want to know more about the complete plumbing system, these 24x36-inch detail sheets will prove very useful. Prepared to meet requirements of the National Plumbing Code, these six fact-filled sheets give general information on pipe schedules, fittings, sump-pump details, water-softener hookups, septic system details and much more. Color-coded sheets include a glossary of terms.

ELECTRICAL

The locations for every electrical switch, plug and outlet are shown in your Blueprint Package. However, these Electrical Details go further to take the mystery out of household electrical systems. Prepared to meet requirements of the National Electrical Code, these comprehensive 24x36-inch drawings come packed with helpful information, including wire sizing, switch-installation schematics, cable-routing details, appliance wattage, door-bell hook-ups, typical service panel circuitry and much more. Six sheets are bound together and color-coded for easy reference. A glossary of terms is also included.

CONSTRUCTION

The Blueprint Package contains everything an experienced builder needs to construct a particular house. However, it doesn't show all the ways that houses can be built, nor does it explain alternate construction methods. To help you understand how your house will be built – and offer additional techniques – this set of drawings depicts the materials and methods used to build foundations, fireplaces, walls, floors and roofs. Where appropriate, the drawings show acceptable alternatives. These six sheets will answer questions for the advanced do-it-yourselfer or home planner.

Plan-A-Home®

Plan-A-Home® is an easy-to-use tool that helps you design a new home, arrange furniture in a new or existing home, or plan a remodeling project. Each package contains:

- More than *700 peel-off planning symbols* on a self-stick vinyl sheet, including walls, windows, doors, all types of furniture, kitchen components, bath fixtures and many more. All are made of durable, peel-and-stick vinyl you can use over and over.
- A reusable, transparent, *1/4-inch scale planning grid* made of tough mylar that matches the scale of actual working drawings (1/4-inch equals 1 foot). This grid provides the basis for house layouts of up to 140x92 feet.
- *Tracing paper* and a protective sheet for copying or transferring your completed plan.
- A *felt-tip pen*, with water-soluble ink that wipes away quickly.

With Plan-A-Home®, you can make basic planning decisions for a new house or make modifications to an existing house. Use with your Blueprint Package to test modifications to rooms or to plan furniture arrangements before you build. Plan-A-Home® lets you lay out areas as large as a 7,500 square foot, six-bedroom, seven-bath house.

House Blueprint Price Schedule and Plans Index

These pages contain all the information you need to price your blueprints. In general, the larger and more complicated the house, the more it costs to design and thus the higher the price we must charge for the blueprints. Remember, however, that these prices are far less than you would normally pay for the services of a licensed architect or professional designer. Custom home designs and related architectural services often cost thousands of dollars, ranging from 5% to 15% of the cost of construction. By ordering our blueprints you are potentially saving enough money to afford a larger house, or to add those "extra" amenities such as a patio, deck, swimming pool or even an upgraded kitchen or luxurious master suite.

To use the index below, refer to the design number listed in chronological order (a helpful page reference is also given). Note the price index letter and refer to the House Blueprint Price Schedule at right for the cost of one, four or eight sets of blueprints or the cost of a reproducible sepia. Additional prices are shown for identical and reverse blueprint sets, as well as a very useful Materials List to accompany your plans.

House Blueprint Price Schedule
(Prices are subject to change without notice)

	1-set Study Package	4-set Building Package	8-set Building Package	1-set Reproducible Sepias
Schedule A	$150	$210	$270	$300
Schedule B	$180	$240	$300	$360
Schedule C	$210	$270	$330	$420
Schedule D	$240	$300	$360	$480
Schedule E	$360	$420	$480	$600

Additional Identical Blueprints in same order ....$40 per set
Reverse Blueprints (Mirror Image) ....$40 per set
Specification Outlines ....$5 each
Materials Lists
     Schedule A-D $35
     Schedule E $45

To Order: Fill in and send the Order Form on page 381 – or call us Toll Free 1-800-521-6797.

Before You Order...

Before completing the coupon at right or calling us on our Toll-Free Blueprint Hotline, you may be interested to learn more about our service and products. Here's some information you will find helpful.

Quick Turnaround
We process and ship every blueprint order from our office within 48 hours. On most orders, we do even better. Normally, if we receive your order by 5 p.m. Eastern Standard Time, we'll process it the same day and ship it the following day. Because of this quick turnaround, we won't send a formal notice acknowledging receipt of your order.

Our Exchange Policy
Since blueprints are printed in response to your order, we cannot honor requests for refunds. However, we will exchange your entire first order for an equal number of blueprints at a price of $20.00 for the first set and $10.00 for each additional set, plus the difference in cost if exchanging for a design in a higher price bracket. (Sepias are not exchangeable.) All sets from the first order must be returned before the exchange can take place. Please add $7.00 for postage and handling via UPS regular service; $10.00 via UPS 2nd Day Air.

About Reverse Blueprints
If you want to build in reverse of the plan as shown, we will include an extra set of reversed blueprints (mirror image) for an additional fee of $40. Although lettering and dimensions appear backward, reverses will be a useful visual aid if you decide to flop the plan.

Modifying or Customizing Our Plans
With over 2,500 different plans from which to choose, you are bound to find a Home Planners' design that suits your lifestyle, budget and building site. In addition, our plans can be customized to your taste by your choice of siding, decorative detail, trim, color and other non-structural alterations.

If you do need to make minor modifications to the plans, these can normally be accomplished by your builder without the need for expensive blueprint modifications. However, if you decide to revise the plans significantly, we strongly suggest that you order our reproducible sepias and consult a licensed architect or professional designer to help you redraw the plans to your particular needs.

Architectural and Engineering Seals
Some cities and states are now requiring that a licensed architect or engineer review and "seal" your blueprints prior to construction. This is often due to local or regional concerns over energy consumption, safety codes, seismic ratings, etc. For this reason, you may find it necessary to consult with a local professional to have your plans reviewed. This can normally be accomplished with minimum delays, for a nominal fee.

Compliance with Local Codes and Regulations
At the time of creation, our plans are drawn to specifications published by Building Officials Code Administrators (BOCA), the Southern Standard Building Code, or the Uniform Building Code and are designed to meet or exceed national building standards.

Some states, counties and municipalities have their own codes, zoning requirements and building regulations. Before starting construction, consult with local building authorities and make sure you comply with local ordinances and codes, including obtaining any necessary permits or inspections as building progresses. In some cases, minor modifications to your plans by your builder, local architect or designer may be required to meet local conditions and requirements.

Foundation and Exterior Wall Changes
Most of our plans are drawn with either a full or partial basement foundation. Depending upon your specific climate or regional building practices, you may wish to convert this basement to a slab or crawlspace. Most professional contractors and builders can easily adapt your plans to alternate foundation types. Likewise, most can easily convert 2x4 wall construction to 2x6, or vice versa. If you need more guidance on these conversions, our handy Construction Detail Sheets, shown on page 377, describe how such conversions can be made.

How Many Blueprints Do You Need?
A single set of blueprints is sufficient to study a home in greater detail. However, if you are planning to obtain cost estimates from a contractor or subcontractors - or if you are planning to build immediately - you will need more sets. Because additional sets are cheaper when ordered in quantity with the original order, make sure you order enough blueprints to satisfy all requirements. The following checklist will help you determine how many you need:

_____ Owner
_____ Builder (generally requires at least three sets; one as a legal document, one to use during inspections, and at least one to give to subcontractors)
_____ Local Building Department (often requires two sets)
_____ Mortgage Lender (usually one set for a conventional loan; three sets for FHA or VA loans)
_____ TOTAL NUMBER OF SETS

 Toll Free 1-800-521-6797

Normal Office Hours:
8:00 a.m. to 8:00 p.m. - Eastern Standard Time
Monday through Friday
10:00 a.m. to 2:00 p.m. - EST Saturday

If we receive your order by 5:00 p.m. EST, we'll process it the same day and ship it the following day. When ordering by phone, please have your charge card ready. We'll also ask you for the Order Form Key Number on the opposite page. Please use our Toll-Free number for blueprint and book orders only.

By FAX: Copy the Order Form on the next page and send it on our International FAX line: 1-602-297-6219.

Canadian Customers

For faster, more economical service, Canadian customers should add 20% to all prices and mail in Canadian funds to:

Home Planners, Inc.
20 Cedar Street North
Kitchener, Ontario N2H 2W8
Phone (519) 743-4169

HOME ORDER FORM

**HOME PLANNERS, INC., 3275 WEST INA ROAD
SUITE 110, TUCSON, ARIZONA 85741**

HE BASIC BLUEPRINT PACKAGE
ush me the following (please refer to the Plans
dex and Price Schedule in this section):

_____ Set(s) of blueprints for
plan number(s) _____. $_____

_____ Set(s) of sepias for
plan number(s) _____. $_____

_____ Additional identical blueprints in same
order @ $40.00 per set. $_____

_____ Reverse blueprints @ $40.00 per set. $_____

MPORTANT EXTRAS
ush me the following:

_____ Materials List @ $35.00 Schedule A-D;
$45.00 Schedule E $_____

_____ Specification Outlines @ $5.00 each. $_____

_____ Detail Sets @ $14.95 each; any two for $22.95;
all three for $29.95 (save $14.90). $_____

☐ Plumbing ☐ Electrical ☐ Construction
(These helpful details provide general
construction advice and are not
specific to any single plan.)

_____ Set(s) of blueprints for
Outdoor Project number(s) _____. $_____

_____ Plan-A-Home® @ $29.95 each. $_____

_____ SUB-TOTAL $_____

ALES TAX (Arizona residents add 5% sales tax;
ichigan residents add 4% sales tax.) $_____

POSTAGE AND HANDLING	1-3 sets	4 or more sets	
UPS DELIVERY (Requires street address - No P.O. Boxes)			
•UPS Regular Service Allow 4-5 days delivery	☐ 5.00	☐ 7.00	$_____
•UPS 2nd Day Air Allow 2-3 days delivery	☐ 7.00	☐ 10.00	$_____
•UPS Next Day Air Allow 1-2 days delivery	☐ 16.50	☐ 20.00	$_____
POST OFFICE DELIVERY If no street address available. Allow 4-5 days delivery	☐ 7.00	☐ 10.00	$_____
OVERSEAS AIR MAIL DELIVERY Note: All delivery times are rom date Blueprint Package s shipped.	☐ 30.00	☐ 50.00	$_____
	☐ Send C.O.D.		

TOTAL (Subtotal, tax, and postage) $_____

OUR ADDRESS (please print)
ame_____
reet_____
ty_____ State_____ Zip_____
aytime telephone number (____)_____

OR CREDIT CARD ORDERS ONLY
ease fill in the boxes below:
redit card number_____
xp. Date: Month/Year_____
heck one ☐ Visa   ☐ MasterCard
gnature_____
rder Form Key   Please check appropriate box:
| V1BP |
☐ Licensed Builder-Contractor
☐ Home Owner

HOME ORDER FORM

**HOME PLANNERS, INC., 3275 WEST INA ROAD
SUITE 110, TUCSON, ARIZONA 85741**

THE BASIC BLUEPRINT PACKAGE
Rush me the following (please refer to the Plans
Index and Price Schedule in this section):

_____ Set(s) of blueprints for
plan number(s) _____. $_____

_____ Set(s) of sepias for
plan number(s) _____. $_____

_____ Additional identical blueprints in same
order @ $40.00 per set. $_____

_____ Reverse blueprints @ $40.00 per set. $_____

IMPORTANT EXTRAS
Rush me the following:

_____ Materials List @ $35.00 Schedule A-D;
$45.00 Schedule E $_____

_____ Specification Outlines @ $5.00 each. $_____

_____ Detail Sets @ $14.95 each; any two for $22.95;
all three for $29.95 (save $14.90). $_____

☐ Plumbing ☐ Electrical ☐ Construction
(These helpful details provide general
construction advice and are not
specific to any single plan.)

_____ Set(s) of blueprints for
Outdoor Project number(s) _____. $_____

_____ Plan-A-Home® @ $29.95 each. $_____

_____ SUB-TOTAL $_____

SALES TAX (Arizona residents add 5% sales tax;
Michigan residents add 4% sales tax.) $_____

POSTAGE AND HANDLING	1-3 sets	4 or more sets	
UPS DELIVERY (Requires street address - No P.O. Boxes)			
•UPS Regular Service Allow 4-5 days delivery	☐ 5.00	☐ 7.00	$_____
•UPS 2nd Day Air Allow 2-3 days delivery	☐ 7.00	☐ 10.00	$_____
•UPS Next Day Air Allow 1-2 days delivery	☐ 16.50	☐ 20.00	$_____
POST OFFICE DELIVERY If no street address available. Allow 4-5 days delivery	☐ 7.00	☐ 10.00	$_____
OVERSEAS AIR MAIL DELIVERY Note: All delivery times are from date Blueprint Package is shipped.	☐ 30.00	☐ 50.00	$_____
	☐ Send C.O.D.		

TOTAL (Subtotal, tax, and postage) $_____

YOUR ADDRESS (please print)
Name_____
Street_____
City_____ State_____ Zip_____
Daytime telephone number (____)_____

FOR CREDIT CARD ORDERS ONLY
Please fill in the boxes below:
Credit card number_____
Exp. Date: Month/Year_____
Check one ☐ Visa   ☐ MasterCard
Signature_____
Order Form Key   Please check appropriate box:
| V1BP |
☐ Licensed Builder-Contractor
☐ Home Owner

Additional Plans Books

The Design Category Series

1.

ONE-STORY HOMES
A collection of 470 homes to suit a range of budgets in one-story living. All popular styles, including Cape Cod, Southwestern, Tudor and French. **384 pages. $8.95 ($10.95 Canada)**

2.

TWO-STORY HOMES
478 plans for all budgets in a wealth of styles: Tudors, Saltboxes, Farmhouses, Victorians, Georgians, Contemporaries and more. **416 pages. $8.95 ($10.95 Canada)**

3.

MULTI-LEVEL AND HILL-SIDE HOMES 312 distinctive styles for both flat and sloping sites. Includes exposed lower levels, open staircases, balconies, decks and terraces. **320 pages. $6.95 ($8.95 Canada)**

4.

VACATION AND SECOND HOMES 258 ideal plans for a favorite vacation spot or perfect retirement or starter home. Includes cottages, chalets, and 1-, 1 1/2-, 2-, and multi-levels. **256 pages. $5.95 ($7.50 Canada)**

The Exterior Style Series

9.

330 EARLY AMERICAN HOME PLANS A heartwarming collection of the best in Early American architecture. Traces the style from Colonial structures to popular traditional versions. Includes a history of different styles. **304 pages. $9.95 ($11.95 Canada)**

10.

335 CONTEMPORARY HOME PLANS Required reading for anyone interested in the clean-lined elegance of Contemporary design. Features plans of all sizes and types, as well as a history of this style. **304 pages. $9.95 ($11.95 Canada)**

11.

TUDOR HOUSES The stuff that dreams are made of! A superb portfolio of 80 enchanting Tudor-style homes, from cozy Cotswold cottages to impressive Baronial manors. Includes a decorating section with colorful photographs and illustrations. **208 pages. $10.95 ($12.95 Canada)**

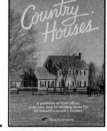

12.

COUNTRY HOUSES Shows off 80 country homes in three eye-catching styles: Cape Cods, Farmhouses and Center-Hall Colonials. Each features an architect's exterior rendering, artist's depiction of a furnished interior room, large floor plans, and planning tips. **208 pages. $10.95 ($12.95 Canada)**

Plan Portfolios

ENCYCLOPEDIA OF HOME DESIGNS
The largest book of its kind — 450 plans in a complete range of housing types, styles and sizes. Includes plans for all building budgets, families and styles of living.

14. 320 pages. $9.95 ($11.95 Canada)

MOST POPULAR HOME DESIGNS
Our customers' favorite plans, including one-story, 1 1/2-story, two-story, and multi-level homes in a variety of styles. Designs feature many of today's most popular amenities: lounges, clutter rooms, media rooms and more.

15. 272 pages. $8.95 ($10.95 Canada)

HOME PLANNERS' STYLE PORTFOLIO
A superb collection of today's most popular styles from Colonials to cool Contemporaries. Incorporates detailed renderings and floor plans with a Chronology of Styles and Glossary of Architectural Terms.

16. 320 pages. $9.95 ($11.95 Canada)

New From Home Planners

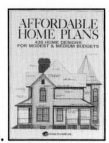

5.

AFFORDABLE HOME PLANS For the prospective home builder with a modest or medium budget. Features 430 one-, 1½-, two-story and multi-level homes in a wealth of styles. Included are cost-saving ideas for the budget-conscious. **320 pages. $8.95 ($10.95 Canada)**

6.

DECK PLANNER 25 practical plans and details for decks the do-it-yourselfer can actually build. How-to data and project starters for a variety of decks. Construction details available separately. **112 pages. $7.95 ($9.95 Canada)**

7.

THE HOME LANDSCAPER 55 fabulous front- and back-yard plans that even the do-it-yourselfer can master. Complete construction blueprints and regionalized plant lists available for each design. **208 pages. $12.95 ($15.95 Canada)**

8.

HOME PLANS FOR OUT-DOOR LIVING More than 100 plans to bring the outdoors in. Features terraces, balconies, courtyards, atriums, and sunspaces for homes of all types and styles. Color photography of homes built. **192 pages. $10.95 ($12.95 Canada)**

13.

COLONIAL HOUSES 161 history-inspired homes with up-to-date plans are featured along with 2-color interior illustrations and 4-color photographs. Included are many plans developed for *Colonial Homes'* History House Series. **208 pages. $10.95 ($12.95 Canada)**

17.

LUXURY DREAM HOMES At last, the home you've waited for! A collection of 150 of the best luxury home plans from seven of the most highly regarded designers and architects in the United States. A dream come true for anyone interested in designing, building or remodeling a luxury home. **192 pages. $14.95 ($17.95 Canada)**

Please fill out the coupon below. We will process your order and ship it from our office within 48 hours. Send coupon and check for the total to:

HOME PLANNERS, INC.
3275 West Ina Road, Suite 110, Dept. BK
Tucson, Arizona 85741

THE DESIGN CATEGORY SERIES – A great series of books edited by design type. Complete collection features 1376 pages and 1273 home plans.

1. _____ One-Story Homes @ $8.95 ($10.95 Canada)		$_____
2. _____ Two-Story Homes @ $8.95 ($10.95 Canada)		$_____
3. _____ Multi-Level & Hillside Homes @ $6.95 ($8.95 Canada)		$_____
4. _____ Vacation & Second Homes @ $5.95 ($7.50 Canada)		$_____

NEW FROM HOME PLANNERS

5. _____ Affordable Home Plans @ $8.95 ($10.95 Canada)		$_____
6. _____ Deck Planner @ $7.95 ($9.95 Canada)		$_____
7. _____ The Home Landscaper @ $12.95 ($15.95 Canada)		$_____
8. _____ Home Plans for Outdoor Living @ $10.95 ($12.95 Canada)		$_____

THE EXTERIOR STYLE SERIES

9. _____ 330 Early American Home Plans @ $9.95 ($11.95 Canada)		$_____
10. _____ 335 Contemporary Home Plans @ $9.95 ($11.95 Canada)		$_____
11. _____ Tudor Houses @ $10.95 ($12.95 Canada)		$_____
12. _____ Country Houses @ $10.95 ($12.95 Canada)		$_____
13. _____ Colonial Houses @ $10.95 ($12.95 Canada)		$_____

PLAN PORTFOLIOS

14. _____ Encyclopedia of Home Designs @ $9.95 ($11.95 Canada)		$_____
15. _____ Most Popular Home Designs @ $8.95 ($10.95 Canada)		$_____
16. _____ Home Planners' Style Portfolio @ $9.95 ($11.95 Canada)		$_____
17. _____ Luxury Dream Homes @ $14.95 ($17.95 Canada)		$_____
Sub Total		$_____
Arizona residents add 5% sales tax; Michigan residents add 4% sales tax		$_____
ADD Postage and Handling		$ 2.50
TOTAL (Please enclose check)		$_____

Name (please print) _____

Address _____

City _____ State _____ Zip _____

CANADIAN CUSTOMERS: Use Canadian prices and remit in Canadian funds to:
Home Planners, Inc., 20 Cedar St. North
Kitchener, Ontario N2H 2W8
Phone: (519) 743-4169

TO ORDER BOOKS BY PHONE
CALL TOLL FREE 1-800-322-6797

V1BK

OVER 2½ MILLION BLUEPRINTS SOLD

"We instructed our builder to follow the plans including all of the many details which make this house so elegant... Our home is a fine example of the results one can achieve by purchasing and following the plans which you offer... Everyone who has seen it has assured us that it belongs in 'a picture book.' I truly mean it when I say that my home 'is a DREAM HOUSE.'"

S.P.
Anderson, SC

"We have had a steady stream of visitors, many of whom tell us this is the most beautiful home they've seen. Everyone is amazed at the layout and remark on how unique it is. Our real estate attorney, who is a Chicago dweller and who deals with highly valued properties, told me this is the only suburban home he has seen that he would want to live in."

W. & P.S.
Flossmoor, IL

"Home Planners' blueprints saved us a great deal of money. I acted as the general contractor and we did a lot of the work ourselves. We probably built it for half the cost! We are thinking about more plans for another home. I purchased a competitor's book but my husband only wants your plans!"

K.M.
Grovetown, GA

"We are very happy with the product of our efforts. The neighbors and passersby appreciate what we have created. We have had many people stop by to discuss our house and kindly praise it as being the nicest house in our area of new construction. We have even had one person stop and make us an unsolicited offer to buy the house for much more than we have invested in it."

K. & L.S.
Bolingbrook, IL

"The traffic going past our house is unbelievable. On several occasions, we have heard that it is the 'prettiest house in Batavia.' Also, when meeting someone new and mentioning what street we live on, quite often we're told, 'Oh, you're the one in the yellow house with the wrap-around porch! I love it!'"

A.W.
Batavia, NY

"I have been involved in the building trades my entire life... Since building our home we have built two other homes for other families. Their plans from local professional architects were not nearly as good as yours. For that reason we are ordering additional plan books from you."

T.F.
Kingston, WA

"The blueprints we received from Home Planners were of excellent quality and provided us with exactly what we needed to get our successful home-building project underway. We appreciate Home Planners' invaluable role in our home-building effort."

T.A.
Concord, TN